Jamie Durie and PATIO have made the concept of a 'designer' garden more accessible. He has enticed a wide audience outside and into the great outdoors with creative and innovative solutions using soft and hard landscaping materials. The result? Gardens that are not just for experiencing but also for living in and, above all, for enjoying.

JANET JAMES, EDITOR
Australian Interiors Magazine

Jamie Durie must be one of the most charismatic landscape designers around, but there's more to him that just looking good on TV. He has a whole body of landscaping knowledge and experience which he's willing to share.

DAVID CLARK, EDITOR
Vogue Living

Recent horticultural lifestyle programs have heightened the awareness of how individuals can improve their own private environments to enhance their leisure pursuits. In a diverse but passionate industry, the contribution of the publications of Jamie Durie and the PATIO team is regarded as significant and complementary.

STEPHEN BOURKE, NATIONAL PRESIDENT
Parks & Leisure Australia

[*The Outdoor Room* is] an inspiring book for anyone wanting to create a small city garden that will blur the boundaries between indoor and outdoor. Excellent photography captures the mood of these spaces and shows how water, light and plants can combine successfully in the urban environment to produce stylish yet practical spaces for relaxed living.

GRAEME PURDY
Herald Sun

Durie's flair with innovative construction techniques and unusual materials is evident on every page [of *The Outdoor Room*].

JENNA REED BURNS
Sydney Morning Herald

Jamie Durie is one of those designer garden designers you see on TV – all gleaming teeth and trendily tousled hair and boyish charm. But boy can he design gardens! Modernists will love the hard-edged landscapes where disciplined arrangements of sculptural plants are set off against impressive water features and dramatic lighting. Jamie insists that it's possible for do-it-yourselfers to achieve the same results and to this end has included plans and plant lists and details such as the paint colours and fabrics and pebbles used.

JANE TURNER
NZ House and Garden

THE SOURCE BOOK
Jamie Durie

Compiled by Sebastian Tesoriero

A Sue Hines Book
ALLEN & UNWIN

First published in 2004

Copyright text ©Jamie Durie 2004
Copyright photography ©individual photographers

A Sue Hines Book
Allen & Unwin Pty Ltd
83 Alexander Street
Crows Nest NSW 2065
Australia
Phone: (61 2) 8425 0100
Fax: (61 2) 9906 2218
Email: info@allenandunwin.com
Web: www.allenandunwin.com

National Library of Australia
Cataloguing-in-publication entry:
  Durie, Jamie.
  The source book.

  Bibliography.
  ISBN 1 74114 428 0.

  1. Gardens – Design. 2. Landscape gardening – Australia.
  3. Landscape design – Australia. 4. Gardening – Equipment
  and supplies – Directories. I. Tesorerio, Sebastian. II.
  Title.

712.6

Designed by Nick Mau
Typeset by Pauline Haas and Nick Mau
Printed in Australia by BPA Print Group
10 9 8 7 6 5 4 3 2 1

PHOTOGRAPHERS' CREDITS

Harriette Rowe: all photographs in the Plant section, except for the photographs by Brent Wilson (listed below); garden photograph on pages 85; all photographs on page 92.

Brent Wilson: photographs of plant numbers 01, 09, 14, 16, 18, 19, 21, 36, 39, 44, 46, 64, 65, 71, 74, 80, 85, 91, 102, 116, 118, 120, 123, 126, 129, 134, 140, 164, 186, 204, 226, 241, 246, 250, 253, 261, 292, 324, 325, 328, 329, 335, 339, 362, 363, 368, 369, 373 and 391.

The photographs that appear on pages 6 and 7 are from the author's private collection.

Siobhan Way: page 21

Simon Kenny: pages 30, 31, 51, 52, 53, 75, 104, 105, 130, 131, 153

David James: pages (ii), (viii), (ix), 20 (lower left), 29 (lower right) 42, 43, 64 (lower left), 65, 81, 123, 141, 163, 169

Motoo Nakagawa: pages 86, 87, 88 and 89.

The author and publisher thank the suppliers who generously provided their images and details for inclusion in the Materials & Products section.

CONTENTS

ACKNOWLEDGEMENTS (vii)

INTRODUCTION (viii)

THE PATIO TEAM {ix}

GROUND WORK 1

PLANTS 9
    HOW TO USE THE PLANTS SECTION 10
    ROOFS & CEILINGS 13
    WALLS 23
    DIVIDERS 33
    FLOORS 45
    ACCENTS 55
    FILLERS 67
    PAINT 77
    WATER 83

MATERIALS & PRODUCTS 91
    HOW TO USE THE MATERIALS & PRODUCTS SECTION 93
    WALLS 95
    FLOORS 107
    OVERHEAD 119
    PAINT 125
    LIGHTING 133
    FURNITURE 143
    ORNAMENTS & ACCESSORIES 155
    POTS & PLANTERS 165

RULES OF ENGAGEMENT 170

HOW TO USE THE SUPPLIER SECTION 171

PLANT DIRECTORY 172

PLANTS: SUPPLIERS 184

MATERIALS & PRODUCTS: SUPPLIERS 191

INDUSTRY ASSOCIATIONS 194

INDEX 196

ACKNOWLEDGEMENTS

Putting this book together was never going to be an easy task but I was supported by a network of extremely talented friends that I am lucky enough to be working with, and without them you would not be holding this beautiful book in your hands.

Without a doubt, one colleague and friend has facilitated the demystification of all the technicality that surrounds good garden making with effortless composure. Our knight in shining armour, Sebastian Tesoriero has painstakingly harvested an incredible amount of information to surround a well thought out, handpicked selection of plants and materials. Seb, you were built for this project – you are not only methodical and meticulous but your attention to detail and your commitment to creating this beautiful template is an achievement that leaves me in awe.

PATIO's right hand, Harriette Rowe – you have executed the vision of this book with pure precision, not only through the lens of your camera but also with every aspect of your generous, courteous and selfless demeanor with every person you touch. Your loyalty and commitment to this project and all other aspects of PATIO are something that I feel blessed to be around. You have managed to turn textbook-style photographs into pieces of art and as always, you continue to fly the flag of our great PATIO culture with your magnificent professionalism … thank you. Michael Conway and Matthew Fishburn – thank you for lending a hand, literally!

Andrea McNamara – this has probably been the most difficult book so far, however without a doubt you have made this the most pleasurable experience. To pull together such a huge amount of information and compile, consolidate and lay it out elegantly and simply, in such a short time frame, is nothing short of spectacular. Your ability to coordinate everyone involved in this project, with such grace and humour, especially where I'm involved (my Mother wants notes!), is a testament to your character. I can't thank you enough for supporting my ideas and for being so generous with your time to make it all happen.

Nick Mau – who would have thought that a 'reference' book could look so damn hot! You've made all of that valuable information sexy – thank you for your incredible inspiration and supporting my ideas, then laying them out so elegantly in the form of beautiful pages. You've outdone yourself again – what a talent! To Pauline Haas, thanks for making it all fit on the page!

Jennifer Castles – once again you've climbed inside my head and turned my gibberish into poetry. Not only is it easy to understand, but you have succeeded in demystifying the technical side of good garden design. Thank you for being such a joy to work with.

Harriette Rowe, Simon Kenny, David James, Brent Wilson (and Wendy Pritchard keeping him organised) and Motoo Nakagawa – your beautiful photography, attention to detail and passion for the final product just leaps from every page.

Sue Hines – thank you for pushing me to do this, I'm so glad you did. The final product makes me so proud and it's a beautiful combination of everyone's efforts. Your dedication, professionalism, enthusiasm and support are qualities that I treasure. Thanks also to Richard Walsh.

To my beloved team at PATIO and JPD Media – Sebastian, Harriette, Julian Brady, Giselle Barron, Matthew Higginson, Grace Mansour, Brandon Wallis – thank you for your patience with my mad schedule and more importantly thank you for your creativity, passion, dedication and loyalty. Nadine Bush, thank you for waving your magic wand over everything we do here – anything it seems to touch just looks beautiful! Belinda Everingham – where do I start! I can't thank you enough for keeping my life in order, thank you for the joy you bring to this office, your incredible professionalism, amazing input into all of my projects no matter how left field they are, and the smiles you bring to the faces of everyone that you deal with. I'd be lost without you.

Sue Forrester, whose advice shaped the direction of the book, thank you.

Stephen Wells – your guidance, support, knowledge, experience and friendship means the world to me. Mike Curnow – thank you for your support and your diligence. Paul Haftke & Annette Park – thank you for giving us all the tools to build great things.

Chris Giannopoulos, Daniel Hill, Greg Hooton and Martin Jolly – thank you for your support, understanding and your guidance.

The Botanic Gardens Trust, Sydney and The Royal Botanic Gardens, Melbourne – thank you so much for your support. It's an honour and a privilege to work so closely with you all. Alpine Nurseries, Collectors Corner, Gardenworld, Plantmark, Lynbrook, Plants Central, Lotus Water Gardens, Daisy's Garden Supplies – thank you for allowing us to photograph your plants and products, and for helping me spread the word about this fantastic industry.

Mary, Joe and the de Pellegrin family – thank you for letting us into your wonderful home. To the Tesoriero family – Angela & Sam, Cath & Nancy, Sebastian & Wendy – thank you for letting us into your beautiful gardens.

All at Channel Nine – David Gyngell, Michael Healy, Stuart Clark, I can't thank you enough for your constant support and guidance. The fantastic publicity team at Nine, thanks for everything. Don and Marea Burke, Rick Spence, Niall Mason, Steve McCann, Scott Cam, Jody Rigby, Nigel Ruck, my beloved Blitz family and all of the team at CTC Productions – thanks for your ongoing support. David Barbour & Julian Cress – thank you for teaching me a whole new art of making television. ACP – John Alexander, Pat Ingram and the rest of the team, thank you for your ongoing support and kind words.

Mum, Dad, Chris, Michelle, Taylor and the rest of my family and friends, thank you for your encouragement and infinite love. To my beautiful Siobhan – thank you for your patience, your guidance, the laughs, your tenacity, your valuable input to all aspects of my life, your loyalty and most importantly your love.

INTRODUCTION

One of the hardest things I found in writing *Patio* and *The Outdoor Room* was deciding what had to be left out. Each time I wanted to include more hands-on information, but there was never enough time or space to do it justice. My publisher would end up saying 'That's another book, Jamie' … well here, at last, is *that* book!

The Source Book is a great companion to the previous two titles, but it's also been written to stand alone as a general resource for anyone interested in creating a garden. And this time it's purely practical: more of the what, how, when and where of designing your own outdoor space and a simple, straightforward but extensive guide for you to access the many resources we've discovered over the years at PATIO.

Every garden is different, and our aim is to encourage you to make decisions based on a sound analysis of the peculiar, complex and unpredictable conditions that are unique to your space. We hope to give you a range of tools to come up with creative solutions in designing a garden that is beautiful, practical and an expression of your personality that makes you deeply proud.

There's no doubt that using imagination and inspiration is a vital – and let's face it, probably the most enjoyable – part of designing a garden. The reality though, is that a very large portion of the work is just slogging away at problem-solving: identifying what your wants and needs are; assessing how much of that is achievable in your particular space; and then using, choosing and combining all the building blocks to bring you the best possible results.

Hopefully, this book will help you in that process and give you the confidence to tackle as many of the tasks involved as you can. Not only will it save you money in the long run, but also give you a stronger sense of ownership and that oh-so-satisfying feeling of personal pride in a job well done. Remember, Rome wasn't built in a day, so don't be disheartened when things go wrong. Accept that it will take a fair bit of trial and error, learn from your mistakes, and move on. And be sure to know your limitations. Excavation, clearing, drainage, set-out, footings, soil preparation and so on can get very technical and usually require special skills, so make sure you get good advice and don't hesitate to bring in the professionals (like the PATIO team!) if it all gets too much.

In the next 200 pages we'll be focusing on plants and materials for contemporary Australian outdoor spaces: how to choose them, how to use them and where to get them. And it wouldn't be a PATIO book without more photographs of the latest gardens designed by myself and the team, a collection of sumptuous images to get those creative juices flowing.

Okay, some might think it's strange that we're giving away our trade secrets, but what's the point of putting all that inspiration out there without providing the tools to bring your dream garden to life? So open your eyes to what's around you every day – plants in your local park, sculpture at the art gallery, shapes and colours of the bush, the beach, the playground, the lights in your favourite café – anything and everything that fires your imagination. Then pick up this book and we'll show you how to bring that inspiration home …

I'd love your feedback on *The Source Book* – let me know what you think when you visit the websites below to find out the latest on what we're up to.

Happy gardening …

Jamie

www.jamiedurie.com
www.thesourcebook.com.au

THE PATIO TEAM

JAMIE DURIE
director/principal designer

As the founder of PATIO, Jamie is an innovative and contemporary designer who does not adhere to one particular style. He has a Diploma of Horticulture and Landscape Design and is an affiliate member of the Australian Institute of Landscape Architects, a board member of The Royal Botanic Gardens Foundation and a member of the Australian Institute of Horticulture Inc. He takes inspiration from the natural environment and the challenges of a client brief to create designs which apply new technologies to traditional materials. He believes that the landscape should be an extension of architecture, that the boundaries of exterior spaces are blurring with living spaces. Jamie has accumulated 19 awards in landscape design both in Australia and internationally, and designs hotel and residential gardens all over the world. His energy and passion for design is endless. Jamie has a media career as the host of Australian television's highest rating lifestyle programs *Backyard Blitz* and *The Block*. He is also the author of two best selling books, *PATIO: Garden Design and Inspiration* and *The Outdoor Room*.

SEBASTIAN TESORIERO
landscape designer/horticulturalist

Seb brings an enthusiasm for detail and order to the job of keeping PATIO organised. He has been largely responsible for collating the vast amount of information needed to put a source book of this kind together and then working out how to deliver it to you, the reader, in a user-friendly way. As a Supreme Court officer and a government lawyer with a passion for plants, Seb shifted into landscape design after collecting a Diploma of Horticulture while studying side by side with Jamie. His broad plant knowledge enhances the creativity of PATIO's planting designs, and he oversees many of our contracts and other written documents. Maintaining the office systems keeps the lawyer in him well satisfied.

HARRIETTE ROWE
senior landscape designer/in-house photographer

Harriette is a fourth-generation architect and has completed a Bachelor of Science (Architecture) and a Bachelor of Architecture. She has also completed a Diploma of Horticulture and Landscape Design with Jamie and a course in Architectural Photography at the Australian Centre of Photography. Her primary roles at PATIO are as senior designer, client consultant and contract liaison, event and media coordinator and photographer. Apart from her impeccable design ability, she remains a huge part of PATIO's soul. Harriette has been responsible for taking 350 of the 400 beautiful plant images you see in this book. She has an artist's eye and is passionate about what she does. Her previous published photographic endeavours appear in books including *PATIO: Garden Design and Inspiration* and *The Outdoor Room*.

ABOUT PATIO

Conceived, founded and lead by Jamie Durie, PATIO provides landscape architecture and design for commercial and domestic outdoor spaces in Australia and internationally. The business has enjoyed enormous success, winning nineteen design awards and exciting interest in its exploration of modern and traditional materials combined with natural plant forms to create a wide range of landscapes.

The PATIO team, handpicked to provide a broad skill set, prides itself on listening carefully to the client's brief and then delivering a unique design which takes into account human interaction with the environment. The team works collaboratively with architects, town planners, engineers and other specialist consultancies and constantly investigates new materials and techniques, thereby keeping the product fresh and effective.

PATIO creates quality designs that inspire, are cost effective, functional and last for many years.

www.patio.com.au

JULIAN BRADY
general manager/senior landscape architect

Julian holds a Bachelor of Arts in Environmental Science and a Bachelor of Landscape Architecture (Honours) and is currently studying a Masters in Business Administration. He is an Associate Member of the Australian Institute of Landscape Architects and a member of the Australian Institute of Landscape Designers and Managers. He brings to PATIO a solid background in business, project and environmental management having worked on environmental, residential, commercial, industrial and government projects of varying scales in Australia, Spain, Thailand and Malaysia. Julian is the driving force behind our elaborate portfolio of work.

GISELLE BARRON
landscape architect

Giselle completed an Interior Design Certificate in 1997, a Bachelor of Landscape Architecture (Honours) in 2001 and is currently studying for a Bachelor of Law. Giselle has made an incredible contribution towards our award winning portfolio.

MATTHEW HIGGINSON
landscape architect

Matthew completed a Bachelor of Landscape Architecture in 2000 and worked as a landscape architect on projects in the UK, Paris, Portugal and Spain. He is a valuable part of our team offering a broad range of skills in CAD and design.

GRACE MANSOUR
landscape architect

Grace has completed both an Associate Diploma in Architectural Drafting and a Bachelor in Landscape Architecture (Honours). Having worked on projects in China and New Zealand, she is one of PATIO's rising stars, working in Malaysia, Spain and Australia.

SIOBHAN WAY
marketing/administration

Siobhan has been instrumental in developing new business and is involved in marketing and events coordination.

BELINDA EVERINGHAM
communications manager

Belinda is the primary point of contact for client liaison and project management and keeps Jamie's hectic schedule between design and media on track.

NADINE BUSH
group creative director

Nadine has been part of PATIO culture since its inception. She now floats between JPD Media and PATIO, overseeing all creative content and production.

GROUND
WORK

Before you get down to choosing a plant or landscape product and finding where to get it from our directories, have a serious think about the job at hand and your precious land and where it's at. Whether you're overhauling the whole yard or just wanting to add a small touch, consider carefully what you're doing and what's the right thing for the job before you buy anything. Preparation is everything.

If you are completely blitzing the backyard, you'd need a certificate in horticulture (at the very least) to scratch the surface of landscape design theory, practice and process. This doesn't mean you can't do the lion's share of the planning and work required, depending on the complexity of your vision. To follow is a basic context to using the landscape elements contained in this book, and some starting points to help you on your way.

Good planning will speed up every step in the process of creating a great garden. It will also give you a better understanding of the tasks involved, a time line as to what stage the various jobs will be completed, and how much they will cost. So take your time to think it all through; do your research and talk to as many experts as possible. Then ask yourself why you're doing this? What do you want to achieve? What do you need? What do you want? How do you want to use your garden? How much maintenance can you afford? What do you like and what do you hate?

Write it all down and there you have it: your brief. These are your guiding principles, the constitution. They will influence your decisions, give you clarity when you're uncertain or losing the plot, or you've forgotten what you're trying to do, or you're trying to do too much …

Site survey

This is where you need to become an outdoor detective and no stone can be left unturned! Look hard at your land and collect its personal information. Get to know it and its relationship to the world. Take measurements and do a mini-survey, noting all the existing elements such as boundaries, steps, levels and slopes, trees and larger plants, underground pipes and overhead wires, neighbouring buildings and vegetation, views, focal points and unsightly blemishes.

Collect as much information as you can about the conditions on your site, and what it's exposed to. Find where north is and think about which areas of the garden get sun, and when and how long they get it. Think about how much rainfall you get on average and watch where the rain runs or collects. Keep in mind the type of climate and temperature range you can expect, where winds come from at different times of the year and whether they are salty winds.

All these details will be really important when you come to the job of choosing plants and products. Choosing won't just be a matter of buying what you like the look of. You want to be confident plants will be happy to grow in and materials will withstand the conditions you've got on offer.

The bit of personal information about your land that is particularly vital to plants is about the soil. Get your hands dirty and do tests for soil structure and PH level and find out exactly what sort of soil you have. To tell whether it's acidic or alkaline soil, buy a PH testing kit at any nursery. To determine the structure do a simple ribbon test: pick up a handful of soil, wet it in your hand and then create a sausage and slowly feed a ribbon of soil between your thumb and forefinger, out of your hand. If the soil is too high in clay, your ribbon will be over 50 mm long. If the soil is too high in sand, you will not be able to make a ribbon.

Good drainage is vital to most gardens and a good soil structure will ensure water and nutrients can flow freely through the soil. If you're really keen, a copy of Kevin Handreck's 'Gardening down under: a guide to healthier soils and plants' will help you get to know your soil intimately.

Constraints and opportunities

Also look for all the good points and possibilities of your site: a pleasant view (from a narrow glimpse to a panoramic sweep), a borrowed landscape (such as the thick foliage of a neighbouring tree), or an indoor room that can be opened up to blend with the outdoors. The trick is to take advantage of these assets and design a landscape that draws attention towards them.

Then be brutal and look for the liabilities of your land too. These come in the form of unsightly buildings visible from the yard, neighbouring windows infringing on your privacy, ugly fences, a relentlessly buffeting wind-tunnel, unhealthy trees, bland, boxy sheds, and garbage and compost bins. These will all work against you so solutions must be found in your design by relocating, screening or deleting them altogether.

Function

What are the most common duties and recreational pursuits that you and the other users of the garden will want or need from the landscape? Will people dine, lounge, swim, meditate, work or even shower there? Now be a bit more specific about what you need: somewhere to have breakfast in the morning sun, somewhere for the kids to play footy, somewhere to hang the washing, somewhere to entertain people. The site survey and analysis will suggest where the appropriate places might be. For instance, the breakfast area should go where there's morning sun, the kids' turf where the land is flat, the clothesline could be good in a sunny spot near the laundry but even better exposed to drying winds, and you'd do well to have the entertaining close to the kitchen.

Vision

Close your eyes and start to paint your space with shapes. Tall shapes that shut out the building next door or mask that unsightly fence, impressive shapes that make a statement or draw the eye, and dense shapes that give the garden a sense of abundance. How about experimenting with levels? Maybe you could raise a section to catch a better view or sink a section to create intimacy and intrigue. Now open your eyes, grab that pencil and paper, and make a rough sketch. No matter how amateur it turns out, this impression can be an invaluable tool when it comes to formulating and communicating your design ideas.

Rules and regs

Your property has a legal relationship to the world. Check with the local council for how building and development regulations affect your site and consult them for their approval (where needed) once you have a plan.

Sense of place

Before the shovel hits the soil you have to make a decision on garden style. Look at the broader context of the setting of your house. If it's located on the edge of a national park, the sense of place suggests you go with an informal design, indigenous if possible. Look at the house itself. If you live in a Federation house, a cottage garden might go well whereas a modern architect-designed house might lend itself to a harder, sparser landscape. Look at the furnishings in the house, its décor, the art on the walls, the materials used. The clues are everywhere. Are there particular fabrics or colours you are drawn to? Are you understated, or into lavish ornamentation, or loud, vibrant colours? How is the interior of the house arranged? Is it built for comfort or is it built for show? Does the family hang out around the kitchen or do they hang out in the lounge room? Where does the main energy in the house derive from and what kind of art or colours run through the house? All of these details will help you create a workable palette of forms, colours and textures.

The principle of sense of place is partly a helpful guiding constraint and partly a liberating opportunity. It involves the responsibility of choosing a style for your garden that fits into its environment but it also allows you the freedom to create a garden that has a style, feeling and special identity all of its own, or of its owner.

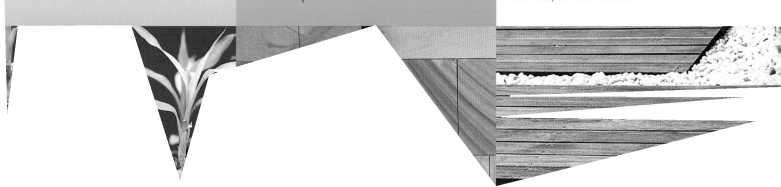

Consistency

Once the decision has been made, stick to it and do it properly. In trying to conjure the sense of a particular place and how it should feel, thoroughly plan the entire composition so that the garden style is sustained and the garden remains unified.

When guests come to your home, the garden should not only fit into its environment, it should also leave your guests with a unique sense of where they have been. Instead of copying something you've seen on holiday or in a book to the last detail, adapt it so your garden is also an expression of yourself. Your garden should have a feel of its own.

Access

Where will the points of entry and exit be? Are you aiming for a meandering journey or will people need to get from A to B as fast as possible? Are there areas where children should be discouraged from playing? Do pool fences, retaining walls or balustrades impinge on the flow of traffic, and if so, how can you overcome this? And are gates, doors and pathways well lit for safety's sake?

Environment

How will the choices you make affect not just your own environment now but that of your children and your children's children? The approach you take in designing your garden can help ease the pressure that development puts on our natural resources.

The recent droughts have sounded the warning bells and taught us a lesson in preparation and planning. Now more than ever, the question for every household shouldn't be whether or not to have a rainwater tank, but where it should go and how much it should hold. Do your research with the local council and have a look at all the wonderful new tank options on the market – there's even one that doubles as a fence!

Grey-water recycling is definitely starting to catch on. Re-using your laundry and bath water in the garden rather than sending it down the drain is a great way to beat water restrictions. And on the subject of drainage: a successful landscape should soak up as much water as possible, so have a look at the 'Floors' section in Materials to give you some good ideas.

What about putting nutrition back in the soil? A worm farm can be a great source of fertiliser for your garden. All it takes is a few steps out the back door with your veggie scraps and a small initial outlay. Worm farms chew through garbage significantly reducing your waste output, and producing a potent, well-formed combination of castings that is a wonderful plant food.

Maybe the lights you install could be solar to help conserve our energy resources. And designing with plants that will grow happily in the natural conditions of your site without much need for fertilisers and pesticides will keep more of those chemicals out of our ecosystems.

Your yard is full of environmentally friendly possibilities. Find spaces and clever ways to incorporate some of them into your plans.

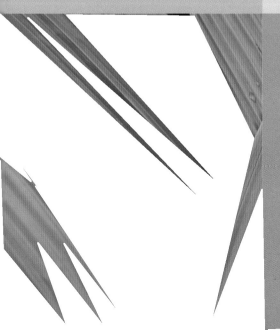

Check list

→ An irrigation system is like an insurance policy that pays priceless dividends.

→ Mulching is an absolute necessity no matter where you live.

→ Put some effort into getting the drainage right. We should all be aiming to retain as much water on site as we can.

→ Be sure to treat pests and diseases as they occur before they get out of hand and wreak havoc.

→ No matter how small your space, be prepared to do a little weeding, a little composting, a little pruning and a little fertilising.

Maintenance

There's no such thing as a maintenance-free garden. Plants, just like people, need love and attention, and if you have any doubts then get a professional to write you a month-by-month hit list of the basic tasks required throughout the year. Decisions you can make in the plant selection stage will greatly affect the amount of upkeep, so be practical and ask yourself if you can provide the level of care that your proposed garden needs. As for the hard stuff, bear in mind that materials like timber decking and furniture need a regular feed of oil to prevent splitting, drains and rills can do with a regular clean out, water features need de-scaling, and mould and mildew forming on any surface should be nipped in the bud before it gets out of hand.

Details

Now it's time to put the flesh on this basic skeleton of a plan: think about how to create these spaces and elements; what they feel like, look like, what they consist of. How do you want to define the spaces – walls, screens or dividers or a combination of all three? Do the spaces have overhead cover? What is the floor made of? How do you want to treat a blank wall: paint, cladding, ornament, lighting, or perhaps a climbing plant? You may have a focal point that needs a feature. Do you prefer statuary, sculpture, lighting, a water feature, or a contrasting accent plant?

This is when this book really comes in handy giving you the goods to explore materials, colours, textures, effects and how they will successfully do what the design needs them to do. It will inform you of the available palette and guide you in the discipline of weighing the considerations when you select and ultimately purchase.

Designing for others

If someone asks you to design a space for them, and you're not a qualified landscape designer, think carefully about what you're taking on.

As designers we all use a combination of theories and tried and tested rules to ensure that whoever looks upon our work will appreciate our efforts, not just now but for many years to come. Successful design is not just creating a combination of plant forms, architecture and structure, it's about balance, harmony, subtlety and accessibility. This can only be achieved with a sound and informative brief from the owner of the garden and a skilled and sympathetic collaborator. At the end of the day, half of being a good designer is about being an astute listener.

If you are designing for an exclusively personal domain, then you need only to cater for your own individual tastes. But if this is a garden to be enjoyed by family and friends – or even a more public space which is constantly being looked upon with fresh eyes – then all of your adventurous choices in terms of plants, materials, scale, integration and overall design, needs to be accessible and acceptable to a wider audience.

USEFUL PLANT REFERENCES

These books also make great gifts.

Gardening Australia's Flora – The Gardener's Bible, ABC Books, Australia, 2004

Botanica: The illustrated A-Z of over 10,000 garden plants, Random House Australia, 1999 (out of print and getting hard to find)

Botanica's Trees & Shrubs: The illustrated A-Z of over 8500 trees & shrubs, Tony Rodd (Chief Consultant), Random House Australia, 2001

Royal Horticultural Society A-Z Encyclopedia of Garden Plants, Christopher Brickell (Ed.), Dorling Kindersley, London, 2003

Australian Native Plants: Cultivation, Use in Landscaping and Propagation, 5th Edition, John W Wrigley & Murray Fagg, New Holland Publishers, Australia, 2003

IDEAS ARE EVERYWHERE – WHEREVER I GO, I TAKE PHOTOS OF COLOURS, PLANTS, SURFACES, TEXTURES, PATTERNS, PEOPLE – ANYTHING THAT CATCHES MY EYE. THESE ARE MY VISUAL MEMORIES, AND THEY'RE REALLY IMPORTANT WHEN IT COMES TO WORKING OUT WHAT I WANT IN DESIGNING OUTDOOR SPACES.

PLANTS

Plants are – and always will be – the heart and soul of every outdoor living space. First and foremost, when it comes to planting, your selection of the right specimens is a crucial part of the process. Where the plant will be placed and how much care you can give it will dictate your choice. Get this right and the hard part's over.

A good place to start is to do your own research. Check out what works well in your local park, botanic gardens or nursery and see if there are any garden tours listed in the newspaper. Don't be afraid to ask questions as you go. The staff at garden centres and nurseries, park rangers, tour guides – basically anyone with a green thumb – are (usually) more than happy to chat and pass on advice.

Then there's the wealth of knowledge to be found in books. Books like 'Botanica' are a good investment and the better quality garden guides can be most helpful, but let's face it, you're already off to a great start with 'The Source Book'!

At PATIO, our plants aren't just chosen because we like the look of them: one of the main priorities is that they serve a structural function. That's why we use structural terminology like roof, floor, divider, wall and so on to categorise plants in the following sections. In this way you'll focus on looking for plants that perform that particular primary function (though you'll often find certain plants popping up in more than one category), so if you need a plant to use as a wall or floor or screen, just go straight to that section.

The second step – and a hallmark of all good planting design – is to look for a plant in that section that will grow well in its place. This is where such elements as dimensions and habit, light, temperature, water needs, soil fertility, salt tolerance and so on come into play. Sounds too technical? Well don't worry, we've got some nifty little horticultural symbols to guide you. They are explained on page 10.

There's a short character profile on each plant to help you in your research and ultimate selection. Once you've made a decision, note the plant number and look it up in the Directory starting on page 172 which will tell you where you can purchase it. Easy! Or take your list down to the local nursery and eyeball the staff.

If you're still finding it hard to narrow down your choice, it's time to apply more detailed design considerations to the final contestants. Ask yourself which plants best suit your garden theme. What's the overall effect you're after? Are particular colours important? Is seasonal shade an issue (i.e. deciduous to let winter light through or evergreen for all-year-round cover)? Do you have a preference for native or exotic plants? Does it matter if the sap is poisonous? (Very important with little kids around.) How quickly does it grow? Will it make a mess on the surface beneath? The plant character profiles will help you with these considerations.

Finally, do you like it? No point in putting in something that fits the bill function-wise, but that you can't stand the sight of. Mind you, this is never the issue for us at PATIO. Spiky, gnarled, blobby, spindly, clumped, bulbous – you name it, we think there's a place for all of them.

HOW TO USE THE PLANTS SECTION

There are thousands of plants to choose from and it was hard to know where to start and even harder to know where to stop. In the end, we included the plants we've found to work well in PATIO designs. In the right place, they can create the kind of architectural effects often found in contemporary landscapes. The details we've given about each plant relate to the broad design style to which they are suited.

Your climatic zone only tells you so much about the conditions on your site – like the temperatures and average rain falls that can be expected over the region. In reality, conditions within a climatic zone can vary dramatically and quickly. One side of a hill can be dry while the other side is moist and the bottom a complete bog. Even within your own backyard, there'll be different micro-climates. Some areas get more sunlight than others. Low-lying, open areas might get frost which other parts don't. You're not positioning a plant in a climatic zone, you're planting it in a particular spot in your yard. And no-one knows more about what's actually happening there than you.

We've designed the horticultural symbols to guide you through the plant growth's basic requirements: light, temperature, water, and nutrient including salt exposure. The symbol indicates what levels or ranges the plant prefers. If you want more detail about a plant's requirements, have a look the books listed on page 5.

light

The 'photo' part of photosynthesis. Plants make and store their own food but most are fairly business-like about doing this – no light, no synthesis in the plant factory. Different plants have adapted to working best with different mood lighting. We've categorised 4 types of light levels:

 HIGH SUN
Exposed to the sun for most of the time it's up, including the late morning and afternoon hours when sensible Australians aren't meant to be in the summer sun.

 SUNNY
Lots of direct sun but not in the late morning and afternoon hours.

 LOW SUN
Direct but soft early morning or evening sun, or direct winter sun when it's lower in the sky, or dappled sun for the whole day.

 SHADY
Little or no direct sun.

temperature

Plants also down tools when it gets too hot or cold. More extreme temperatures will destroy their cells – just like sunburn or frostbite. You'll be wasting money unless the micro-climate suits your plant's limits.

They might be starting to sound fussy but plants can be adaptable and forgiving. They don't have their own fixed and absolute temperature range so we've used 4 grades to indicate their different temperature preferences.

 ALWAYS WARM
T-shirt weather all the time

 NO FROST
Gets cold but frosts are unusual

 LIGHT FROST
Light frosts are to be expected

 HEAVY FROST
Heavy frosts are to be expected

water

Water is another element of photosynthesis. A thirsty, wilted plant has shut down production and growth. If it gets a drink, it will resume work; if left longer, it could desiccate and die.

Water is an element that could be modified to suit your plant selection by using irrigation or drainage, but doing either will cost money and resources. It's more practical and economical to select your plants according to the site's natural moisture conditions.

Moisture levels are affected by rainfall, runoff and irrigation, and how well the soil holds on to water. Flat, clayey soils will stay moist longer than sloping and sandy soils. It's the condition of the soil your plants will be rooted in rather than rainfall levels that you're looking at. We've defined 5 different categories.

 DRY
Soil is dry for extended periods

 DRY PERIODS
Irregular soil moisture

 MOIST
Constant soil moisture

 BOGGY
Poorly drained or flooded soil

 WATER
Aquatic conditions

nutrient and soil

Nitrogen, phosphorus, potassium, calcium and various other nutrients are the ingredients from which plants produce food. Some plants grow healthily only on rich diets while others prefer lean meals.

Native plants are adapted to the natural soil character of your area, which in Australia is typically old, tired and thin. But these days soils in most gardens have already been excavated, scraped, compacted, cultivated, fertilised, imported or conditioned at some point.

Nutrient levels and soil condition are site factors that should be modified to some extent. Some soil preparation – like cultivating deeply and adding organic matter – goes a long way to getting plants established and performing well, while improving efficient penetration and water use. But there are issues about how much soil and fertiliser can and should be imported.

The inter-relationship of soil fertility, texture, structure, pH, profile and drainage is a science in itself. We'll remind you which plants prefer naturally fertile or improved soil conditions by marking them with the following symbol:

The following two symbols indicate a useful tolerance some plants have to conditions found in many gardens of our coastal cities.

S [1] **FRONT LINE**
Direct exposure to salt wind and air

S [2] **SECOND LINE**
On or near the coast but protected from direct exposure to salt wind and air

The symbols tell you the requirements for the plant's wellbeing.

This number defines the plant in the directory that starts on page 172. You will find where to get this plant in each state in Australia.

The shape of the plant. See right, for description.

The measurement of the plant at maturity.

001

Abies spp. **FIR** This conifer comes in many shapes, colours and sizes but especially offers geometric structure and blue-grey leaf colour for large gardens with a formal or Asian theme. Big specimens will create dense shade in the landscape. **50m x 10m**

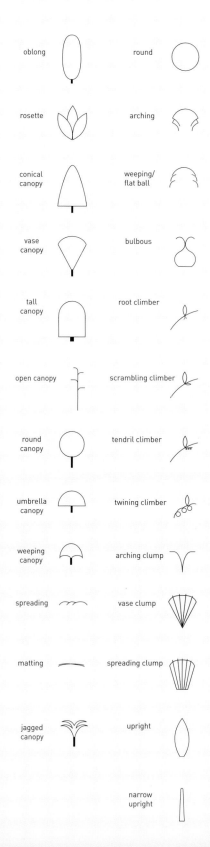

canopy
living
filtering

alfresco

shelter

cosiness

ROOFS & CEILINGS

Shade is a must in the Australian climate. Pergolas, awnings, sails and trellises are wonderful for instant overhead protection, and you'll see a lot of them about, especially in public places. But there's something really special about a living shelter. If space and growing conditions allow, take a moment to imagine yourself swinging lazily in a hammock or reclining on a lounge gazing up through fronds of green or a canopy of natural dappled light. Then read on!

A big tree is what we would characterise as a roof: tall, strong and wide spreading. These are major natural structures that affect the character of our suburbs and have an impact on our fauna and ecosystems. Large evergreen specimens have permanent canopies but the low sun can get underneath when you need it to warm the yard in winter. Deciduous trees filter the light when the sun is high in summer and shed their cloak to let through the winter sun.

Many people are reluctant to take on a big tree because of bad press. First there's the fear of roots interfering with cables, pipes or building foundations. Plumbing's come a long way – we now build PVC, not terracotta, pipes. Then there's the danger of dropping branches on heads or leaves in the gutters, for example. But like any plant, it's a question of finding the right spot – you just need to take a bit more care locating it.

If you require something less robust, check out the smaller trees that work as a ceiling more than a roof. These are the varieties that enclose a space, making it more intimate by providing an overhead frame that visually defines all or part of the outdoor area.

Once you've identified the function of your tree, consider the quality and density of the shade you're after. Some trees cast heavy shade while others are more open. Deciduous trees lose their leaves at different times in the season. Whether it is evergreen or deciduous don't forget that either type will drop leaves, from a light spatter to a thick blanket. It's part of nature and makes great mulch.

Then there are aesthetic qualities. Think about the trunk shape, and the colour and texture of its bark. And consider the sensual pleasures of a tree that can be found over the seasons: the sight and fragrance of delicate spring blossoms, the taste of perfectly fresh, ripe fruit, the blaze of autumn leaves, the tangy aroma of gum leaves, especially after a rain shower.

If trees are not your thing, or you don't have the space to accommodate them, then don't forget climbers and vines can work in just the same way as trees. You'll find them in the Paint chapter, starting on page 77.

All climbers will initially need a structure of some sort (pergola, arbour, loggia or portico) to provide support. Of course the bougainvilleas and wisterias of the world can be trained to eventually stand up by themselves, but they require a lot of patience (about 15 to 20 years) to reach their full potential. Be ruthless with pruning and keep them under control or they can take over.

As a general rule of thumb, exposure to sun in the cooler months is desirable so if you don't mind a bit of seasonal sweeping up (nothing good comes easy) the deciduous types let those precious winter rays shine through. Then when you need protection in the summer, their once naked stems have been 're-born' with a fresh blanket of luscious leaves. Some great players in this category are wisteria and *Vitis vinifera* (ornamental grape).

001

Abies spp. **FIR** This conifer comes in many shapes, colours and sizes but especially offers geometric structure and blue-grey leaf colour for large gardens with a formal or Asian theme. Big specimens will create dense shade in the landscape. **50m x 10m**

002

Acacia baileyana **COOTAMUNDRA WATTLE** Heavy seeding and widespread planting means this native is becoming weedy in its own country. Grey leaves and masses of bright yellow winter flowers are too beautiful not to use — safely away from bush areas. 'Purpurea' has purple-red new leaves. **7m x 7m**

003

Acacia binervia **COASTAL MYALL** A canopy of sickle shaped blue-silver leaves gives this native the feel of an olive tree but with the bonus of fragrant, light yellow flowers and dark, furrowed bark. Fits comfortably in Mediterranean and coastal designs. **15m x 10m**

004

Acacia elata **CEDAR WATTLE** The creamy yellow balls of fragrant flowers appear among the dark, ferny foliage in summer. A long-living native wattle and forest tree, appropriate in tropical, Asian and Mediterranean garden designs. **20m x 12m**

005

Acer palmatum **JAPANESE MAPLE** A primary element in Asian garden designs. Various cultivars of this deciduous tree feature cooling limy, purple or variegated five-fingered leaves which fire up into brilliant autumn colours in areas where autumn is chilly. **5m x 4m**

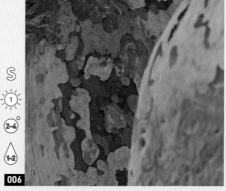

006

Angophora costata **SYDNEY RED GUM** Sheds messy flakes of bark in spring and suddenly drops branches but these are only reasons to be careful in finding a place for this large iconic tree with gnarled, salmon and grey limbs. **25m x 15m**

007

Araucaria bidwillii **BUNYA BUNYA** The domed form of this native conifer seems integrally related to historic houses. Few spaces are large enough; where the large cones dropping and pointy leaves aren't a hazard. But shouldn't be forgotten altogether. **30m x 15m**

008

Araucaria heterophylla **NORFOLK ISLAND PINE** An instantly recognisable silhouette, especially in beach suburbs. A warm climate alternative to large northern hemisphere conifers for those gardens where there's room. The low horizontal branches frame a view beautifully. **45m x 15m**

009

Arbutus unedo **STRAWBERRY TREE** Twisted branches with cinnamon coloured flaky bark, leaves like a bay laurel, pink-white urn-shaped flowers from autumn and rough, round fruit, red when ripe. Not a big tree or a quick grower so suited to small gardens. **8m x 7m**

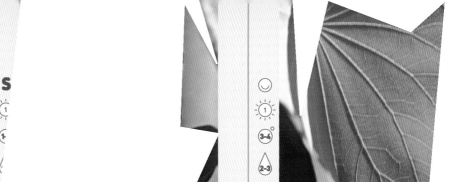

012

Archontophoenix alexandrae **ALEXANDRA PALM** Grey trunk slightly bulbous at the base and ringed up to a bright green crownshaft. For formal designs, plant in rows, or looser designs in groups. The Bangalow Palm, *A. cunninghamiana*, is green rather than white under its leaves. **15m x 4m**

Banksia integrifolia **COAST BANKSIA** A good native tree to sit under and look up at the woolly white under each dark green leaf. Fragrant lemon-white flowers appear for the first half of the year — in Australia. It tolerates strong salt winds. **15m x 15m**

Bauhinia variegata **ORCHID TREE** Butterfly leaves and light to purple pinks, or white orchid flowers for tropical or Asian designs. The cooler its winter conditions, the more leaves are lost and sun let in. *B.* x *blakeana* with purple-pink flowers is more evergreen. **10m x 10m**

013

014

015

Betula pendula **SILVER BIRCH** Loved for its white bark, yellow autumn leaves and purple winter haze of drooping branchlets. Adapted to, and looks best in, group plantings. Cultivars of differing habits and colouring. Try *B. nigra* the 'Tropical' or 'River Birch' in warmer areas. **15m x 8m**

Brachychiton acerifolius **ILLAWARRA FLAME TREE** Can't be missed when flowering — which happens more reliably in grafted plants. A deciduous native tree appropriate for tropical or Mediterranean themes, though a lawn of the fallen flowers has an Asian feel. **15m x 8m**

Brachychiton rupestris **QLD BOTTLE TREE** Deciduous native with ferny foliage held above a trunk that gets fatter and funnier the older the tree gets. Flowering isn't much of a show but is followed by canoe-shaped pods. Try it in Asian or arid gardens with space. **10m x 6m**

016

017

018

Buckinghamia celsissima **IVORY CURL FLOWER** A tall native rainforest tree but much smaller when domesticated. Can even be trained as a screening shrub. Long, milky flower brushes in late summer and glossy leaves make a dazzling tropical or Mediterranean effect. **12m x 9m**

Callistemon viminalis **WEEPING BOTTLEBRUSH** Furrowed patterns of the bark are a feature of this native tree often overlooked for the weeping habit and red brush flowers. Try 'Dawson River', 'Hannah Ray' or 'King's Park Special' where there are wires overhead. **10m x 5m**

Calodendrum capense **CAPE CHESTNUT** Dense clouds of dark, glossy leaves set off pink clusters of orchid-like flowers from late spring. A sheltering canopy for cooling shade though it will thin and lose leaves in winter under conditions at the cool end of its range. **10m x 10m**

019

Castanospermum australe **BLACK BEAN** A fire of yellow to red flowers along the branches from late spring is inflamed by the sight of parrots getting drunk on its nectar. A native for shading tropical, Asian or Mediterranean schemes but not where falling pods will find heads. **12m x 12m**

020

Citrus cultivars **CITRUS** Loved by pests as much as by people but worth the effort to keep them in good health and fruiting well. Careful selection must be based on not only which fruit is desired but on the conditions of the site. **5m x 5m**

021

Elaeocarpus reticulatus **BLUEBERRY ASH** Fragrant, white fringed bell flowers from mid-spring, then blue berry fruit. 'Prima Donna' is pink. Flashes of reddish new and old leaves. For tropical Mediterranean or Asian designs. Use the upright bushy form of this native tree as a wall. **8m x 5m**

022

Eucalyptus citriodora **LEMON SCENTED GUM** Nobody cares that botanists now reckon this isn't a *Eucalyptus* but a *Corymbia*. A big native tree, that drops branches and is becoming weedy. Too beautiful not to be used although careful consideration must be given to its placement. **30m x 15m**

023

Eucalyptus ficifolia & hybrids **RED FLOWERED GUM** Grafted & hybrid cultivars overcome the species' problems of erratic flower colour & limited range. 'Summer Beauty' is pictured. Look for 'Summer Glory', 'Summer Red', 'Summer Snow' & 'Orange Splendour'. **8m x 8m**

024

Eucalyptus haemastoma **SCRIBBLY GUM** Screwy trunk with mottled and scribbly bark is characteristic of this native tree. Lots of light through its thin canopy of blue-green leaves. Looks good in clumps as an informal element in arid and Mediterranean designs. **12m x 10m**

025

Eucalyptus maculata **SPOTTED GUM** Another naughty, iconic tree. From NSW and Queensland, it is only for the biggest landscapes where branch drop and self seeding are not a risk. Individual trees stay narrower and look good planted in a group. **35m x 25m**

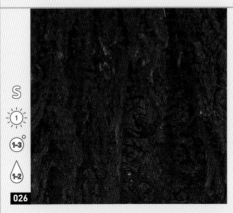

026

Eucalyptus sideroxylon ssp. *sideroxylon* **MUGGA IRON BARK** Leaves are variably blue-grey-green and the flowers unpredictably white, pink to red some time between late autumn and early spring. The bark is usually near-black and furrowed on a straight tall trunk. **25m x 10m**

027

Fraxinus angustifolia 'Raywood' **CLARET ASH** The leaves are finer than the 'Golden Ash' and dark green then red-purple in autumn. As ever, best autumn colouring comes under cooler conditions but tolerates more heat and drier conditions than many deciduous trees. **20m x 12m**

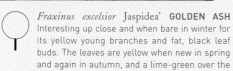

028

Fraxinus excelsior 'Jaspidea' **GOLDEN ASH** Interesting up close and when bare in winter for its yellow young branches and fat, black leaf buds. The leaves are yellow when new in spring and again in autumn, and a lime-green over the rest of the season. **12m x 12m**

Ginkgo biloba **MAIDENHAIR TREE** Slow to mature height, which is substantial. Apple green leaves turn yellow in autumn. Even better if the garden design allows space below the tree for the yellow fallen leaves to remain as a beautiful carpet. Cultivars of different form. **30m x 10m**

030

Gleditsia triacanthos 'Sunburst' **GOLDEN HONEY LOCUST** A deciduous tree, colourful even in warmer areas. Ferny leaves are yellow when young in spring and again in autumn; lime-green the rest of the season. Tolerant of difficult conditions and fast-growing to create an irregular canopy. **15m x 12m**

031

Gordonia axillaris **GORDONIA** Slow-growing small tree. Can be kept trimmed to a screening shrub at the expense of beautiful patchy orange-brown trunks. Autumn to winter flowers are a show on the tree or carpeting the ground, but are slippery on wet hard surfaces. **5m x 4m**

032

Jacaranda mimosifolia **JACARANDA** Plant where there will never be need for pruning which encourages uncharacteristic erect shoots. Place where fallen flowers can be left to extend the show. Winter sun might get under its branches but leaves retained through winter may provide unwanted shade. **15m x 15m**

033

Lagerstroemia indica **CREPE MYRTLE** Fits comfortably into any landscape style. Graceful spreading shape, twisted low-branching trunk, mottled bark, prolific flowering and autumn leaf colour. Modern hybrids come with a broader habit and flower colour range and improved disease resistance. **8m x 6m**

034

Liriodendron tulipifera **TULIP TREE** Green tulip-shaped flowers with an orange maple leaf pattern on each petal are showy up close but indistinct in the landscape. 'Aureo-marginatum' has leaves with a yellow margin. 'Fastigiata' has narrower form. **30m x 20m**

035

Macadamia tetraphylla **MACADAMIA** Dense native tree with dark, prickly leaf whorls flushed bronze when young. Masses of long, pink or white chains of fragrant flowers in spring. Hard-shelled nuts follow as will cockatoos. Plant where nuts and birds can make a mess below. **15m x 8m**

036

Magnolia denudata **YULAN MAGNOLIA** Pure, white chalice flowers provide fragrance when the branches are bare in the middle of winter. Delicate new shoots are then vulnerable to frost. Integral to Asian designs, but not out of place in Mediterranean or tropical schemes. **10m x 8m**

037

Magnolia grandiflora **BULL BAY MAGNOLIA** Beautiful dark, shiny leaves with rusty fur below and fragrant flowers from late spring. Overall effect is of a brooding tree that grows slowly to eventually create dense shade. Suits formal, Asian, Mediterranean and tropical schemes. **20m x 20m**

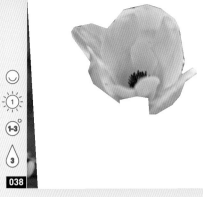

038

Magnolia x *soulangeana* **MAGNOLIA** A hybrid developed into cultivars with fragrant flowers in all shades between the white and purple of the two original ancestors. Flowers from late winter through spring depending on the cultivar. Usually another light flush in summer. **7m x 7m**

039

Malus x *floribunda* **JAPANESE FLOWERING CRABAPPLE** Broad canopy for summer shade and winter sun. Small, red-yellow fruit falling isn't dangerous but could be annoying in some positions. Dark pink flower buds in early spring fade to pink and white. A delicate Japanese or Mediterranean effect. **4m x 6m**

040

Melaleuca quinquenervia **BROAD LEAFED PAPER BARK** Layers of papery bark and lots of cream flowers especially in autumn. Provides a not too dense shade for Mediterranean and coastal designs but plant only where roots will be away from paths, pipes and services. **20m x 6m**

041

Melia azedarach **WHITE CEDAR** A native tree for summer shade in tropical, Mediterranean or Asian designs. Fragrant white and purple flowers in late spring. Yellow fruit brightens up bare winter branches but is toxic. The hard seeds are dangerous on hard surfaces. **10m x 9m**

042

Mespilus germanica **MEDLAR** Slow-growing into a tree with tortured-looking, sometimes thorny branches. Creates deep shade before leaves colour in autumn, then fall. Flowers like a white rose in late spring and edible brown fruit. For Mediterranean and Asian designs. **6m x 8m**

043

Olea europaea var. *communis* **OLIVE** Very Mediterranean design element. Can be trained as a screen or a topiary in formal designs. Quite informal as a tree, developing gnarled trunk and branches with age and suckering from the base. Don't plant where fruit drop will annoy. **7m x 7m**

044

Parrotia persica **PERSIAN IRONWOOD** Broad, deeply veined leaves are bronze when new and turn through various autumn colours before browning and falling. Mottled flaking bark on multiple, low-branching trunks. Slow-growing to having a canopy for summer shade. **10m x 6m**

045

Pittosporum undulatum **SWEET PITTOSPORUM** Problematic native being ornamental, fast-growing, fragrant, food-providing for fauna but weedy even in its natural habitat. Cream flowers in spring and berries in autumn and winter in tropical and Mediterranean designs. **8m x 6m**

Plumeria obtusa **WHITE FRANGIPANI** The success of this tree is more confined to areas with tropical conditions where it's reliably evergreen. But can be used over the same range of garden schemes as *P. rubra*. Intensely fragrant flowers over a long season. **8m x 6m**

Plumeria rubra **FRANGIPANI** *P. r.* var. *acutifolia* is the white one with yellow centres. It's getting easier to get cultivars in reds, pinks and various mixes as well. Fits into tropical, Mediterranean, Asian and succulent designs. This deciduous tree keeps its leaves well into winter. **8m x 6m**

Podocarpus elatus **PLUM PINE** This native conifer can also be kept trimmed as a screen or sculpted into other shapes as an accent in formal designs. As a tree, it suits tropical, Asian or Mediterranean garden schemes where it will create dense shade. **15m x 10m**

049

Prunus cerasifera 'Nigra' **PURPLE LEAFED PLUM** Simple, soft pink flowers are among the early blossoms to appear. But the real show is the dome of red-purple leaves that makes a canopy of dappled summer shade and looks wonderful lit up by sunlight. **8m x 5m**

050

Pyrus calleryana 'Capital' **CAPITAL CALLERY PEAR** With upright form like a scaled-down poplar, this deciduous tree can also be used as an accent in formal, Asian and Mediterranean designs. Fine white spring blossom turns into small brown fruit while the leaves turn into autumn colours. **12m x 4m**

051

Robinia psuedoacacia 'Frisia' **GOLDEN ROBINIA** Eye-catching lime foliage, turning deep yellow in autumn, can jar with subtle bush colours. This deciduous tree can still be comfortably placed in an Asian, Mediterranean and tropical garden theme. Some wisteria-like, fragrant white flowers in spring. **15m x 10m**

052

Sapium sebiferum **CHINESE TALLOW TREE** A deciduous tree that colours well outside the cool conditions usually required for an autumn show. Colour can vary so select for leaf colour in autumn, if possible. Sits well in Asian designs. Becoming weedy in some areas. **10m x 7m**

053

Schefflera actinophylla **QLD UMBRELLA TREE** Often starts as a pot plant. If a home needs to be found in the ground, don't plant close to anything the roots might damage. Drooping leaf fingers form a textured canopy with red antennae flower spikes from late summer. **12m x 6m**

054

Schinus molle var. *areira* **PEPPER TREE** So adaptable that, across the country, most of us have experienced the magic of sitting under the weeping, ferny canopy of a Pepper Tree. Peppercorns are best in drier areas but the roots are always a threat to pipes. **15m x 10m**

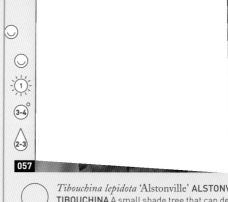

055

Spathodea campanulata **AFRICAN TULIP TREE** A beautiful big tree for tropical designs but only if the hazard of its branches becoming hollow and brittle with age is carefully managed. Also weedy and banned from sale in Qld and restricted in WA. **20m x 15m**

Stenocarpus sinuatus **QLD FIREWHEEL TREE** A natural choice for tropical schemes but would also fit comfortably into Mediterranean or Asian designs. The firewheels appear mostly through summer and autumn. Fairly upright and will need training to create a shade canopy. **12m x 6m**

Tibouchina lepidota 'Alstonville' **ALSTONVILLE TIBOUCHINA** A small shade tree that can develop a dense, rounded canopy that doesn't produce much mess. The vivid flowers appear from late summer through autumn. Good for a tropical effect or in a Mediterranean design. **6m x 4m**

058

Tristaniopsis laurina **WATER GUM** This native tree ultimately develops a good shade canopy, with some bronze-red tints, suitable for almost any garden theme. Vigorous roots but slow to mature. Often multi-trunked with flaky bark. Flower clusters appear from late spring to early summer. **15m x 8m**

Ulmus parvifolia **CHINESE WEEPING ELM** Gets autumn colouring but is not entirely deciduous in mild winters. Variable in habit and presence of attractive brown-orange and grey mottled bark. 'Churchyard' has mottling and reliable weeping habit. 'Todd' is more regular and upright. **15m x 10m**

Washingtonia spp. **COTTON PALM** Slow in making their mark on a skyline but stately when they do. The two species both keep a skirt of dead leaves around their trunks. *W. filifera* is shorter and stouter to 15m. *W. robusta* has a thinner, taller trunk. **25m x 8m**

Other plant options for roofs & ceilings

WALLS 63-*Acca sellowiana* 64-*Acmena smithii* 71-*Calliandra haematocephala* 72-*Camellia sasanqua* 81-*Ficus benjamina* 82-*Grevillea* 'Moonlight' 85-*Hibiscus tiliaceus* 87-*Laurus nobilis* 88-*Luma apiculata* 90-*Metrosideros kermadecensis* 96-*Photinia glabra* 'Rubens' 104-*Strelitzia nicolai* 105-*Syzygium australe* 106-*Syzygium leuhmannii* 108-*Thuja plicata* 109-*Viburnum odoratissimum* 111-*Waterhousia floribunda* ACCENTS 225-*Acer platanoides* 'Globosum' 237-*Bismarckia nobilis* 241-*Camellia japonica* 242-*Citrus x meyeri* 'Meyer' 254-*Dracaena draco* 258-*Dypsis decaryi* 263-*Ficus lyrata* 267-*Howea forsteriana* 279-*Pandanus tectorius* 281-*Phoenix canariensis* FILLERS 306-*Angophora hispida*

Other plant options for pergola ceilings:

PAINT 362-*Akebia quinata* 366-*Bougainvillea* cultivars 367-*Cissus hypoglauca* 369-*Clytostoma callistegioides* 375-*Pandorea jasminoides* 378-*Passiflora coccinea* 381-*Thunbergia grandiflora* 383-*Vigna caracalla* 384-*Vitis vinifera* 'Alicante Bouchet' 385-*Wisteria sinensis*

If you look hard enough, you'll find a plant that will provide any shape, size and habit that you need to create a particular effect. For example, sometimes a natural canopy can be the best roof or ceiling you could possibly choose. This is one of my favourite places in Indonesia – we ate lunch and dinner under the tree every day. It's a great example of how clever design has made the most of the natural surroundings.

enfolding

sanctuary

nurturing

warming

intimacy

retreat

Spatially, walls are about creating rooms: either providing boundaries for entire yards or creating rooms within yards. They set the perimeter of the space, form the backdrop to all that's within, and can play a big part in dictating the theme of the room. Plants that work as walls grow tall enough and dense enough to close a space off visually because they can't be looked over or through.

If you need a reasonable level of security or a strong safety barrier, it's easy to assume that only hard man-made substances are appropriate to the task. On the contrary, some of the sturdier plant options are more than up to it, so consider the idea of a green wall. A well established arrangement of hedging shrubs can be some of the best security around: difficult to climb, impossible to walk through and they'll grow as high as you require. You'll find a range of suitable plants in this section including tall shrubs, clumping palms, bristling fortresses of bamboo and large, dense-growing perennials.

First establish how high you need your wall. How thick do you need it to be? Do you have the luxury of at least a metre for your walls to spread? If so, then shrubs like photinia, camellias, hibiscus, oleander, and various conifers and viburnums can all do the job. When space is an issue you will need to look for a more vertical habit in your plant, such as Sacred Bamboo or cultivars of pittosporum, Lady Palm. Also decide if a neat, clipped hedge is the right look for your design or whether your wall should be less formal.

Some plants give you the effect of a light screen rather than a solid wall. Although tall, these plants are less substantial specimens with thinner trunks or more sparse or delicate leaf cover that allow light in and air to circulate. They are great for introducing the 'suggestion' of intimacy and privacy which is perfect for spas and outdoor showers. And because of their semi-transparent qualities, they interact more with the elements: filtering sunlight into delicate patterns and rippling gently in the breeze.

A green wall doesn't give you the instant gratification of a brick or timber structure that can be erected in a couple of days, so you must take growing time into account. Some may take several years to reach full maturity, but like any long-term investment, the rewards are substantial.

Abelia x *grandiflora* **GLOSSY ABELIA** Leaf colouring and the calyces left after the summer-to-autumn flowers give this shrub an all-over bronze effect. Good for Mediterranean and Asian garden themes. 'Francis Mason' has golden variegation. 'Sunrise' has gold-cream variegated leaves with red autumn tints. **2m x 2m**

Acacia vestita **HAIRY WATTLE** A weeping habit and hairy grey-green triangular leaves give this native shrub a soft look and year-round interest that could be used in Mediterranean and Asian designs. The golden-yellow flowers appear through spring. **6m x 5m**

Acca sellowiana **PINEAPPLE GUAVA** Grey underneath, the dark leaves of this adaptable shrub or small tree gives it a Mediterranean feel but its red and white summer flowers have a tropical look. Produces edible fruit in autumn. **3m x 3m**

064

065

066

Acmena smithii **CREEK LILLYPILLY** Shrubby native tree with glossy leaves flushed red when young that make a good background in tropical and Mediterranean designs. Fluffy white flowers in spring are followed by edible white, pink or mauve fruit. 'Hot Flush' is smaller with bright pink new growth. **10m x 8m**

Acokanthera oblongifolia **WINTER SWEET** Neatly arranged foliage and wonderfully fragrant pink-tinged white flowers in spring followed by fruit that looks like olives. Good for Mediterranean and Asian garden designs. All parts of this plant are poisonous. But so many plants are. **5m x 3m**

Alpinia zerumbet **SHELL GINGER** A robust ginger that can take a bit of cold. Drooping sprays of pink-tipped, waxy white buds open fragrant and yellow with red markings. 'Variegata' is shorter and has leaves dramatically splashed with light yellow. **3m x 1m**

067

068

069

Backhousia anisata **ANISEED MYRTLE** A big bush tucker rainforest tree with white flowers and wavy leaves that smell of aniseed. Smaller in cultivation and can be kept to a dark, drooping background shrub in a tropical or Asian garden design. **12m x 9m**

Backhousia citriodora **LEMON SCENTED MYRTLE** Can be trained as a tree or a shrub but the flowers and leaves of this native myrtle smell of lemon rather than aniseed. Snowball flower-heads appear near Christmas and remain interesting after the stamens have fallen. **8m x 8m**

Bambusa multiplex cultivars **HEDGE BAMBOO** Different heights and habits, culm diameters, colouring or striping available. 'Goldstripe' is gold on green and 'Alphonse Karr' (pictured) green on gold. Ferny leaf forms of this clumping bamboo are better for screening. **10m x 3m**

S

070

073

S

074

075

S

076

077

S

078

Banksia ericifolia **HEATH BANKSIA** Fine leaves & warm coloured flowers in cooler months make a native shrub with Mediterranean & tropical effects. 'Limelight' has lime leaves & 'Golden Girl' has blue-green with gold flowers. 'Burgundy' for burgundy flowers. **5m x 5m**

Calliandra haematocephala **POWDERPUFF TREE** Can be pruned into a small tree but the knobby buds and flowers, in reds of different intensity or white, set on ferny leaves have a stronger impact when kept trimmed to shrub size. **6m x 4m**

Camellia sasanqua **SASANQUA CAMELLIA** Can make a small feature tree but quicker repeat-planted and manipulated into a glossy screen. Less formal than the japonicas, there are centuries worth of cultivars to choose from for flower colour, form and time. For acidic soils. **8m x 5m**

Cephalotaxus harringtonia **JAPANESE PLUM YEW** A conifer that doesn't get too big but can be used for screening in formal or Japanese garden designs, even in humid, wet or low light situations. The branches of 'Fastigiata' are upright and crowded. **5m x 3m**

Ceratopetalum gummiferum **NSW CHRISTMAS BUSH** Pretty masses of cream starry flowers are followed by the real show. Cultivars have reliable sepal colour including 'Albery's Red' dark red; 'Wildfire' from pink to red; 'White Christmas' in green-white while 'Christmas Snow' has cream blotched leaves. **5m x 3m**

Chamaerops humilis **MEDITERRANEAN FAN PALM** Very useful palm that will clump enough — although slowly — to be used as a screen or divider and also bring a tropical effect to garden designs in cold climates. Handsome on its own as an accent. **3m x 4m**

Coprosma repens **LOOKING GLASS PLANT** Leaves so shiny they're unaffected by salt air. Older cultivars have yellow variegations. Newer ones like 'Pink Splendour' and 'Rainbow Surprise' are smaller and as colourful as crotons. 'Karo Red' and 'Yvonne' have dark bronze-reds. **4m x 3m**

Cupressus glabra **ARIZONA CYPRESS** A conifer that tolerates drought and doesn't mind being down on the coast where it has a columnar rather than conical habit. Cultivars have aromatic leaves like coral formations from blue-grey in 'Blue Ice' to lime-gold in 'Limelight'. **15m x 8m**

x *Cuprocyparis leylandii* **LEYLAND CYPRESS** Conifer for a quick, dense screen in formal, Asian or Mediterranean designs. Regular maintenance is needed. 'Castlewellan' has yellowish foliage aging bronze-green. 'Naylor's Blue' is blue-grey. 'Leighton Green' is pictured. **35m x 8.5m**

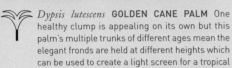

079

Dypsis lutescens **GOLDEN CANE PALM** One healthy clump is appealing on its own but this palm's multiple trunks of different ages mean the elegant fronds are held at different heights which can be used to create a light screen for a tropical design. **9m x 6m**

080

Euphorbia pulcherrima **POINSETTIA** Usually seen as a small feature in a pot disposed of after losing its Christmas colour. When not artificially forced, this show comes in winter with red, pink, cream, white, marbled and double bracts with a tropical or Asian effect. **4m x 4m**

081

Ficus benjamina **WEEPING FIG** Features as a potted topiary and attractive as a tree. Safer kept small and with roots restricted. Screening for Asian and tropical themes. 'Baby Ben' is naturally smaller. 'Bushy Prince' is denser, as is 'Bushy King' but with yellow leaf edges. **20m x 15m**

082

Grevillea 'Moonlight' **MOONLIGHT GREVILLEA** A native hybrid for a small tree or screening shrub with a Mediterranean effect. 'Sandra Gordon' with grey-green leaves & yellow flowers has a similar feel. Try 'Honey Gem' with dark leaves & gold flowers for tropical themes. **4.5m x 3m**

083

Gunnera manicata **GIANT RHUBARB** Especially dramatic where the giant, rough-textured leaves will be reflected in water, but only for reliably moist or boggy positions where the leaves will have enough space. Appropriate for Asian and tropical gardens and as a contrasting element in formal designs. **2.5m x 4m**

084

Hibiscus rosa-sinensis **HIBISCUS** From all the tropical over-bred flowers available, choose just one hybrid for tall, vigorous and bushy form that will make a good screen. These shrubs can flower well yet still look scrappy unless given favourable growing conditions. **3.5m x 3.5m**

085

Hibiscus tiliaceus **COTTONWOOD** A dense native tree that can be kept as a screening shrub in large tropical or Mediterranean designs. Selections with red-purple leaves are easier to control. Long-flowering but mostly in summer. Tolerates front-line salt winds. **8m x 8m**

086

Juniperus chinensis 'Spartan' **SPARTAN JUNIPER** Its dark, dense, geometric form is a garden accent. But as a fast-growing, textured conifer, it can be used in formal, Mediterranean or Asian designs as a screen that won't need as much trimming as other bigger conifers. **5m x 2m**

087

Laurus nobilis **BAY LAUREL** Can make a tree or feature topiary but inevitably suckers into a fuller shape. Often kept as a mobile divider in troughs in Europe. For formal or Mediterranean gardens, 'Aurea' has gold-green leaves when grown in plenty of sunlight. **8m x 4m**

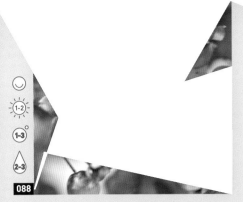

088

○ *Luma apiculata* **TEMU** Aromatic screening plant for formal or Mediterranean schemes. Small white flowers in spring and summer followed by purple-red winter fruit. Can be grown as a small tree with mottled bark. 'Glanleam Gold' is smaller with cream and pink variegation. **8m x 4m**

089

○ *Megaskepasma erythrochlamys* **BRAZILIAN RED CLOAK** A shrub for a tropical effect with its broad, prominently veined leaves and plumes of crimson-red bracts with white flowers from late autumn into winter. Makes a quick-growing and dense screen. **3m x 2m**

090

○ *Metrosideros kermadecensis* **KERMADEC POHUTUKAWA** Not quick to take on the shape of a tree so easy to keep as a shrub for screening. Suitable for coastal and Mediterranean themes. Variegated cultivars with strong yellow in the centre of the leaf or on the margin. **8m x 5m**

091

○ *Michelia figo* **PORT WINE MAGNOLIA** Dense, slow shrub that can be shaped as a topiary accent. Purple-cream flowers in spring are noticed for their strong, sweet smell. Cultivars and hybrids available that are more compact or with whiter, more open flowers. **4m x 3m**

092

○ *Murraya paniculata* **MURRAYA** A valued shrub also trained as a topiary accent or smaller divider. Bright green new leaves on dark older leaves with flushes of citrus flowers, especially in late spring and autumn. Suits Mediterranean, Asian and tropical designs. **3m x 3m**

093

○ *Nandina domestica* **SACRED BAMBOO** Not actually a bamboo. Ferny foliage on erect canes in winter with shades of red, purple and yellow for screening in Asian, Mediterranean or tropical designs. 'Richmond' is bushier with many red berries if cross-pollinated. **2.5m x 1.5m**

094

○ *Nerium oleander* **OLEANDER** Of all the poisonous plants in gardens, this one has been singled out for special attention. Characteristic of Mediterranean countries where it is planted widely in public places. Could also be used in tropical, coastal and Asian designs. **4m x 4m**

095

○ *Persoonia pinifolia* **PINE-LEAFED GEEBUNG** A graceful native shrub with upright and pendulous branches and leaves like pine needles. Flower bunches appear in late summer and turn into green berries. Appropriate for screening in Asian or Mediterranean designs. **4m x 3m**

096

○ *Photinia glabra* 'Rubens' **SMALL LEAFED PHOTINIA** Red new growth mostly in spring or after pruning. Flower clusters appear mostly in spring. For formal, Asian or Mediterranean designs. Can also be kept to a lower height as a divider or trained into a small tree. **5m x 4m**

Phyllostachys nigra **BLACK BAMBOO** Culms emerge green but within months darken and turn black if grown in sun. Especially suited to Asian and tropical designs but only after taking serious precautions to prevent escape. An aggressive running bamboo banned from sale by many councils. **10m x 10m**

Pittosporum tenuifolium cultivars **PITTOSPORUM** Leaves in shades and variegations of green, silver, cream and yellow that produce different effects to match house colour and garden theme. Green and glossy for tropical, silvery for Mediterranean. Many lower growing cultivars for dividers. **8m x 4m**

S

099

Plumbago auriculata **PLUMBAGO** Can be trained against a wall or left to spill over. Plant where suckering and vigorous growth won't be a problem. Even with space, it looks better pruned occasionally. 'Royal Cape' is darker blue and less vigorous while 'Alba' is white. **3m x 3m**

100

Punica granatum **POMEGRANATE** Multi-stemmed but not dense deciduous shrub with orange-red funnel flowers from late spring through summer. Fruit like baubles full of jewel-like seeds need a hot dry summer to ripen. A fertility symbol in Mediterranean gardens. **6m x 5m**

101

Rhaphis excelsa **LADY PALM** Another slow, clumping palm that's useful to provide screening down low when other palms have shot upward. The fingers on this palm spread wide and hang elegantly. Also an accent for pots and for an Asian, Mediterranean or tropical feel. **5m x 2.5m**

102

Rhododendron Large Leaf Hybrid **RHODO-DENDRON** Large dark leaves and flower clusters have a tropical feel. Only for acidic soils. Many hybrids available with different peak flowering seasons in spring and in a huge colour range. Some stay small enough for a divider. **4m x 4m**

103

Schefflera arboricola **MINIATURE UMBRELLA TREE** Often an indoor pot plant, but can make a dense screen with enough space in tropical designs. 'Jacqueline' and the smaller 'Madame de Smet' have variegations for a brighter effect. Not for planting where roots can do damage. **4m x 4m**

104

Strelitzia nicolai **GIANT BIRD OF PARADISE** Ultimately a tree with a fan of banana-like leaves on a thin trunk. Unless space is available, better to restrict strong roots and growth within planters or other confined areas. White and blue bird flowers can appear any time. **10m x 5m**

105

Syzygium australe **SCRUB CHERRY** Dense native tree for topiary or screen in most designs. Young leaves flush bronze. Edible fruit follow summer flowers. 'Hunchy', 'Elite' & 'Southern Aussie' get to 5m. 'Aussie Copper' is smaller still. **8m x 5m**

Syzygium leuhmannii **RIBERRY** Drooping pink-red new growth stands out against the green of this native tree. Can be trained as a wall in Mediterranean, tropical and Asian designs. White flowers followed by red fruit. 'Royal Flame' is a smaller cultivar for a divider. **10m x 5m**

Thevetia spp. **YELLOW OLEANDER** Frequently has fragrant yellow or apricot flowers but mostly over summer. Suits tropical, Mediterranean, coastal or Asian designs. Poisonous and weedy under tropical conditions. *T. peruviana* is banned from sale in Queensland. *T. thevetioides* is pictured. **5m x 3m**

Thuja plicata **WESTERN RED CEDAR** A conifer that can be left to grow into a big conical tree but usually kept trimmed into a topiary shape or hedge. A place could be found for it in formal, Mediterranean or Asian themes. Cultivars in many sizes and variegations. **30m x 10m**

109

110

111

Viburnum odoratissimum **SWEET VIBURNUM** Fast, low-branching shrub with glossy, cheery green leaves for background plantings in formal, tropical, Mediterranean and Asian designs. Fragrant, white late spring flowers followed by red berries turning black. Can also be trained into a small dense-canopied tree. **5m x 5m**

Viburnum tinus **LAURISTINUS** Fragrant flower-heads appear from autumn and into spring, followed by blue-black berries on a dense shrub. Appropriate in Mediterranean and Asian designs. 'Lucidum' has shiny leaves. 'Variegatum' is slower with cream leaf margins. **3m x 3m**

Waterhousia floribunda **WEEPING LILLYPILLY** Tall native tree that can be trained as a large screen for formal, tropical, Mediterranean or Asian designs. Weeping branchlets are a show of bronze-red new leaves. Creamy flowers like wattle in summer. Susceptible to leaf damage by psyllids. **20m x 5m**

Other plant options for walls
ROOFS 2-*Acacia baileyana* 16-*Buckinghamia celsissima* 20-*Citrus* cvs 21-*Elaeocarpus reticulatus* 31-*Gordonia axillaris* 43-*Olea europea* var. *communis* 48-*Podocarpus elatus* 107-*Thevetia* spp. DIVIDERS 115-*Agonis flexuosa* 'After Dark' 151-*Ixora coccinea* 153-*Leucadendron* spp. 160-*Myrtus communis* 168-*Pittosporum tobira* 170-*Protea neriifolia* ACCENTS 240-*Callitris columellaris* 241-*Camellia japonica* 263-*Ficus lyrata* 273-*Magnolia grandiflora* 'Little Gem' 291-*Synadenium compactum* 'Rubrum' 292-*Telopea speciosissima* FILLERS 308-*Bauhinia galpinii* 316-*Cordyline stricta* 323-*Elettaria cardamomum*

Instead of overpowering the side aspect of this home, a number of elements were employed to disguise and beautify the built wall without compromising security. Several metres were clad with sandstone tiles, the delicate swirling patterns in the stone emerging as water slides down the face in smooth sheets from evenly spaced emitters. The stone expanse is suddenly broken by foliage as a green wall takes over in the form of Waterhousia floribunda which also serves to soften the hard lines of the adjacent dwelling.

Hugging the pool-side another green wall thrives. This one is lusher and designed for width more than height with cascading fronds of Dypsis lutescens providing colour and texture contrast to the sharp geometric cubes of the brilliant blue tiles.

Large format pavers unify the busy entertainment area and walkways and timber highlights inject a note of warmth wherever possible. Silky smooth on bare feet, they make up a path of pontoons beside mulched beds sprinkled with a liberal dose of Aspidistra elatior and Liriope muscari. Around the pool, timber decking is hinged in places so sections can tip up into a lounge recliner position.

composing

linking

vista

defining

relaxing

framing

Dividers are the next tool you use in partitioning a space. They work like a wall by marking out a space or reinforcing a line – but they're not tall enough to completely hide the other spaces. They create smaller rooms within a big room.

Because their job is to define a space the main thing about these dividers is that they stay in their place and maintain their shape. They are the smaller, compact or slow-growing shrubs–like the Hebes, Pittosporum tobira 'Miss Muffett', and Buxus. They include grassy clumping plants (like Liriope or Pennisetum) and specimens that have a more wandering habit but look their best when trimmed and tidy like Alternanthera dentata and Teucrium fruticans. So if you're wanting to lay out a line, a block, a curve or any other shape you desire, these are the plants you're after.

Using groups of plants to stand in rows or blocks of contrasting foliage colour is one of the hallmarks of contemporary planting design and the more vivid the contrast the better. With green the predominant shade you might go for the subdued greys of Artemisia 'Powis Castle' or Correa alba, or go vibrant with the crimson of Iresine herbstii or limes and golds of Duranta.

Use a row of these dividers to edge a path, form a low hedge or create a series of parterres. In a high-activity space they can direct traffic like witches hats or roundabouts, discouraging jaywalkers and guiding little feet away from no-go areas.

As you'll see from the specimens listed on the following pages, if left unsupervised some of them can grow as tall as a common wall, but these tend to look their best and do their best 'work' when they are kept lower and compact.

Ensure as you go, that you keep the general style and feel of the room in mind when you make your selection. Dividers are part of a whole scheme and need to harmonise visually and stylistically with all the other elements in the garden.

112

113

114

Acacia cognata 'Lime Magik' **BOWER WATTLE** Begging to be fondled, weeping lime foliage rather than flowers is the appeal of this native. 'Mop Top' with aromatic leaves and fragrant, light yellow flowers has purplish new leaves. Good as features in a pot or in Asian designs. **3m x 2m**

Acmena smithii var. *minor* **SMALL LEAFED LILLYPILLY** A native *Buxus* substitute with glossy leaves, coppery when young. Fluffy white spring flowers followed by fruit. Sculpt into shapes as an accent in formal designs. 'Hedgemaster' is smaller and more compact, as is 'Allyn Magic' but with orange new leaves. **4m x 3m**

Aechmea spp. & cvs **BROMELIAD** One plant — with architectural leaves in grey, burgundy through yellow-orange, with or without bands or stripes, and flowers like a firecracker — is enough for an accent. Will multiply itself and can be used massed as a tropical divider or filler. **1m x 1m**

115

116

117

Agonis flexuosa 'After Dark' **AFTER DARK AGONIS** From late winter are not the feature of this form of the native willow myrtle. Leaves are a red-purple that's deepest in full sun and brilliant seen with sunlight coming from behind. **5m x 2m**

Aloe arborescens **CANDELABRA ALOE** Flat rosettes of toothed leaves multiply to provide useful structure or mass to succulent garden designs. The torches of red-orange or yellow flowers are, however, a real tropical touch in winter. **3m x 3m**

Alternanthera dentata cultivars **JOY WEED** Various cultivars with leaves in the purple, burgundy, copper range to make a block of year-round colour that can contrast with or complement a pot, a paint scheme or other plants. **0.6m x 0.6m**

118

119

120

Anthurium spp. **FLAMINGO FLOWER** Handsome specimens alone in a pot, *A. scherzerianum* or *A. andraeanum* can also be massed with their large heart-shaped leaves and red, orange, pink, white or partly green plastic-looking flowers making a show. **1m x 0.7m**

Artemisia 'Powis Castle' **POWIS CASTLE WORMWOOD** A quick-growing, multiple-branching sub-shrub with delicately divided and aromatic silver leaves. Useful for Mediterranean designs and contemporary bands of different foliage colours. Can take some salty air. **0.6m x 1m**

Arthropodium cirratum **RENGA LILY** From a clump of strappy but slightly twisted, agave-green leaves come sprays of starry white flowers with yellow and purple touches in summer which are stunning when massed. Resistant to salt air but watch out for snails. **0.75m x 0.5m**

121

Aspidistra elatior **CAST IRON PLANT** One clump of these curving leaves is an elegant accent on its own but also good massed. Useful for difficult, dry and shady positions in tropical and Asian garden themes. Cultivars come with various creamy-white streaks or speckles. **0.6m x 0.6m**

122

Aucuba japonica **GOLD DUST PLANT** A dense shrub with big, dark, glossy leaves speckled or splashed with yellow, depending on the cultivar. Useful as a *Codiaeum* of the south — for tropical garden designs in cooler climates or gardens with an Asian theme. **2.5m x 2.5m**

123

Banksia spinulosa & cvs **HAIRPIN BANKSIA** Variety in this native shrub for botanists involves leaf margin details. Everyone else will only care that forms come with flowers in golds, oranges, yellows and reds. 'Giant Candles' (pictured) is a hybrid with *B. ericifolia*. **3m x 3m**

124

Berberis thunbergii **JAPANESE BARBERRY** Flowers and fruits in cooler climates only, where autumn leaf colouring is also best. A deciduous shrub with cultivars in purples, reds or limy-gold for leaf contrasts through the season even in warmer conditions. Sharp spines a hazard or security asset. **2m x 2m**

125

Brunfelsia australis 'Sweet & Petite' **YESTERDAY TODAY TOMORROW** Unlike the species, this cultivar is not much of a flowerer. But its round, compact form and neatly arranged, apple-green leaves are useful for formal designs in climates too warm for *Buxus* or *Nandina*. **1m x 1m**

126

Burchellia bubalina **SOUTH AFRICAN POMEGRANATE** Leaves are a serious green but the clusters of orange-red bell flowers with yellow dongers are a party in spring and summer. Easy to manage as it's slow to reach its full size. **3m x 3m**

127

Buxus sempervirens 'Suffruticosa' **DUTCH BOX** There are many other Boxes to do the same job. This is an especially low, slow one for parterres, garden edges or other divisions in a formal garden design. Bright green leaves develop orange tones in cooler seasons. **1m x 1m**

128

Callistemon viminalis 'Little John' **LITTLE JOHN BOTTLEBRUSH** A compact native shrub with a dense cover of two-toned leaves; new shoots a bluish grey-green over dark older foliage. Flowers in a saturated red with gold tips good for tropical and Mediterranean effects. **1.5m x 1.5m**

129

Chaenomeles speciosa **FLOWERING QUINCE, JAPONICA** Blossom on bare thorns. A single plant is a feature in flower in late winter. Suckering stems and spines make an impenetrable thicket for the security conscious. Cultivars available in red, white and various pinks. **2.5m x 2.5m**

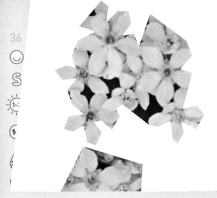

○ *Choisya ternata* **MEXICAN ORANGE BLOSSOM** A bushy relative of the citrus fruits with fragrant, white flowers, mostly in spring. Like the citrus, it demands excellent drainage. 'Sundance' needs protection from the hottest sun. Yellow new leaves turn more green with age. **2m x 2m**

Chorizema cordatum **HEART-LEAFED FLAME PEA** The form of this quick-growing native shrub with wonderfully vulgar flowers can vary so the slender stems lightly scramble, arch or remain compact. The open forms are good for filling, spilling over and container planting. **1m x 1.5m**

○ *Codiaeum variegatum* **CROTON** Noisy enough as an individual accent. Choosing just one of the many cultivars to repeat plant as a divider is enough for a tropical riot. Fine, broad, lobed or divided foliage and variegations in green, yellow, orange, red and white. **2m x 1.5m**

133

134

135

○ *Coleonema pulchellum* **DIOSMA** One of those South Africans that readily fits in with the locals. Fine aromatic foliage is kept more compact with light pruning after the flowers — from winter to spring in shades of pink from almost white to red. **2m x 2m**

○ *Correa alba* **WHITE CORREA** Fuzzy, round leaves and starry flowers from late autumn to spring work well in coastal and Mediterranean themes. Variable native shrub, so *C. a.* var. *pannosa* is more spreading while 'Blush' and 'Pinkie' are faintly pink flowering White Correas. **1.5m x 1.5m**

○ *Crassula ovata* **JADE PLANT** Multi-branched succulent like a miniature tree. 'Tricolor' and 'Hummel's Sunset' have red and yellow colouring. Suitable for pots or cactus gardens. Could be used in tropical or Japanese gardens with its glossy leaves and natural bonsai look. **1.75m x 1m**

136

137

138

Cuphea hyssopifolia **MEXICAN HEATHER** Fine, shiny foliage and masses of flowers in white and shades of pink in late spring and summer. Other cultivars come with golden leaves. Another shrub that fits well with natives or as an edging in a Mediterranean design. **0.5m x 0.6m**

Dietes bicolor **YELLOW PEACOCK FLOWER** Upright leaves more yellowish and refined than *D. vegeta* and it seems to self-seed less. One clump makes an accent but its spreading habit makes a good divider or filler. Flowers appear mostly in late spring and summer. **0.8m x 1m**

Dodonea viscosa 'Purpurea' **PURPLE STICKY HOP BUSH** Leaves are red-purple in sun but turn black-purple then green with shade. Purple-red seed capsules are a summer feature. This native shrub can get high enough for screening. Suits most design themes. **3m x 1.5m**

141

Duranta erecta 'Sheena's Gold' **PIGEON BERRY** Weedy species in warmer climates. Growing cultivars in clipped forms for their colourful leaves rather than the flowers encourages pruning before the orange berries can get into the bush. 'Variegata' and 'Sheena's Lime' come with softer greens. **4m x 4m**

Echium fastuosum **PRIDE OF MADEIRA** Can get tall enough to be a wall and should be given some width to spread. Architectural hairy grey-green leaves in rosettes and striking spires of pinky-blue flowers mainly through spring. Not long-lived but quick-growing. **1.8m x 2.5m**

Escallonia spp. & cvs **ESCALLONIA** A long-flowering shrub with glossy leaves and dense form. 'Apple Blossom' is pale pink and white. 'Hedge With An Edge' and 'Pink Pixie' are smaller and bright pink. Gold leaves of 'Gold Brian' need more sun protection. **3m x 3m**

142

143

144

Euphorbia milii **CROWN OF THORNS** Fascinating in a pot as a feature. Succulent stems have leaves in a spiral only at the tips but are covered in spines. New hybrids in colours and combinations from red, pink to cream. Drought and somewhat salt tolerant. **1m x 2m**

Euryops pectinatus **BRIGHT EYES** Hair on the deeply divided leaves turns them grey and protects this shrub from salt air. Suited on the coast where light reduces the intensity of this sunny yellow. 'Little Sunray' is a compact form. 'Viridis' has green leaves. **1.2m x 1.2m**

Fatsia japonica **FATSIA** Dark, deeply lobed and glossy foliage is a tropical or Japanese element even in cool shady conditions. Counter its open habit by repeat-planting as a screen. White balls of flowers from mid-autumn. Cultivars available with yellow or white variegations. **3m x 3m**

145

146

147

Gardenia augusta **GARDENIA** 'Florida' (pictured) is a classic for bringing fragrance from late spring to autumn. 'Aimee Yoshiba' is larger, 'Radicans' is smaller and prostrate while 'Ocean Pearl' is smaller and compact. 'Veitchii' is upright and dense with many flowers. **1.5m x 2m**

Hebe 'Wiri Mist' **WIRI MIST HEBE** One of many compact *Hebe* cultivars and species to use as a divider. Crowded leaves are interesting year-round — each one with an outline that accentuates the pattern of their arrangement around the stem. White summer flowers. **0.6m x 0.6m**

Hemerocallis Hybrid Cultivars **DAY LILY** Clumps of arching, strappy leaves come in various heights. Not all are evergreen. Mass plant as a filler or a divider. Wiry stems hold a succession of short-lived flowers in various colours and combinations mostly over summer. **1m x 1m**

Hydrangea macrophylla **HYDRANGEA** A deciduous shrub so visual effect as a divider is seasonal. Find a strong cultivar. Vigorous and prolific under favourable conditions. Gives a wet feel to any garden theme and has quite a tropical effect in cooler conditions. **2m x 2m**

Iresine herbstii **BEEFSTEAK PLANT** May need renewing after a few years but is a quick-growing perennial for strong tropical foliage effect. 'Brilliantissima' is more vibrant purple-crimson. 'Aureo-reticulata' has yellow and green leaves with red flashes and stems. 'Purple Lady' is a groundcover. **1.5m x 1.5m**

Isopogon formosus **ROSE CONEFLOWER** Traces of colour and divided foliage provide year-round interest. Sparklers of purple-pink flowers appear in winter to spring and leave behind conical seed heads. Dry, sandy conditions may increase the reliability of this WA shrub in eastern states. **1.75m x 1m**

151

152

153

Ixora Hybrid Cultivars **JUNGLE FLAME** *I. coccinea* with orange-red flowers is a species tall enough for a wall in a tropical or Asian design. The various hybrids appearing are smaller but come in many shades of red, orange, pink, yellow and white. 'Prince of Orange' is pictured. **2.5m x 2m**

Lavandula stoechas **ITALIAN LAVENDER** An aromatic shrub. The species is weedy in some Victorian districts. Many new cultivars in different colours and sizes to be planted with some care. 'Avonview' is purple and compact. 'Willowbridge Wings' is white. 'Somerset Mist' is purple and pink. **0.75m x 1m**

Leucadendron spp. & cvs **LEUCADENDRON** Various South African shrubs suitable for those with native gardens who aren't purists. 'Safari Sunset' with leaves flushed red and red bracts in autumn is often seen as a cut flower. 'Safari Small Strike' is smaller with yellow winter-spring bracts. **2.5m x 1.8m**

154

155

156

Leucophyta brownii **SILVER CUSHION BUSH** A bizarre, tangled mound that can make a feature in a pot or planted as a single specimen in the garden. A native shrub for coastal or succulent garden designs. 'Silver Nugget' is a small, compact form. **0.75m x 1m**

Liriope muscari **LILY TURF** Suitable for Asian, tropical and Mediterranean designs as a floor, filler or divider. Cultivars with violet, pink or white flowers in late summer. 'Variegata' has pale yellow leaf margins. 'Evergreen Giant' is an elegant tall grower. **0.45m x 0.45m**

Lonicera nitida **BOX LEAFED HONEYSUCKLE** Often trained as a topiary accent. Can be planted out and trimmed into dividing shapes in formal, Asian and Mediterranean gardens. 'Aurea' has yellow leaf colouring. 'Silver Beauty' is smaller with silver leaf margins. **3.5m x 3m**

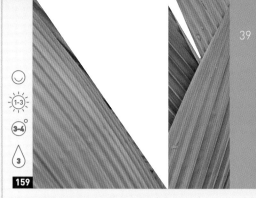

159

Lophomyrtus x *ralphii* **LOPHOMYRTUS** Hybrid shrubs with round puckered leaves that colour strongest in cooler conditions. 'Kathryn' is coppery-red. 'Little Star' is smaller and has a variegation with an overall pink effect. New leaves of 'Black Stallion' (pictured) are red in spring but black-red in winter. **2m x 1.25m**

Loropetalum chinense 'Rubrum' **CHINESE FRINGE FLOWER** Also available as 'China Pink' or 'Burgundy'. Purple-red new foliage turns bronze-olive with age. Feathery flowers appear mostly from late winter through spring. 'Blush' is more compact as is 'Razzleberri' but with strong bronze colouring in the cooler months. **2.5m x 3m**

Molineria capitulata **WEEVIL LILY** Broad arching straps of pleated leaves make a textural display when massed. Especially effective when given more visual depth on a slope. A native perennial for tropical or Asian designs. Leaf edges can get ratty if conditions aren't favourable. **1m x 1m**

160

161

162

Myrtus communis **MYRTLE** A typical shrub of Mediterranean gardens. Leaves are aromatic when crushed. Pink-backed, fragrant white flowers in summer are followed by blue-black winter berries. The species is large enough to use as a wall while 'Compacta' is smaller. **3m x 3m**

Nandina domestica 'Nana' **DWARF SACRED BAMBOO** A geometric ball shape looks odd as a single specimen. 'Firepower' is a compact dwarf cultivar, with red-purple winter colour. 'Moonbay' has lime foliage turning scarlet. 'Gulfstream' has leaves like Sacred Bamboo. 'Harbour Dwarf' is more spreading for a filler. **0.5m x 0.5m**

Odontonema strictum **FIRESPIKE** Broad, bright green leaves over erect cane-like stems contrast strongly with the red flower spikes which appear mostly in autumn but over a long season. A shrub for tropical gardens although it could work well in an Asian design. **2m x 1m**

163

164

165

Pelargonium x *hortorum* **ZONAL GERANIUM** Many hybrids with various flower colours and forms, variegations, leaf shapes and sizes. The red geranium in a terracotta pot is a classic Mediterranean accent. Multiple plant as a divider and tip-prune to improve density. **0.75m x 0.75m**

Philodendron 'Xanadu' **XANADU PHILODENDRON** A well-behaved philodendron, mass-planted as a low divider. The dense clumps of deeply lobed, glossy leaves are a tropical statement, best where the red tinges underneath can be appreciated. **0.9m x 1.2m**

Phlomis fruticosa **JERUSALEM SAGE** Upright stems on a spreading sub-shrub with yellow flowers in summer. The felty grey-green aromatic leaves with crimped, silvery margins reinforce the plant's Mediterranean origin. Prune back each year to maintain shape. **1m x 1.5m**

166

167

168

Phormium cookianum **MOUNTAIN FLAX** Species has arching leaves and is a parent of many hybrid cultivars. Foliage straps in a range of colours and striped combinations, heights and forms. Taller, straighter, more colourful ones are accents. Smaller, grassier, arching ones can be fillers. All can be dividers. **2m x 3m**

Pieris japonica **JAPANESE PIERIS** Bronze-red new shoots age to dark green. Pendulous sprays of white upturned urn flowers in winter and spring. Various cultivars with variegated leaves or flowers in white, pink and red. Only for acid soils. **3m x 2m**

Pittosporum tobira **JAPANESE MOCK ORANGE** Dense and dark shrub with cream-white flowers in late spring. Tall enough to slowly make a wall in formal, Asian, Mediterranean or coastal designs. 'Miss Muffett' (pictured) is smaller, more compact and has less flowers. 'Creme de Mint' is variegated. **5m x 3m**

169

170

171

Pogonatherum paniceum **MINIATURE BAMBOO GRASS** Clumping balls of this grass can be used massed as a filler or groundcover, or kept in a pot as an accent if given enough water. Appropriate to Asian and tropical designs. 'Monica' (pictured) is more lime than the species. **0.6m x 0.6m**

Protea neriifolia **OLEANDER LEAFED PROTEA** High enough for a wall but pruning for bushiness and cutting the long-lasting flowers for the vase should keep it lower. Suited with many natives in style and growing conditions. Also appropriate to Mediterranean and even Asian designs. **3m x 3m**

Punica granatum 'Nana' **DWARF POMEGRANATE** Spiny deciduous shrub spotted with vivid orange-red funnel flowers from late spring through summer followed by fruit like baubles. Also makes a good bonsai specimen or accent in a pot without such training, in Asian or Mediterranean designs. **1m x 1m**

172

173

174

Rhaphiolepis indica cultivars **INDIAN HAWTHORN** The species is wall-size and weedy. Smaller cultivars for Asian or Mediterranean schemes are 'Springtime' to 1.5m with white flowers and 'Apple Blossom' to 1m in deep pink. Smaller still is 'Ballerina' in light pink. **1.5m x 2m**

Rhododendron Indica & Kurume Hybrids **AZALEA** There's one for most conditions except lime soil. Select only from those suitable for the conditions, not for the flowers. Choose for tolerance to heat, cold, humidity, shade, sun or disease and size as relevant. **2.5m x 2.5m**

Salvia corrugata **RIBBED SAGE** The dark leaves of this shrubby sage have an interesting bubbly texture and a rusty felt on the back and up the stems which sets off the blue autumn and winter flowers beautifully. Suitable for Mediterranean garden designs. **1.5m x 1.5m**

Santolina chamaecyparissus **COTTON LAVENDER** An aromatic little shrub like a silvery coral. A good foil for other colours in the garden. Yellow or lemon button flowers held on long, thin stalks appear in summer. Suitable for coastal or Mediterranean garden designs. **0.5m x 1m**

Strelitzia reginae **BIRD OF PARADISE** One thick clump of these paddle leaves and exotic flowers can be an accent, but good to repeat — plant as a divider for a tropical, Mediterranean or Asian theme. Flowers from autumn through spring. 'Mandela's Gold' has orange-yellow instead of orange. **1.5m x 1.5m**

Teucrium fruticans **BUSH GERMANDER** Dense tangle of thin stems and leaves, covered in white hairs that turn this aromatic shrub grey. Lilac-blue flowers in summer. Although the stems are always shooting, it can easily be sculpted into shapes. Suitable for Mediterranean and formal designs. **1.25m x 2m**

178

179

180

Tibouchina 'Jules' **JULES TIBOUCHINA** Dark little shrub with velvety, veined leaves and flowers from late summer through autumn. Can also be used in a pot as a feature when flowering. Good for a tropical effect but could be placed in a Mediterranean design. **0.6m x 0.75m**

Tulbaghia violacea **SOCIETY GARLIC** An essentially evergreen, prolific-flowering bulb that quickly multiplies into dense clumps. When mass planted, 'Variegata' (pictured) will create a whiter overall effect compared to the grey-green leaves of the species. Both smell of garlic and have a Mediterranean feel. **0.3m x 0.2m**

Westringia fruticosa **COAST ROSEMARY** Long-flowering, dense native shrub for Mediterranean, coastal and formal designs. The grey-green foliage effect is even softer in compact, variegated cultivars 'Smokie' and 'Morning Light'. 'Wynyabbie Gem' is a hybrid with lilac flowers. **1.75m x 2m**

181

Zephyranthes candida **STORM FLOWER** An evergreen bulb multiplying quickly into clumps of grassy leaves. Flowers in successive flushes late summer to mid autumn. Good for small gardens and most Mediterranean, tropical, Asian, coastal and succulent themes. **0.2m x 0.2m**

Other plant options for dividers

WALLS 76-*Coprosma repens* cultivars 92-*Murraya paniculata* 96-*Photinia glabra* 'Rubens' 98-*Pittosporum tenuifolium* cultivars 105-*Syzygium australe* cultivars 106-*Syzygium leuhmannii* cultivar FLOORS 186-*Bergenia* spp. & cvs ACCENTS 235-*Astelia chathamica* 239-*Buxus microphylla* var. *japonica* 246-*Crinum pedunculatum* 253-*Doryanthes excelsa* 265-*Hebe albicans* 266-*Hebe* 'Emerald Green' 268-*Hymenocallis* spp. 271-*Kniphofia* spp. & hybrids 275-*Moraea robinsoniana* 283-*Phormium tenax* 285-*Protasparagus densiflorus* 'Myersii' 288-*Spathiphyllum* Hybrid Cultivars 295-*Vriesea* spp. & cvs 298-*Zamia furfuracea* FILLERS 301-*Agapanthus praecox* 307-*Anigozanthos flavidus* hybrids 311-*Carex* spp. 312-*Chamaedorea elegans* 313-*Clivia miniata* 315-*Coprosma* x *kirkii* 319-*Dianella ensiformis* hybrids 320-*Dianella* spp. & cvs 322-*Dietes vegeta* 324-*Eranthemum pulchellum* 329-*Hebe diosmifolia* 331-*Helichrysum petiolare* 336-*Isolepis nodosa* 338-*Jasminum sambac* 'Grand Duke of Tuscany' 341-*Lomandra longifolia* 345-*Neoregelia* spp. & cvs 347-*Ophiopogon japonicus* 350-*Pennisetum alopecuroides* 353-*Poa labillardieri* 355-*Rosmarinus officinalis* 359-*Tradescantia spathacea* WATER 386-*Acorus gramineus* 392-*Juncus usitatus*

This multi-function outdoor room is jam-packed with hard forms so the organic elements need to work hard. Stands of Miscanthus sinensis 'Zebrinus' fulfil the task admirably with graceful arching stems not so much screening as interrupting the lines and adding the suggestion of intimacy appropriate to the act of bathing.

Fresh green clumps of the non-native Miscanthus appear in spring with yellow stripes that darken through the season. All turns a burnished gold as the seed heads shoot skyward and burst like mini-fireworks, hovering for some months as reflections of the curved sweep of the timber lounge. The space looks amazing at night – see page 141.

growing

cultivating

enhancing

tactile

earthed

connection

FLOORS

Lawn is the major player when it comes to green base cover and they're really important when you have kids around. With water restrictions applying almost everywhere, the less water-needy turf varieties are the ones to go for. But lawns are for walking on and we see too many that are fed, watered, mowed and not used.

At PATIO we're far more inclined to use other forms of outdoor 'carpet' to characterise and decorate the horizontal plane where the ground isn't going to be used for play or picnics. The right groundcovers will stay looking better through a dry spell longer than any turf.

What we're talking about here are the plants that spread out over a bit of ground, in a variety of different ways. They are runners, trailers, creepers and prostrate plants that reach out with a net of stems. They include the low spreading shrubs and small perennials and succulents that clump out and multiply in dense groupings.

Floor plants don't just 'cover the slab' but they 'protect the floorboards' while making sure the space stays low and open. They act as a sort of living mulch that keeps the sun and weeds out and the moisture in. Groundcovers discourage foot traffic which has two benefits. These are living, breathing elements of the garden so we are less inclined to step on them if there is a choice between organic or inorganic substance. In this way groundcovers can gently keep the pedestrian flow on a path. And because people are kept away, the ground doesn't become so compacted. Where paved or compacted surfaces lead to runoff and erosion problems, a rug of groundcovers will save your soil from trampling and let more rain soak down into it.

If you do have an expanse of man-made floor, it can be softened with plant 'floors'. Break up a stretch of cobbles or pavers, or fringe a path with streams of green. And disguise any unsightly gaps or crevices with a small matting plant.

Many floor plants shouldn't be restricted to the lower reaches but can be planted in pots, hanging baskets or retaining walls, to spill over the side in a cascade of contrasting colour and texture.

A few final tips: groundcovers come in various heights and spreads, so take this into account when you position them in relation to each other. Also, be aware that some can climb trees and walls which might not suit your space. The more rampant varieties should be confined to planters, enclosed courtyards or isolated beds so that they don't take over. As for the more slow-growing varieties, be sure not to plant them in competition with more vigorous neighbours as they will eventually be starved of the light and nourishment they need to survive.

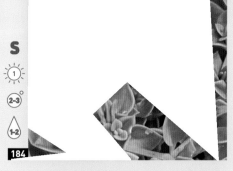

Acacia pravissima 'Kuranga Cascade' **OVENS WATTLE** An adaptable native shrub with interesting sail-shaped leaves and sunny yellow flowers in spring. It can be used as a spillover or groundcover in a design for a Mediterranean or coastal feel. 'Little Nugget' or 'Golden Carpet' for golden leaves. **0.5m x 4m**

Ajuga reptans **CARPET BUGLE WEED** Choose from many cultivars to creep out and cover a constantly moist area or fill between pavers with green, purple-brown, pink or cream variegated leaves. Small spires of purple-blue, sometimes white or pink flowers displayed from late spring. **0.2m x 1.5m**

Aptenia cordifolia **HEARTLEAF ICE PLANT** Bright green leaves and intense pink flowers are equally suited to tropical or succulent garden designs; covering the ground or spilling over walls and tubs. **0.05m x 2m**

185

186

187

Banksia spinulosa 'Birthday Candles' **BIRTHDAY CANDLES BANKSIA** Native shrub like a ready-made bonsai. Several plants can make a mounding groundcover but one is a feature in Japanese designs or a pot. Also try 'Coastal Cushion', 'Cherry Candles', 'Honeypots' & 'Stumpy Gold' in different golds. **0.5m x 1m**

Bergenia spp. & cvs **BERGENIA** Big, round leaves are glossy and evergreen, some flushed with brown or purple. Flowers in light to purple pinks and white in spring. Good for a tropical theme in cooler climates or cottage gardens. **0.4m x 0.4m**

Cerastium tomentosum **SNOW IN SUMMER** Hidden under white summer flowers. White hairs covering the leaves give this plant its silvery, Mediterranean look and help it tolerate coastal conditions but also make it liable to suffocate in humid, wet conditions. Consider also for arid garden designs. **0.2m x 3m**

188

189

190

Chrysocephalum apiculatum **YELLOW BUTTONS** This widespread native perennial differs depending on where it comes from. Use those with greyer leaves and creeping habit in arid and Mediterranean garden designs. Gold flowers appear in late spring and summer. **0.2m x 1.5m**

Cissus antarctica **KANGAROO VINE** As a plant used indoors, this native climber doesn't need much light. Outdoors it can be left to make a jungle of cover under a dense tree canopy. Can and will climb up those trees or a fence if allowed. **12m**

Convolvulus sabatius ssp. *mauritanicus* **GROUND MORNING GLORY** Small grey-green foliage and purple-blue flowers make a good foil in coastal, arid and Mediterranean designs as a ground-cover or spillover plant. The flowers, from late spring to autumn, close in the shade. **0.3m x 1.5m**

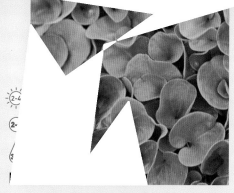

192

193

Dichondra repens **KIDNEY WEED** Matting native useful for a surface block of green or around steppers in dark, moist positions where turf won't grow. Unlike turf it's not really for pedestrian traffic and doesn't need mowing but can be invasive if allowed to spread. **0.1m x 1m**

Doodia aspera **PRICKLY RASP FERN** A small native fern that will spread to make a groundcover even in sunny positions. Fishbone fronds are bronze-red when young. *D. media* is similar but not quite as tolerant of sunny and dry conditions. **0.3m x 0.3m**

Echeveria elegans **MEXICAN SNOWBALL** Lustrous, pearly balls. Widely available and develop into clumps of multiple rosettes which can be useful over the surface of succulent garden designs. *E. glauca* is an alternative producing a more jagged texture. **0.15m x 0.4m**

194

195

196

Erigeron karvinskianus **SEASIDE DAISY** Wiry, fine-leafed stems and sea of flowers over a long season. Suits arid and Mediterranean designs. Species self-seeds readily and can be weedy. Well-behaved cultivars are the compact 'Daisy Spray' and 'Spindrift' and 'LA Pink' with only pink flowers. **0.3m x 0.6m**

Evolvulus glomeratus **BLUE DAZE** Well-behaved spreading or spillover sub-shrub with a Mediterranean feel. Slightly grey-green leaves and blue flowers mix well with other colours. Flowers appear through summer and autumn but they close when not in sunlight. **0.3m x 0.75m**

Gazania Hybrid Cultivars **TREASURE FLOWER** Various colours, combinations and forms in flower, leaf and habit. All salt wind tolerant. Grey leaves and gold, yellow and white flowers for arid, coastal or Mediterranean designs; green leaves and reds, purples and oranges for tropical. Flowers close without sunlight. **0.2m x 0.8m**

197

198

199

Graptopetalum paraguayense **MOTHER OF PEARL PLANT** In succulent or arid garden themes, stems can be allowed to lengthen and spread as a groundcover or spillover. Otherwise prune in winter for dense re-growth. Leaves can readily take root as new plants. **0.2m x 0.8m**

Grevillea 'Bronze Rambler' **BRONZE RAMBLER GREVILLEA** A living mulch or spillover. 'Fanfare', 'Poorinda Royal Mantle' & 'Raptor' have broader leaves. Try 'Copper Crest' or 'Bedspread' for more tropical look. All are natives with blushing new foliage & long season of pinky-red flowers. **0.3m x 5m**

Hedera helix **ENGLISH IVY** Effective low cover around trees if kept from climbing trunks. Cultivars with different leaf shapes, various greens and variegations of yellow, white and purple. Weedy in some areas. Supervise its attachment to vertical surfaces. **0.05m x 5m**

200

Juniperus conferta **SHORE JUNIPER** A thick, weed-suppressing groundcover or spillover and a good foil for other plants in coastal, formal, Mediterranean or Asian designs. A tough conifer that can generally be left alone and tolerates front-line salt winds. **0.5m x 3m**

201

Juniperus horizontalis 'Douglasii' **WAUKEGAN JUNIPER** This creeping juniper has much the same design use as the Shore Juniper but in a different colour. Its blue-grey foliage develops purple-flushed tips in winter. Other cultivars come in other blues, greys and greens. **0.3m x 2m**

202

Kalanchoe pumila **FLOWER DUST PLANT** A plant made for a world with water restrictions as the powdery leaves resent watering. Designer colour combination of the leaves with pink spring flowers to loosely spread in a succulent or Mediterranean garden design. **0.2m x 0.45m**

203

Lamium maculatum cultivars **DEAD NETTLE** Creates less work planted where suckers and spreading stems will be confined. Silver, white, lime and green blotched leaves and summer flower spikes in white or various pinks brighten dark areas in Mediterranean, Asian or tropical schemes. 'Beacon Silver' is pictured. **0.2m x 1m**

204

Lampranthus spp. **ICE PLANT** Succulent sub-shrubs for covering some ground in a cactus or coastal garden design. Smothered in spring flowers. *L. auranticus* is pictured. *L. spectabilis* has grey-blue leaves and bigger, vivid purple-pink flowers. *L. roseus* has pale pink flowers and is short-lived. **0.1m x 1m**

205

Lantana montevidensis **TRAILING LANTANA** Trailing shrub with lavender-pink flowers most of the time. 'Alba' is pictured. Use also as a divider. Spreads broadly enough to spillover, but no signs of being noxiously weedy like its relative. Still, entry to WA prohibited and sale banned in Queensland. **1m x 3m**

206

Mammillaria spp. **PINCUSHION CACTUS** Hundreds of species and forms with patterned spines in a range of colours, textures and combinations. Small accent in pots but ability to fill out and spread by offsets will be important for floors in cactus gardens. **0.5m x 0.5m**

207

Mentha suaveolens **APPLE MINT** Safest to restrict runners by using this herb to fill or cover in a planter or in other confined areas. Good for Mediterranean garden designs and for making tea. 'Variegata' (pictured) has pineapple rather than apple aroma of the species. **0.6m x 1m**

208

Nymphaea spp. & cvs **WATERLILY** A floor for water. Tropical and cold-hardy forms available in a range of flower colours, some fragrant. Some tropicals are day-blooming, some night blooming. Magical anywhere but especially for Asian or tropical schemes. **0.3m x 3m**

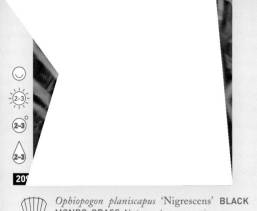

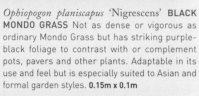

209

210

Ophiopogon planiscapus 'Nigrescens' **BLACK MONDO GRASS** Not as dense or vigorous as ordinary Mondo Grass but has striking purple-black foliage to contrast with or complement pots, pavers and other plants. Adaptable in its use and feel but is especially suited to Asian and formal garden styles. **0.15m x 0.1m**

Origanum vulgare **OREGANO** A strong-growing, aromatic groundcover or filler in the garden doubles as a handy herb for the kitchen. A haze of pink, purple or white flowers in summer. 'Aureum' has lime-gold leaves. Good for Mediterranean garden designs. **0.3m x 0.9m**

Reineckea carnea **REINECKEA** A greener, le[ss] formal version of its relative — Mondo Grass[.] Sends out short runners to cover the ground [in] tropical or Asian themes. Little pink flower spik[es] in summer are hard to see and are followed [by] red berries. **0.2m x 0.4m**

212

213

214

Sagina subulata **PEARLWORT** A small-scale mossy looking mat for Asian and tropical garden designs in cooler conditions. Can be used between pavers where there won't be competition from bigger plants. Little white flowers in summer. 'Aurea' (pictured) has lime rather than green colouring. **0.05m x 0.2m**

Scaevola aemula cultivars **FAN FLOWER** Long-flowering native perennials for coastal, Mediterranean & Asian designs. 'Fan Dancer' is pictured. 'Mauve Clusters' is low & suckering. 'New Wonder' in blue & 'Purple Fanfare' are vigorous trailers. **0.4m x 1m**

Scleranthus biflorus **SCLERANTHUS** A moss-like native for Asian and tropical designs. Widely distributed but forms from alpine areas are denser than those from the coast. Good for use in small gardens between pavers and among rocks where there won't be competition from bigger plants. **0.02m x 0.4m**

215

216

217

Sedum rubrotinctum **JELLY BEAN PLANT** Quick-growing and multiple-branching succulent can covers ground in arid designs and wouldn't be out of place in tropical schemes. Red intensifies under sunnier, colder, drier conditions. 'Aurora' has pink-red colouring and more of it. **0.25m x 0.5m**

Sempervivum tectorum **HOUSELEEK** Widely available and develops into clumps of multiple, dense rosettes which can be useful in succulent garden designs. These plants hybridise freely. Cultivars come with tints, tips or whole of the leaves in various purple-reds. **0.15m x 0.5m**

Senecio serpens **BLUE CHALK STICKS** A white powdery coating over the blue-green succulent leaves is an unusual colour. Naturally suited to arid garden designs but also good in coastal and Mediterranean schemes. Can also be featured in a pot, like most succulents. **0.25m x 0.6m**

218

S
219

220

Soleirolia soleirolii **BABY'S TEARS** Can provide a unifying cover in the landscape, between pavers or in crevices but best used where its rampant spread can be readily contained. It works well in tropical, Asian and Mediterranean designs. 'Aurea' has more yellow green colouring. **0.05m x 2m**

Stachys byzantina **LAMBS' EARS** A perennial to let run over the ground of a Mediterranean, coastal or succulent garden design. Furry spikes of pink-purple flowers in summer. 'Big Ears' is not as grey but has bigger leaves and flower spikes. **0.3m x 0.9m**

Thymus spp. & cvs **THYME** There are many of these aromatic kitchen herbs to choose from with gold, silver or bronze colouring and white, pink, mauve or purple flowers in spring or summer. Especially good between pavers in Mediterranean and coastal designs. **0.5m x 1m**

221

222

223

Tradescantia pallida 'Purpurea' **PURPLE HEART** A sprawling, fleshy perennial with a rare colour for the garden that's most intense in full sun. Especially suited to tropical garden designs. Pink flowers in continual flushes appear mostly through summer and in the mornings. **0.2m x 0.4m**

Tradescantia zebrina **SILVER INCH PLANT** A quick cover as its stems take root where they touch the ground. Foliage and purple-pink flowers in spring and summer are especially tropical but could work in a Mediterranean or Asian design. Must be contained. **0.25m x 1m**

Vinca minor **LESSER PERIWINKLE** Takes root where stems touch the ground. For tropical, Mediterranean or Asian designs where it will be contained. Cultivars available with blue, purple, violet or white flowers and cream variegated leaves. 'Darts' Blue' is pictured. **0.1m x 2m**

224

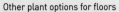

Viola hederacea **NATIVE VIOLET** This native creeper can comfortably fit into tropical, Mediterranean, Asian and coastal schemes, covering a lot of territory with its runners. Will find its way into crevices and fill around steppers but can get out of hand if happy. **0.1m x 2m**

Other plant options for floors
DIVIDERS 142-*Euphorbia milii* 149-*Iresine herbstii* cultivar 155-*Liriope muscari* 169-*Pogonatherum paniceum* 314-*Convolvulus cneorum* 331-*Helichrysum petiolare* 346-*Nepeta x faassenii* 347-*Ophiopogon japonicus* WATER 394-*Pratia pedunculata*

An impressive display of combination flooring is found in this inner-city yard. Pavers and pebbles are broken up by the juicy cabbage-like leaves of *ajuga reptens cv*, its deep mauve hues echoing the purples, magentas and violets of the predominant colour theme.

Beneath a tulip tree the silvery foam of *Gazania* bleeds into a bed of snowy pebbles, blurring the transition between soil and stone.

Such an imposing wall could easily overwhelm the space, but instead becomes a stunning feature with the addition of a simple timber sculpture that ties in with the folding concertina door separating indoors from out. Olive trees soften the effect of the wall. A diversity of materials (stone planters and sculpture, stainless steel furniture and timber pieces), trees and shrubs makes for a garden brimming with character and interest.

Garden 'staging' at its finest. We designed this drought-tolerant permanent sculpture garden for the succulent section of Sydney's Royal Botanic Gardens. Here the slopes, steps and thrust platforms are studded with hundreds of cacti and succulents embedded in a rainbow of mulches, gravels and lateral spreading groundcovers. With their wildly varying forms, from statuesque and elegant to tortured and sometimes even grotesque, cacti and succulents maintain their shape year after year – they are indeed the accent plant extraordinaire. Solo, they can hold their own in any setting, but as you can see here, multiple plantings make a truly spectacular display. See pages 130 and 131 for other views of these plants and their surrounds.

soul

spontaneity

invigorate

colour

focus

stimulate

ACCENTS

These are the stars that can put on a solo show. The bold, brash centre-pieces that shout 'Look at me!' like an original painting on the wall, an exotic sculpture in a recess, a distinctive piece of furniture in a minimalist setting or, of course, a water feature.

Contemporary landscape design is marked by the feature or accent plant. Residential architecture is getting edgier and we're seeing more hard, minimalist landscapes with just the odd well-placed accent plant. These plants are so interesting that just one will attract attention. They might have unusual or striking, year-round architectural structure and colour like Cordyline fruticosa and Bismarckia nobilis or a habit that acts like an exclamation mark in the landscape like a bird's nest fern or Cleistocactus strausii. It might just look good singled out in a pot like most citrus. Others like Buxus or conifers are really plain individuals but they are commonly dressed up into spectacular topiary shapes. One thing's for sure: the accent plant will always be eye-catching.

A lot about accent plants is to do with their staging – setting them up in the right pot or against a wall painted the right colour as a backdrop or locating them in a focal point. Sometimes the right position will be obvious, but study the viewing points from inside the house, the entry ways to the garden and from the garden seating area to find your most important focal points.

Sometimes accents are planted in multiples, like a row of yuccas or pencil pines or a dotting of Macrozamias. Still, each plant is given its own space to show off its form rather than being planted close together into a group like the 'walls', 'floors' and 'fillers'.

56

225

226

227

Acer platanoides 'Globosum' **NORWAY GLOBE MAPLE** An adaptable deciduous tree in a lollipop shape for a formal garden design. New spring leaves are bronze before turning green then yellow in autumn. **5m x 4m**

Adenium obesum **IMPALA LILY** Not out of place in a tropical design with its red, bright pink or white flowers twice a year. Also use in a cactus garden with its bulbous succulent trunk base. **1.5m x 1m**

Aeonium arboreum **AEONIUM** The green species doesn't have the impact of forms with burgundy rosettes on branching succulent stems. For beds or pots in succulent or tropical designs. Leaves turn greener with increased shade. 'Zwartkop' (pictured) can be temperamental. **1m x 1m**

228

229

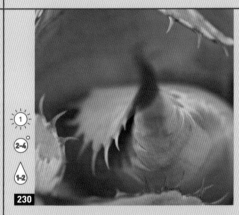

230

Agave americana **CENTURY PLANT** With toothed leaf margins and spiky tips, keep the tentacles of this succulent well away from pedestrian traffic and where the rosette form can develop freely. Blue or grey-green leaves can come with various yellow stripes. **1.8m x 2.5m**

Agave attenuata **AGAVE** The rosette of grey-green leaves unfurling from a tight central growing point makes a reliable living sculpture in a pot or in the garden. Appropriate to almost any design scheme. **1m x 2m**

Agave parryi **PARRY'S AGAVE** A rosette so tight as it ages that each leaf bears a thorny imprint from its neighbours. The arrangement of blue or grey green leaves trimmed with red-brown teeth and purple spike is a formal presence in the landscape. **0.6m x 1m**

231

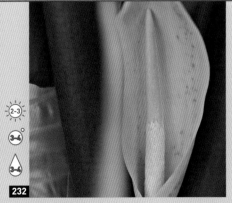

232

233

Alluaudia comosa **ALLUAUDIA** Not for positions near curious hands or unsuspecting elbows but the arrangement of leaves and thorns on erect, succulent stems demands close attention. Also try *A. procera* or *A. dumosa*. **10m x 1m**

Alocasia brisbanensis **CUNJEVOI** Wonderful bold, ribbed leaves in this native for tropical garden designs make you overlook that it's poisonous and somewhat weedy. The fragrant flower spike has a green-yellow spathe followed by red fruit. Also looks good massed. **2m x 1.5m**

Aloe plicatilis **FAN ALOE** A small succulent tree that grows up slowly. Even when young, the multiple branches, each holding a fan of grey-green leaves like long tongues, are a feature in a pot or a succulent garden design. **2m x 1.5m**

234

235

236

Asplenium australasicum **BIRD'S NEST FERN**
A sculptural accent with its crinkled rays of broad, leathery leaves: bright green with a dark mid-rib. Use in a tropical garden design or as a formal element in a pot. *A. nidus* is similar but better adapted to warmer conditions. **1.5m x 2m**

Astelia chathamica **SILVER SPEAR** The leaves are a metallic silver but look more like a sword than a spear. Can be massed like a grass when small but it matures into a striking individual clump. Red-orange berries on female plants. **1.5m x 1.5m**

Beaucarnea recurvata **PONYTAIL** The fountain of sharp edged leaves falling back on the swollen trunk base can be used in a pot or in the ground as an accent in tropical, Mediterranean, formal or succulent garden designs. **8m x 3m**

237

238

239

Bismarckia nobilis **BISMARCK PALM** An eye-catcher as a young or mature specimen. Suitable for a tropical effect, like any palm. The blue-silver of the pleated leaves help it fit into arid or Mediterranean designs. Plenty of structure for a formal effect. **12m x 4m**

Blechnum nudum **FISHBONE WATER FERN** A native cycad-like fern with its graphic wheel of deeply dissected fronds provides a formal element in the garden. The exotic *B. brasiliense* and *B. gibbum* have red new fronds but will need warmer conditions. **0.75m x 0.75m**

Buxus microphylla var. *japonica* **JAPANESE BOX** Even the plainest plants can make a feature. This one has many design uses — like other boxes and their many cultivars — and can be shaped into topiaries or standards, in the ground or a pot in formal designs. **2m x 1.5m**

240

241

242

Callitris columellaris **SAND CYPRESS PINE** Not as dark or geometrically rigid as the Italian Cypress but still formal for an Aussie as an accent conifer in those Tuscan garden designs. Or repeat plant and trim as a hedge. *C. glaucophylla* for a more blue-grey effect. **20m x 6m**

Camellia japonica **CAMELLIA** Thousands to choose from with varying qualities, though still none for lime soils. Dense habit and neatly arranged flowers have a formal effect although those with frilly bi-coloured flowers are like a tropical hibiscus for cooler climates. **5m x 4m**

Citrus x meyeri 'Meyer' **MEYER LEMON** One of the smaller, more prolific and cold tolerant lemons, actually genetically half orange. Other small citrus like cumquats and limes can also be used in a large pot as a feature for formal or Mediterranean designs. **3m x 2.5m**

243

Cleistocactus strausii **SILVER TORCH CACTUS** White spines among a coat of hair and deep pink flowers in spring or summer decorate these poles, branching from a common base. Don't crowd the roots but place several less-branched plants together for a quick succulent garden accent. **3m x 1m**

244

Cordyline australis **NZ CABBAGE TREE** Single or multiple trunks, each with a fountain of slender green leaves. Several cultivars including 'Purpurea' with purple-brown leaves. 'Red Star' is more red, 'Red Sensation' is more purple, 'Albertii' has cream stripes and red tinges and 'Sundance' is pictured. **6m x 3m**

245

Cordyline fruticosa cultivars **TI PLANT** Many cultivars of this eventually multi-stemmed shrub for upright tropical fountains of foliage. Some leaves are finer and more arching, others broader and more clustered. Colours and streaks range through green, purple, red, pink, yellow and cream. **4m x 2m**

246

Crinum pedunculatum **SWAMP LILY** Often mass planted but this evergreen native bulb matures into a substantial accent of bright strappy leaves. The spidery white flowers are fragrant and appear late spring through summer. Watch young plants for snails and caterpillars. **1.75m x 1.75m**

247

Cupressus sempervirens **PENCIL PINE** Seed grown plants can lose their shape. Get a tight form of 'Stricta' like 'Nitschke's Needle' for that dark, vertical icon of Tuscan landscapes. Other forms have brighter greens through to the gold of 'Swanes Golden'. **15m x 5m**

248

Cyathea australis **ROUGH TREE FERN** Widespread native fern that is quite a formal element. Keep clothes away from annoying papery scales at the top of the trunk until it's overhead. *C. cooperi* is elegant with its coin-spotted trunk and has more particular requirements. **10m x 4m**

249

Cycas revoluta **SAGO PALM** A cycad with symmetrical arrangement of fishbone fronds is appearing often in contemporary gardens. Low, slow and valued for its year-round architectural form. Eventually develops one or more trunks and decorative cones. **2m x 2m**

250

Cymbidium Hybrid Cultivars **CYMBIDIUM ORCHID** Choose from the many flower colours and shapes that fit the overall design. Enjoy the plant outside flowering season for its clumps of slender, arching leaves which are appropriate to formal and tropical schemes. **1m x 1m**

251

Dicksonia antarctica **SOFT TREE FERN** Slow, architectural native fern providing a formal element with its form, and texture contrasting with its divided foliage, even in shady and wet positions. Best structure depends on fronds not being lost to hot, dry or windy conditions. **5m x 3m**

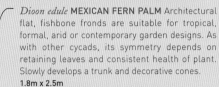

252

Dioon edule **MEXICAN FERN PALM** Architectural flat, fishbone fronds are suitable for tropical, formal, arid or contemporary garden designs. As with other cycads, its symmetry depends on retaining leaves and consistent health of plant. Slowly develops a trunk and decorative cones. **1.8m x 2.5m**

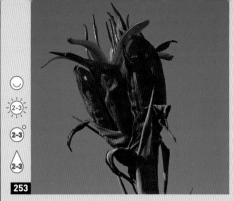

253

Doryanthes excelsa **GYMEA LILY** Mass planting this evergreen native like a tall grass restricts its growth. But it can mature into a magnificent accent of bright sword leaves. The stately torches of red lilies appear mostly in late spring or summer. **2.4m x 4m**

254

Dracaena draco **DRAGON TREE** With their multi-stemmed, succulent branches and umbrella canopy of bunched, stiff grey leaves, these eventually become dramatic trees for arid and Mediterranean designs. Patience or money required for mature specimen but architectural even when small. **10m x 8m**

255

Dracaena fragrans 'Massangeana' **HAPPY PLANT** In conditions where it will be really happy, this plant can be planted densely to make a screen. More often used individually in a pot, inside or out, or in the ground for a tropical or formal foliage accent. **4m x 1.5m**

256

Dracaena marginata **RED EDGE DRACAENA** A fountain of slender green leaves edged red on the end of each stem. The single then multiple stems marked with leaf scars can be erect or meandering. 'Tricolor' has additional cream-white stripes. **4m x 2m**

257

Dracaena sanderiana **LUCKY BAMBOO** The plant found in Chinatown with its stem trained in spirals and growing in nothing but water. The slightly twisted leaves held out from the erect stem are an elegant vertical accent in tropical and Asian designs. **1.5m x 0.8m**

258

Dypsis decaryi **TRIANGLE PALM** Erect grey-green fronds are arranged in three vertical columns. Purple-rusty fur at the bottom of the fronds turns into a grey-white bloom. Appropriate as a feature where its form can be clearly seen in arid, Mediterranean and tropical themes. **10m x 3m**

259

Echeveria agavoides **RED EDGE ECHEVERIA** A waxy accent in a small package. As with the many others of the genus, this is perfectly formed and holds its own as a feature in a pot. Cultivars have varied amounts of lipstick around the leaf edges. **0.15m x 0.3m**

260

Echinocactus grusonii **GOLDEN BARREL CACTUS** Green ball with longitudinal ribs studded with starry spines along the ridges that pick up and reflect light. Slow but eye-catching form, texture and colour, singly or in groups, in a pot, succulent or formal gardens. **0.8m x 1m**

261

262

263

Encephalartos altensteinii **PRICKLY CYCAD** Slow-growing but always architectural cycad. Bright green fronds are stiffly held out from a sturdy trunk patterned like a Canary Island Date Palm. A formal statement alone in a contemporary garden or in tropical, arid or Mediterranean designs. **5m x 3.5m**

Ensete ventricosum **ABYSSINIAN BANANA** Live fast and die young. Best form is where lush, untorn growth from sheltered, warm, moist, rich conditions can be assured. Dramatic in a tropical courtyard design. Restricted in commercial banana-growing areas where conditions would suit. **6m x 5m**

Ficus lyrata **FIDDLE LEAF FIG** As with most figs, placement should be considered carefully before selecting this plant. Safest confined to large pots and planters where the handsome display of glossy, crinkled leaves can be appropriately featured in tropical garden designs. **25m x 2m**

264

265

266

Gahnia sieberiana **RED-FRUITED SAW SEDGE** Like a smaller version of Pampas Grass but with blackish plumes of seed. Each has leaves with razor edges but *Gahnia* is native and makes its impact as an accent even in partly shaded and poorly drained sites. **2.5m x 1.5m**

Hebe albicans **HEBE** Compact shrub with crowded leaves, each one outlined to highlight the pattern of their arrangement around the stem. Good up-close and near seating where this texture can be observed. Heads of white flowers appear in summer. **0.5m x 0.75m**

Hebe 'Emerald Green' **EMERALD GREEN HEBE** Like a little round conifer, this can be a bright accent on a small scale in a pot or in formal and Japanese garden designs. The compact form also lends itself to multiple planting in geometric patterns. **0.3m x 0.3m**

267

268

269

Howea forsteriana **KENTIA PALM** A native palm slow to develop its ringed trunk but elegant even as a young plant with arching fronds and drooping leaflets. Effective when mature if planted in groups. For tropical, Mediterranean and formal landscapes and planters. **15m x 5m**

Hymenocallis spp. **SPIDER LILY** Fragrant flowers in summer or autumn and leaves like a clivia are evergreen in *H. speciosa*, *H. caribaea* and *H. littoralis*. *H. x festalis* and *H. narcissiflora* take cooler conditions but are deciduous. For Asian and tropical designs. **0.6m x 0.3m**

Juniperus virginiana 'Skyrocket' **SKYROCKET JUNIPER** Almost out of proportion it's such a skinny conifer. Good for narrow spaces. Dense, but outline isn't geometric unless trimmed. Vertical impact in the landscape is accentuated by foliage colour. Tolerant of neglect. **6m x 0.6m**

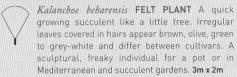

270 *Kalanchoe beharensis* **FELT PLANT** A quick growing succulent like a little tree. Irregular leaves covered in hairs appear brown, olive, green to grey-white and differ between cultivars. A sculptural, freaky individual for a pot or in Mediterranean and succulent gardens. **3m x 2m**

271 *Kniphofia* spp. & hybrids **RED HOT POKER** Various torch flowers of red, orange, yellow and green-white, alone or in combinations. Clumps come in different heights and can be massed as a divider. Not all are evergreen. For tropical, Asian, succulent and coastal designs. **1.25m x 1m**

272 *Macrozamia communis* **BURRAWANG** Appears spectacularly massed in eucalypt forests. Sculptural native cycad in a pot or in the ground, as a single specimen or repeated. Slow to develop one or more trunks. Fits into formal, Asian, Mediterranean or tropical designs. **2m x 2m**

273 *Magnolia grandiflora* 'Little Gem' **LITTLE GEM MAGNOLIA** Dark, glossy leaves with brown suede contrast underneath. Combined with creamy-white fragrant flowers, makes a feature for Asian, tropical or Mediterranean gardens. 'Exmouth' has leaves and flowers on a bigger scale. 'St Mary' is smaller with wavy leaves. **6m x 3m**

274 *Melianthus major* **HONEY BUSH** Fast-growing, suckering shrub has a place in Mediterranean, Asian and possibly tropical designs. Heavily carved leaves and nectar-rich red-brown flowers in late spring. Leaves have an unpleasant odour if damaged. Weedy in areas of WA and SA. **3m x 1m**

275 *Moraea robinsoniana* **WEDDING LILY** Could be used as a filler or divider but one specimen of this native iris grows into an elegant clump of upright and arching strappy leaves. Appropriate to Asian, tropical and Mediterranean schemes. Stems of white flowers in late spring. **1.2m x 1m**

276 *Musa velutina* **PINK VELVET BANANA** Yellow flowers exposed by unfurling pink bracts develop into bunches of self-peeling, pink bananas. Vertical fan of broad leaves is a tropical accent in the garden. Banned in Queensland and restricted in NSW commercial banana-growing areas. **2m x 2m**

277 *Nelumbo nucifera* **SACRED LOTUS** Multiplies into a filler where it's happy and has the space. Some space is needed even for a single plant as an accent in a water feature. Glamorous leaves, flowers and seed pods for Asian, tropical or Mediterranean gardens. **1.5m x 2m**

278 *Pachypodium lamerei* **MADAGASCAR PALM** Not a palm but a deciduous succulent shrub. Has a swollen trunk with a pattern of thorns topped by a ring of leaves. Summer flowers look and smell like frangipanis. Suitable for cactus, tropical, Mediterranean and formal themes. **6m x 2m**

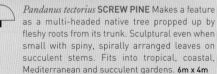

279

280

281

Pandanus tectorius **SCREW PINE** Makes a feature as a multi-headed native tree propped up by fleshy roots from its trunk. Sculptural even when small with spiny, spirally arranged leaves on succulent stems. Fits into tropical, coastal, Mediterranean and succulent gardens. **6m x 4m**

Pedilanthus tithymaloides **DEVIL'S BACKBONE** An open succulent shrub with zigzag stems and milky sap to be avoided. Deciduous in cooler areas. An informal curiosity for a pot or for succulent or tropical gardens. 'Variegatus' with cream and pink colouring is pictured. **1.5m x 0.5m**

Phoenix canariensis **CANARY ISLAND DATE PALM** Magnificent palm makes a landmark in any landscape. Leaf bases have rigid spines to be avoided for a long time until the crown rises. Susceptibility to fusarium wilt is a serious selection consideration. Suits the style of almost any design. **20m x 10m**

282

283

284

Phoenix roebelenii **PYGMY DATE PALM** Feathery looking palm fronds but their stems are lined with sharp spines. Pattern of pegs develops if dead fronds are not removed too close to the trunk. Can be placed in formal, tropical, Mediterranean, Asian or succulent garden designs. **3m x 3m**

Phormium tenax **NZ FLAX** Species has upright leaves and is a parent of many hybrid cultivars. Foliage straps in a range of colours and striped combinations, heights and forms. Taller, straighter, more colourful ones are accents. Smaller, grassier, arching ones can be fillers. All can be dividers. **2.5m x 2.5m**

Platycerium superbum **STAGHORN FERN** A nest of sterile shield fronds attach to a mount with one growing point for the fertile, antler fronds. Makes an unusual and dramatic sculptural accent on a wall, tree or post in informal, tropical garden schemes. **2m x 2m**

285

286

287

Protasparagus densiflorus 'Myersii' **FOXTAIL FERN** Upright or twisting cylindrical plumes make a sculptural alternative to *Sansevieria* in a limey green. White starry flowers in summer followed by red berries. Good mass-planted but safest used away from bush areas. **0.9m x 1m**

Restio tetraphyllus **TASSEL CORD RUSH** Foliage of this native is used in floral arrangements. Short, clumping runners and arching stems make it a useful filler. But the generally erect habit and fine, waving branchlets in bright green can make an Asian-style accent. **1.2m x 0.5m**

Sansevieria trifasciata **MOTHER-IN-LAW'S TONGUE** Architectural succulent also massed as a filler or divider. 'Laurentii' is pictured but the species doesn't have the yellow trim. Suits most garden themes. Cultivars with squat, rosette form are silver, gold and green. **1.5m x 0.5m**

288

289

290

Spathiphyllum Hybrid Cultivars **PEACE LILY** Luxuriant foliage clumps can also be massed as a divider or filler. Flowers well inside so it's useful outside in deep shade in tropical or Asian designs. 'Sensation' has stately dark, ribbed foliage. Leaves of 'Metallica' have a silver sheen. **1m x 1m**

Strelitzia reginae var. *juncea* **RUSH-LIKE STRELITZIA** Only one of this dramatic Bird of Paradise is needed for a big effect in a Mediterranean, Asian or tropical design. There are no leaves or only a small leaf on some tips of the stems. **1.8m x 1.8m**

Stromanthe sanguinea **STROMANTHE** The dark green and grey-green pattern on the paddle leaves is interesting to look down at. But it's the maroon colouring underneath that needs to be visible when placing this plant. Use in tropical garden designs. **1.5m x 1m**

291

292

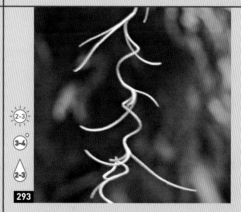

293

Synadenium compactum 'Rubrum' **RED AFRICAN MILK BUSH** Succulent shrub with glossy leaves in green, red or splashes of both all on the one plant. Fits into tropical and succulent garden designs. Its habit can be quite open but avoid its milky sap if pruning for density. **4m x 2m**

Telopea speciosissima **WARATAH** Hard to grow well as a spring flowering feature. 'Corroboree' is red. 'Wirrimbirra White' is white. Try 'Shady Lady' hybrids in 'Red', 'Crimson', 'Pink' & 'White' or 'Braidwood Brilliant' for more flowers & compact, rounded habit. **3m x 3m**

Tillandsia usneoides **SPANISH MOSS** A bromeliad that's not like anything else. Tangled grey curls hang from branches of trees in nature and can be mounted the same way or on anything else in arid, tropical or Mediterranean designs. **0.5m x 0.1m**

294

295

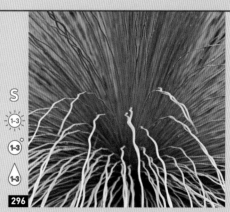

296

Trachycarpus fortunei **CHINESE WINDMILL PALM** Only slow but this palm withstands snow. Retains its dead fronds but a pattern of pegs develops if they're not removed too close to the fibre-covered trunk. Fits in formal, tropical, Mediterranean, Asian or succulent garden designs. **10m x 3m**

Vriesea spp. & cvs **BROMELIAD** As with other bromeliads, this will multiply and can be used massed as a filler or divider. On top of the architectural arrangement of strappy leaves, with variegations, the long-lasting inflorescences set this one apart as a feature. **1m x 1m**

Xanthorrhoea spp. **GRASS TREE** Even when young, these icons of the Australian bush can be sculptural in most design themes & send up amazing flower spears. It can take 30 years for a trunk to develop but salvaged specimens are available. **2m x 1.5m**

297

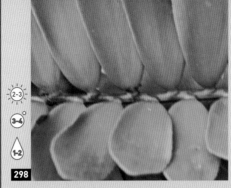

298

Yucca guatemalensis **GIANT YUCCA** Also known as *Y. elephantipes* and Spineless Yucca as the leaves don't have the typical rigid tips. Often repeat-planted but with enough space to highlight the highly architectural form of each. Works in succulent, Mediterranean, coastal, tropical and formal designs. **6m x 2m**

Zamia furfuracea **CARDBOARD PALM** This cycad has an irregular clumping form but the bronze-olive leaves are so sculptural that it still makes a good accent plant. Can be used for succulent, tropical, Asian and Mediterranean garden designs. Even young plants form interesting cones. **1m x 2m**

Other plant options for accents
ROOFS 1-*Abies* spp. 5-*Acer palmatum* 13-*Betula pendula* 50-*Pyrus calleryana* 'Capital' 60-*Washingtonia* spp. WALLS 69-*Bambusa multiplex* cultivars 75-*Chamaerops humilis* 79-*Dypsis lutescens* 80-*Euphorbia pulcherrima* 86-*Juniperus chinensis* 'Spartan' 97-*Phyllostachys nigra* 101-*Rhaphis excelsa* 104-*Strelitzia nicolai* DIVIDERS 112-*Acacia cognata* cultivars 114-*Aechmea* spp. & cvs 116-*Aloe arborescens* 117-*Anthurium* spp. 129-*Chaenomeles speciosa* 132-*Codiaeum variegatum* cultivars 137-*Dietes bicolor* 154-*Leucophyta brownii* 166-*Phormium cookianum* 176-*Strelitzia reginae* FILLERS 304-*Alpinia purpurata* 307-*Anigozanthos flavidus* hybrids 310-*Calathea zebrina* 317-*Ctenanthe setosa* 'Grey Star' 322-*Dietes vegeta* 330-*Hedychium gardneranum* 335-*Iris x germanica* 345-*Neoregelia* spp. & cvs 360-*Xanthosoma violaceum* 379-*Platycerium bifurcatum* WATER 386-*Acorus gramineus* 388-*Colocasia esculenta* 389-*Cyperus papyrus* 390-*Cyperus prolifer* 391-*Iris* Louisiana Hybrids 392-*Juncus usitatus* 395-*Thalia dealbata* 397-*Zantedeschia aethiopica*

Other plant options for pot subjects
ROOFS 20-*Citrus* cvs 53-*Schefflera actinophylla* WALLS 103-*Schefflera arboricola* DIVIDERS 121-*Aspidistra elatior* 135-*Crassula ovata* 142-*Euphorbia milii* 163-*Pelargonium x hortorum* 169-*Pogonatherum paniceum* FLOORS 185-*Banksia spinulosa* 'Birthday Candles' 206-*Mammillaria* spp. 359-*Tradescantia spathacea*

Other plant options for topiary subjects
ROOFS 43-*Olea europea* var. *communis* 48-*Podocarpus elatus* WALLS 81-*Ficus benjamina* 87-*Laurus nobilis* 88-*Luma apiculata* 91-*Michelia figo* 92-*Murraya paniculata* 105-*Syzygium australe* cultivars 108-*Thuja plicata* DIVIDERS 113-*Acmena smithii* var. *minor* 127-*Buxus sempervirens* 'Suffruticosa' 156-*Lonicera nitida* 177-*Teucrium fruticans* 180-*Westringia fruticosa*

When it comes to accents, this startling marriage of plants and material says it all. Rods and coils of Lucky Bamboo culminate in a starburst of tapering green and gold leaves. Every detail of its structure is enhanced by the rich ripe tomato tones in the rear painted wall. The pure simple lines of the clear glass vase complete the composition, and, when lit creatively, contribute an element of understated style that sets off the dominant players to perfection. For more details of this stunning space see page 81.

contrast

essence

layering

balance

encompass

Don't go thinking these are the boring, uninteresting plants. Just because fillers do the bulking out of your garden beds doesn't mean that they're dull, disposable or unimportant. These plants do put on a show but they tend to do it together as a collaboration.

Mass planting is another one of the prominent features of contemporary garden design. Think of a field of Pennisetum with its feathery seed heads all fluttering together in the wind. Imagine not just a couple of clumps of clivias or Japanese anemones but a whole sweep of them in full flower. One specimen of *Ctenanthe* could work as an accent if placed among low groundcovers but plant it in multiples and it definitely won't get lost in the crowd.

Other 'filler' plants aren't as spectacular but they still have important functions. They have the role of supporting the 'accent' stars; providing the backdrop colour and texture that makes the diva plants, and even other features like statues, look so good. And after all the walls, paved areas, paths and other plantings have gone into your landscape plan, there'll usually still be plenty of garden bed space to fill. Your choice is either to leave the gaps bare with nothing but a cover of mulch or else use filler plants that won't look too busy and fight with the stars.

These plants don't travel as far as 'floor' plants but their habit is more random and spreading than wall and divider plants. They are more open and arching, giving you a lot more coverage bang for your buck. Or they steadily thicken out from a central clump with their runners; this means they give good coverage and that they're usually easy to propagate and therefore inexpensive, so they can be purchased in large quantities. Or they're listed here just because they look really good massed.

299

300

301

Acanthus mollis **ACANTHUS** A perennial with spires of purple and white flowers late spring to mid-summer and striking leaves that inspired the design of the Corinthian column. Handsome alone, best when massed. Suits tropical, Asian and Mediterranean gardens. **1m x 1m**

Adiantum raddianum **DELTA MAIDENHAIR FERN** Many varieties of this native fern with leaves of differing textures, and some variegated. But all of them are for constantly moist, shady positions as a delicate-looking underplanting in tropical, informal garden designs. **0.4m x 0.5m**

Agapanthus praecox **AGAPANTHUS** A massed sweep of lush strappy leaves and the blue or white flowers — or now bi-coloured — around Christmas is a show. Try the deep blue of 'Black Pantha'. Not for planting close to the bush and definitely no dumping. **0.8m x 1m**

302

303

304

Ajania pacifica **GOLD & SILVER** Year round interest in this spreading perennial comes from its lobed leaves arranged like a rosette; the grey underside showing as a silver outline to each leaf. Also buttons of gold-yellow flowers in autumn. **0.4m x 0.9m**

Alpinia coerulea **NATIVE GINGER** Strappy leaves arranged stepping up erect stems give a useful textural contrast in a tropical design. White summer flowers are only small but followed by edible blue berries. Typically green, look for forms of this native with red-purple backed leaves. **2m x 1.5m**

Alpinia purpurata **RED GINGER** A single clump is attractive with its bright green leaves, stepped leaf arrangement and flames of flower bracts but it looks best when the clumps are massed. Cultivars with red or pink flower spikes. **3m x 1m**

305

306

307

Anemone x *hybrida* **JAPANESE WIND FLOWER** Slow to start but the clumps of lobed leaves held on elegant, wiry stems will fill and spread. Drifts of white, pink or rose, single or double flowers in early autumn are spectacular in informal cottage or Asian designs. **1.5m x 1.5m**

Angophora hispida **DWARF APPLE** Open-limbed native with leaves arranged opposite each other around the stem. Young leaves and flower buds are covered with red hairs. White flowers after Christmas, when not much else is flowering, are followed by interesting fruit capsules. **3m x 3m**

Anigozanthos flavidus hybrids **KANGAROO PAW** A stand of these strappy leafed natives in flower is a show as a divider or accent also, in tropical or Mediterranean designs. The 'Bush Gem' series offers an improved and varied range of leaf & flower colours & sizes. **2m x 1m**

308

309

310

Bauhinia galpinii **PRIDE OF THE CAPE** Orange-red flowers and slightly grey green, butterfly leaves are both features of this sprawling shrub. It can be trained for a Mediterranean, Asian or tropical theme to climb, be pruned to shape, or left to cover ground and spillover. **3m x 4m**

Brachyscome multifida **CUT LEAF DAISY** A native daisy with mauve, pink, white or lemon flowers, mostly from spring to autumn. It's good for mass planting in cottage gardens or Mediterranean designs. 'Break O' Day' is less pastel, with darker foliage and flowers. **0.15m x 0.4m**

Calathea zebrina **ZEBRA PLANT** One clump of its broad leaves make a feature composition for pots or as an indoor plant. But makes a really lush, tropical effect with its jungle stripes when planted out in stretches in landscapes with warm, moist conditions. **1m x 1.2m**

311

312

313

Carex spp. **SEDGE** Mass plant New Zealand's evergreen sedges for contemporary sweeps of tone and texture. *C. comans* 'Frosted Curls' (pictured). *C. testacea* has an unusual orange haze around its tips but is banned, along with other species, in Tasmania. **0.75m x 0.75m**

Chamaedorea elegans **PARLOUR PALM** Small, slow and single-stemmed, this palm looks best when many seeds have germinated close together to make it look like one clump. It can be a useful filler or groundcover repeating this effect around the bare legs of taller palms. **2m x 1.5m**

Clivia miniata **CLIVIA** The orange that has always been 'in'. Now this plant is available — not widely or cheaply — in warm tones from cream and yellow through red. Dark straps of foliage grow well in dry shade but flowers better with some sun. **0.5m x 0.5m**

314

315

316

Convolvulus cneorum **SILVERBUSH** The neatly arranged silver foliage is a good foil in coastal, arid and Mediterranean designs with airy, free-draining conditions. Yellow-centred white disc flowers from spring to summer close in low light to reveal pink flushes on their backs. **0.6m x 0.9m**

Coprosma x *kirkii* **SMALL LEAFED LOOKING GLASS PLANT** Not a remarkable looking individual but useful for covering a lot of ground or as a spillover in difficult conditions. Not out of place in Asian garden designs. 'Variegata' has leaves with cream margins. **1m x 3m**

Cordyline stricta **SLENDER PALM LILY** Starts as a single-stemmed fountain of slender leaves, good as an accent. Matures into a multi-stemmed shrub with purple flowers in summer followed by black berries. Good native for narrow spaces in tropical or Asian designs. **5m x 2.5m**

317

Ctenanthe setosa 'Grey Star' **CTENANTHE** Slim stems hold grey-green paddle leaves with green ribs and purple underneath. Elegant as a feature. When mass planted its clumps will thicken into blocks of grey tones that can be a useful contrast in tropical garden designs. **1.5m x 1m**

318

Cyperus involucratus **UMBRELLA SEDGE** Often too quick to make itself at home in some areas. Harness that vigour for difficult gardens spots where its growth will be more restricted. Triangular stems are taller and the leaf spokes more graceful in shadier positions. **1.2m x 1m**

319

Dianella ensiformis hybrids **FLAX LILY** Variegated clumping perennials for an accent of foliage colour in dark spots or mass planting in tropical, Asian or Mediterranean designs. 'Border Silver' is pictured. Yellow stripes of 'Border Gold' are more sensitive to sunburn. 'Border Emerald' has bright green stripes. **1m x 0.6m**

320

Dianella spp. & cvs **FLAX LILY** Grassy natives of different heights & leaf colours; all with sprays of blue & yellow flowers in spring & summer then blue berries. Try 'Little Jess', 'Little Rev', 'Tas Red', 'Cassa Blue', 'Breeze' & variegated 'Peninsula Perfection'. **1.25m x 0.7m**

321

Dichorisandra thyrsiflora **BLUE GINGER** Glossy leaves arranged in spirals around canes like bamboo. Upright but will branch and spread into a clump for tropical or Asian designs with rich and moist soils. Deep purple-blue flowers in autumn even in deep shade. **2.5m x 1m**

322

Dietes vegeta **WILD IRIS** Prolific and not native. Flushes of flowers on wiry stems over a long season even in difficult conditions. Position thoughtfully and remove seed heads to reduce self-seeding. Flower stems of *D. grandiflora* don't stretch as high above its leaves. **1m x 1m**

323

Elettaria cardamomum **CARDAMOM** Makes a dense, textural clump of arching stems. Dark, stepped leaves smell of the spice when brushed. Ultimately high enough for a wall in warm conditions where flowers and pods will appear. Fits into Asian and tropical designs. **2.5m x 2.5m**

324

Eranthemum pulchellum **BLUE SAGE** The leaves are textured and attractively arranged yet really quite sombre. But the plant is useful to quickly cover even quite shady areas although there won't be as many of the blue flowers appearing in mid-autumn and winter. **1.2m x 1.2m**

325

Farfugium japonicum 'Aureomaculatum' **LEOPARD PLANT** Gold-yellow flowers in autumn to winter are not the feature of this moisture-loving perennial with bold, glossy leaves spotted yellow. Tropical-looking plant for cooler gardens. Also for Asian designs. **0.75m x 0.75m**

326

327

328

Festuca glauca **BLUE FESCUE** This evergreen grass is swamped by others when planted on its own but looks terrific mass planted. An arrangement of these compact blue tufts makes a textural and tonal composition. Try cultivars 'Elijah Blue' and 'Peninsula Blue'. **0.25m x 0.25m**

Gaura lindheimeri **BUTTERFLY PLANT** Airy, informal sub-shrub with many wiry, upright stems that flutter their flowers in the slightest breeze. Self-seeds readily. Cultivars in pure white, pink and crimson. 'Whirling Butterflies' is smaller, more compact and has sterile pink-flushed white flowers. **1.2m x 1.2m**

Hardenbergia violacea **NATIVE SARSAPARILLA** Shrubby native climber with dark, eucalyptus-like leaves to cover ground or spillover. 'Happy Wanderer' & 'Sweet Heart' are purple. 'Free 'N' Easy' is near-white. 'Happy Duo' is both. 'Mini Ha Ha' (pictured) is compact. **2m x 2m**

329

330

331

Hebe diosmifolia **HEBE** Dense but slightly spreading shrub with fine, neatly arranged foliage. The faintly lilac flowers appear from late winter through summer but mostly in spring. Highly tolerant of salt winds and can also be used as a divider. **1m x 1.5m**

Hedychium gardneranum **KAHILI GINGER** Glossy leaves stepped up erect canes and fragrant summer flowers. An eye-catching accent as an individual clump but looks a bit thin unless massed. A tropical element that survives cooler conditions but can be weedy in areas where conditions suit. **2m x 1.5m**

Helichrysum petiolare **LICORICE PLANT** Fast-growing sub-shrub with hairy grey leaves making a tangled mound that can be trimmed as a divider. Suitable for coastal and Mediterranean themes. 'Limelight' (pictured) has a more tropical colour. It is more sprawling and better without strong sunlight. **0.5m x 2m**

332

333

334

Heliotropium arborescens **HELIOTROPE** A wiry, open shrub that looks goods sprawling and contrasting with plants of similar vigour. Flowers from spring until autumn smell like vanilla. 'Aureum' is pictured. 'Lord Roberts' has purple flushed leaves and dark purple flowers. **1m x 1.5m**

Helleborus orientalis **HELLEBORE** Clumps of glossy, dark leaves with nodding winter or spring flowers in purple, pink, green and white held above. Slow to establish but effective as a massed planting in Asian and tropical themes under cooler conditions. **0.4m x 0.4m**

Imperata cylindrica 'Rubra' **JAPANESE BLOOD GRASS** Erect grass with tips coloured a red that spreads down the blades and intensifies through the season. Brilliant effects when mass planted in a sweep which can be backlit by low sun. Suited to Asian and tropical designs. **0.4m x 0.3m**

335

S

336

S

337

Iris x germanica **BEARDED IRIS** Handsome fans of grey-green foliage look good in small clumps as an accent but a spectacular show in flower planted as a divider or filler. Broad range to choose from for site conditions, height and colour. **0.8m x 0.6m**

Isolepis nodosa **KNOBBY CLUB RUSH** Tough native sedge that can take front-line salt winds and dry or boggy soils. Best when clumps are massed to allow the grassy stems topped with flower and seed head clusters to arch over each other. Suits most design themes. **0.6m x 0.4m**

Isopogon anemonifolius **BROAD-LEAFED DRUMSTICKS** This native shrub is generally upright and good as a divider. 'Little Drumsticks' and 'Woorikee 2000' are smaller, compact selections to mass plant as fillers. Explosions of yellow flowers through spring and summer leave cone fruits behind. **1.75m x 1m**

338

339

340

Jasminum sambac 'Grand Duke of Tuscany' **DOUBLE ARABIAN JASMINE** An open, shrubby climber that can be trained onto a trellis or pole, pruned into a fuller shrub or massed and left to sprawl over itself. Growth isn't strong but the fragrance is. Flowers open white and age to pink through summer. **2m x 2m**

Kalanchoe blossfeldiana **FLAMING KATY** Commonly grown house plant and as good in a pot outdoors. Can be repeat-planted on a small scale in succulent and tropical designs for a winter display of flowers in hot pink, orange, red, yellow or white. **0.3m x 0.3m**

Kalanchoe tomentosa **PANDA PLANT** High return succulent for little investment. Thrives under hostile conditions producing sculptural and touchable rosettes of blue-grey furry leaves with rusty dots around the tip and margin. Spreads as stems lengthen and flop over. **0.4m x 0.2m**

341

342

343

Lomandra longifolia **SPINY-HEADED MAT RUSH** A mass of this native fits into tropical, Asian, Mediterranean and coastal schemes. 'Tanika' is a refined cultivar. 'Cassica' has rigid, bluish leaves and is adapted to sandy soils. 'Katrinus' is more arching, adapted to heavy soils. **1m x 0.8m**

Miscanthus sinensis cultivars **MISCANTHUS** White leaf stripes in 'Variegatus' (pictured) give it a silvery, Mediterranean look. It can flop. Shorter is 'Sarabande' with a sea of flowers and strong autumn colouring. 'Gracillimus' is shorter and finer still with elegantly arching foliage. **2.5m x 1m**

Miscanthus sinensis 'Zebrinus' **ZEBRA GRASS** Green arching leaves on upright stems develop lemon bands. Works well in tropical, Asian or Mediterranean designs as a mass. Silver-pink flower and seed plumes and autumn colouring before dying back in winter. **2.5m x 1m**

344 *Monstera deliciosa* **FRUIT SALAD PLANT** Can climb by attaching its roots to vertical surfaces — in which case it'll need strong support. Best kept off trees. Left to sprawl, the big Swiss cheese leaves can cover a lot of ground in tropical garden designs. **15m x 5m**

345 *Neoregelia* spp. & cvs **BROMELIAD** Flowers aren't as spectacular as in other bromeliads. But form, leaf colour and pattern are strong enough to make an accent. Foliage colour and pattern can be used effectively massed in tropical garden designs. **0.6m x 0.8m**

346 *Nepeta* x *faassenii* **CATMINT** An informal sprawling perennial for Mediterranean designs. Combination of aromatic grey leaves and lavender-blue flowers, appearing in flushes from spring through autumn, goes well with most other colours. 'Six Hills Giant' is bigger, for further back in the border. **0.3m x 0.6m**

347 *Ophiopogon japonicus* **MONDO GRASS** Can be easily categorised for use as a floor or divider also. Fine dark arching leaves are a tough but delicate-looking textural display when massed. For Asian, formal and Mediterranean designs. 'Nana' makes a shorter and less spreading tuft. **0.2m x 0.15m**

348 *Osteospermum* Hybrid Cultivars **OX-EYE DAISY** Tough, spreading sub-shrubs for Mediterranean and coastal designs. Increasing number of hybrids available. Flowers in white, purple, pink, red, orange, yellow and combinations, with or without pinched petals over a long season. But they close when not in direct sun. **0.75m x 1.5m**

349 *Pelargonium peltatum* **IVY LEAFED GERANIUM** Trailing perennials which can sprawl, spillover or even be trained to climb. Flowers in many pinks, reds, purples and white or combined with white. Waxy looking leaves are variegated in some. Good for Mediterranean or maybe tropical designs. **0.75m x 2.5m**

350 *Pennisetum alopecuroides* **SWAMP FOXTAIL GRASS** A native grass. Spring leaves yellow through season. Flower & seed heads over time may pose threat to bushland. 'Purple Lea' & 'Nafray' produce little viable seed. 'Black Lea' is smaller with black seed heads. **1.5m x 1.2m**

351 *Philodendron selloum* **TREE PHILODENDRON** Dramatic divided leaves attract attention and are something of an accent. Strong growth and aerial roots can be dealt with by using it as a filler where it can sprawl over itself. A tropical, jungle-like element in the garden. **3m x 4m**

352 *Plectranthus argentatus* **SILVER SPUR FLOWER** Handles damp shady conditions — unusual for a furry, grey-leafed plant. Useful in gardens with a Mediterranean feel. This native sprawls. Sacrifice its plain spires of lilac summer flowers and tip-prune occasionally for denser growth. **0.6m x 1.2m**

353 *Poa labillardieri* **TUSSOCK GRASS** A fine-leafed native grass forming a grey-green clump. Makes a textural display when massed in coastal or Mediterranean schemes. 'Eskdale' is a hardy, blue-green cultivar. Use *P. poiformis* as a shorter alternative; 'Kingsdale' is also blue and 'Courtney' is green. **1m x 0.5m**

354 *Rhipsalis cereuscula* **CORAL CACTUS** Looks more like a fern than a cactus from a distance. Long, thin stems arch and divide into a mounding mesh of short, barrel shoots. White, starry flowers appear in spring. Useful filler or spillover in succulent garden designs. **0.6m x 0.4m**

355 *Rosmarinus officinalis* **ROSEMARY** A shrubby herb for the kitchen and for remembrance. And several cultivars for filling or trailing, depending on their density and habit. Use more compact forms to prune into a divider. Blue, pink or white flowers from autumn through spring. **2m x 2.5m**

356 *Russelia equisetiformis* **CORAL PLANT** Arching canes have the grace of Asian designs, the never-ending flowers a colour of the tropics, and the wiry branchlets the fine look of a Mediterranean plant. Especially good where the branches and bells can spill and hang. **1.5m x 2.5m**

357 *Salvia sinaloensis* **SINALOA SAGE** Suckers will increase the density of a massed planting with purple tints in the leaves that grow stronger with more light and less water. Flowers appear mostly through summer and autumn. Good for Mediterranean garden themes. **0.3m x 0.4m**

358 *Trachelospermum jasminoides* 'Tricolor' **VARIEGATED STAR JASMINE** More compact, slower and fewer flowers than ordinary star jasmine. Not grown for its flowers but the cream and pink new leaves which become variegated and then green with age. Adaptable to Asian, tropical and Mediterranean designs. **2m x 2m**

359 *Tradescantia spathacea* **RHOEO** Fleshy perennial which quickly divides from its base into clumps of two-toned rosettes. Small but architectural as a feature in a pot. Or use as a divider for a tropical effect. 'Vittata' has yellow stripes. Could be weedy under tropical conditions. **0.3m x 0.3m**

360 *Vinca major* **GREATER PERIWINKLE** Can be weedy as it suckers taking root where the stems flop and touch the ground. For Mediterranean or tropical designs only where it will be contained. The species is all-green with blue spring flowers. 'Variegata' is pictured. **0.4m x 2m**

361 *Xanthosoma violaceum* **BLUE TARO** Like *Alocasia* and *Colocasia*, this makes a handsome accent planting in tropical designs but is easier to use as a filler as it will spread itself anyway. The purple stems have a white bloom. Potentially weedy under tropical conditions. **2.5m x 2m**

This award-winning garden helps put to bed the notion that filler plants have to be boring. A mound of deep scarlet azaleas bring bulk, softness and bold colour to this outdoor bath finished with brushed stainless steel tiles. Discreet lighting picks out the planes and edges of surrounding plant structures and makes the pearly white marble tiles of the day bed shimmer. Creamy candles, single and en masse, flicker warmly in the descending twilight.

Other plant options for fillers

WALLS 66-*Alpinia zerumbet* 99-*Plumbago auriculata* DIVIDERS 114-*Aechmea* spp.& cvs 120-*Arthropodium cirratum* 121-*Aspidistra elatior* 131-*Chorizema cordatum* 136-*Cuphea hyssopifolia* 137-*Dietes bicolor* 139-*Duranta erecta* cultivars 147-*Hemerocallis* Hybrid Cultivars 155-*Liriope muscari* 158-*Loropetalum chinense* 'Rubrum' 159-*Molineria capitulata* 161-*Nandina domestica* cultivars 166-*Phormium cookianum* 169-*Pogonatherum paniceum* 175-*Santolina chamaecyparissus* 179-*Tulbaghia violacea* ACCENTS 232-*Alocasia brisbanensis* 259-*Echeveria agavoides* 275-*Moraea robinsoniana* 283-*Phormium tenax* 285-*Protasparagus densiflorus* 'Myersii' 286-*Restio tetraphyllus* 288-*Spathiphyllum* Hybrid Cultivars 295-*Vriesea* spp. & cvs PAINT 363-*Allamanda cathartica* 365-*Aphanopetalum resinosum* 366-*Bougainvillea* cultivars 367-*Cissus hypoglauca* 372-*Hibbertia scandens* 374-*Mandevilla sanderi* 375-*Pandorea jasminoides* 378-*Passiflora coccinea* 382-*Trachelospermum jasminoides* WATER 387-*Colocasia esculenta* 388-*Cyperus papyrus* 389-*Cyperus prolifer* 391-*Iris* Louisiana Hybrids 392-*Juncus usitatus* 395-*Thalia dealbata* 397-*Zantedeschia aethiopica*

blooming

energy

hue

welcoming

perfume

being

Real paint is about covering up and decorating a surface and 'paint' plants do the same thing. If you have an ugly shed, a neighbour's blank wall that's crying out for visual relief or a small courtyard without enough space for a screening hedge, a treatment with a splash of plant paint might just be the answer.

These plants are mostly climbers – plants that grow up to a fair height without being able to support themselves. The weak stems of climbing plants find support by attaching themselves to stronger neighbours in various ways. Some have tendrils that wrap their fingers around whatever comes within reach, like passionfruit and grape vines. Others, like bougainvillea, have hooks that let the plant scramble upwards. The stems of twining climbers such as star jasmine at least do some work by twisting their way around and up even thick trunks and posts. Then there are those climbers like creeping fig that attach themselves to surfaces with what are called adventitious roots, or little roots that come out of the stems. Boston ivy is especially good at climbing because it has tendrils that also have suction cups which stick just like adventitious roots.

It's important to set up the right kind of support for your climber of choice. Wire isn't any use to a root climber which can make its own way straight up a brick wall. But a twiner won't have anything to wrap around along a brick wall unless some lattice or wires are rigged up.

All climbers need a support that's strong enough to carry the extra weight. Some, like Stephanotis floribunda, are only light and might climb up any old pole and be happy not to go much further. Others are rampant and will buckle fences and trellises that aren't up to the job. These are the ones to look for when you're planning to use a climber to go up and extend overhead on a pergola (See Roof and Ceiling sections starting on page 13).

Most climbers will need discipline.

They've adapted to move upwards in search of light and will climb wherever the wind happens to blow them. If you don't want all your vine growing along the top of a fence, give it some help to do the job you want by training it to spread out down low and climb where you want it to grow.

Espalier is a wonderful way to 'paint' a wall, but it's an art that requires a great deal of skill as you have to discipline the plant into an unnatural two-dimensional shape (though the elegant results are truly rewarding). Fruit trees are especially desirable for this process because the lateral spread encourages maximum fruit yield, particularly when growing against a warm wall.

Also consider epiphytes like the staghorn and elkhorn ferns and Tillandsia which attach themselves to other plants in nature without being parasitic. Along with lithophytes, or plants that grow on rocks, these plants can be mounted and hung as wall decoration just like a painting.

362 *Akebia quinata* **CHOCOLATE VINE** The strong growth and five-fingered leaves of this semi-deciduous twiner work well in tropical designs for cooler climates. Fragrant brown-purple flowers are followed by sausage fruit if cross-pollinated. **8m**

363 *Allamanda cathartica* **GOLDEN TRUMPET** Can be trained against a wall or massed in tropical and Mediterranean designs as a loose, open shrub to fill a space with its bright glossy leaves and yellow trumpet flowers through summer and autumn. **5m**

364 *Ampelopsis glandulosa* var. *brevipedunculata* **PORCELAIN VINE** A deciduous twiner much like a grape vine except the fruit are a fantasy of metallic blues and purples in autumn. 'Elegans' has an interesting white speckled variegation but at the expense of the fruit. **5m**

365 *Aphanopetalum resinosum* **GUM VINE** A shrubby native climber that can also be allowed to sprawl as a filler or a spillover. Bracts like a white NSW Xmas Bush appear among the glossy leaves in late spring. Compatible with tropical, Mediterranean or Asian themes. **2m**

366 *Bougainvillea* cultivars **BOUGAINVILLEA** The vibrant bracts of this scrambler are a standard of tropical or Mediterranean designs. The well-behaved 'Bambino' range comes in less saturated colours and can be used as groundcovers or in pots. **8m**

367 *Cissus hypoglauca* **WATER VINE** Five fingered glossy leaves like those of an Umbrella Tree give this native climber a rainforest feel. Let the plant climb high enough to reveal the blue-green colouring under the leaves. **10m**

368 *Clerodendrum splendens* **FLAMING GLORYBOWER** Robust-looking, rippled leaves but a good-mannered climber to bring flaming colour to a warm, small space over a long period. The flowers are also likely to bring butterflies in to feast on their nectar. **3m**

369 *Clytostoma callistegioides* **ARGENTINE TRUMPET VINE** Soon becomes a robust climber needing room and solid support. Among glossy leaves, the lilac and white of the purple-veined trumpet flowers in late spring are unusually pastel for a distinctly tropical-looking vine. **10m**

370 *Ficus pumila* **CREEPING FIG** Fig with vigorous roots and radically different adult habit. Consider carefully before selecting. Usefully attaches itself to and covers any surface even in shade. Several miniature and variegated cultivars. Immediately prune growth coming off surface. **10m**

371

S

372

373

Gelsemium sempervirens **CAROLINA JASMINE** Strong-growing but light climber for smaller spaces and trellises. The fragrant flowers appear over a long season but mostly over winter and spring. Growth is more shrubby with more sun exposure. The plant has toxic properties. **5m**

Hibbertia scandens **SNAKE VINE** Variable native with a shrubbier habit in full sun where useful as a filler. Most flowers in spring but appear over a long season. Compatible with tropical, Mediterranean, coastal or Asian themes if the yellow flowers won't jar with other colours. **4m**

Hoya carnosa **HOYA, WAX FLOWER** A strong but light, tropical-looking climber with waxy leaves. For a smaller space or around a pole where the fragrance of the waxy, pink or white summer flowers can be enjoyed. Waxy leaves also, may be variegated or crumpled. **2m**

374

375

376

Mandevilla sanderi **CHILEAN JASMINE** Not an aggressive climber. Easy to restrict in small areas or train up a post. It can also be kept low and shrubby for a filler. Cultivars with yellow-throated flowers in red, pink and white. For tropical and Mediterranean designs. **4m**

Pandorea jasminoides **BOWER OF BEAUTY VINE** Native climber with dark-throated trumpet flowers in pinky-white, or mid-dark pinks, through spring and summer. 'Lady Di' is white with a yellow throat. 'Charisma' has yellow variegated leaves. Strong enough to get over a pergola or use as a groundcover. **6m**

Parthenocissus henryana **SILVER VEIN CREEPER** Self-clinging and with five-fingered leaves like the Virginia Creeper. Not as vigorous and new leaves are bronze-flushed, developing silver veins with purple underneath. Plants in sun lose their silver but plants in the shade don't colour as red before falling. **8m**

377

378

379

Parthenocissus tricuspidata **BOSTON IVY** Layers of maple-like leaves give an established look to walls in formal or Asian designs. Tendrils attach this deciduous vine to surfaces with pads that are hard to remove. 'Veitchii' has bronze flushed new leaves which colour purple-red in autumn. **15m**

Passiflora coccinea **RED FLOWERING PASSION-FRUIT** An at times overly-vigorous tropical climber that can also be used as a groundcover if nothing else will be in its way. Foliage has a bronze tinge and the fascinating flowers appear through summer and autumn. **9m**

Platycerium bifurcatum **ELKHORN FERN** Not the usual decoration for a wall or post but makes a big impact. Shield fronds attached to a mount will multiply and spread, each with a growing point for the fertile, antler fronds. For informal, tropical schemes. **1m x 1m**

380

381

382

Stephanotis floribunda **MADAGASCAR JASMINE** A light climber that doesn't need much support. Good for a post, trellis or wires and for Asian, tropical or Mediterranean schemes. Beautiful fragrance as it continues to flower from late spring and through autumn. **4m**

Thunbergia grandiflora **SKYFLOWER** Strong, heavy vine that needs that be kept at a safe distance from everything except a solid support. Casts dense shade but flowers most of the time. So vigorous it's a Class 2 weed in Queensland and entry to WA is prohibited. **10m**

Trachelospermum jasminoides **STAR JASMINE** Slow to start but becomes a dense cover of dark green. Main flush of fragrant flowers is from late spring. Suitable for a tropical, Mediterranean or Asian effect. Also a groundcover but stems should be prevented from twining into ropes. **6m**

383

384

385

Vigna caracalla **SNAIL FLOWER** Looks much like an ordinary bean until the fragrant flowers appear, first white then colouring, through summer and autumn. Once established, quickly covers a big area on a wall or pergola in a tropical or Mediterranean garden design. **8m**

Vitis vinifera 'Alicante Bouchet' **ORNAMENTAL GRAPE** Grape vines are a very Mediterranean element in the landscape. Also used in bonsai and their ancient looking stems and maple-like leaves could work in Asian designs. This cultivar has particularly good autumn colouring before the leaves fall. **6m**

Wisteria sinensis **CHINESE WISTERIA** Plenty of room, support and discipline needed to enjoy the benefit of the spring flowering show in lavender, purple, pink or white. Use in Mediterranean, Asian or as an informal element in formal schemes. Suckers persistently where roots are disturbed. **10m**

Other plant options for paint
WALLS 99-*Plumbago auriculata* FLOORS 189-*Cissus antarctica* 199-*Hedera helix* ACCENTS 284-*Platycerium superbum* 293-*Tillandsia usneoides* FILLERS 308-*Bauhinia galpinii* 328-*Hardenbergia violacea* 338-*Jasminum sambac* 'Grand Duke of Tuscany' 344-*Monstera deliciosa* 349-*Pelargonium peltatum* 351-*Philodendron selloum* 358-*Trachelospermum jasminoides* 'Tricolor'

Spanish Moss or tillandsia usneoides *is a wonderful paint plant that survives on moist air. Here it takes centre stage – a bizarre hairy clump that looks straight out of a sci-fi movie. Suspended against a deep red backdrop on a thin stainless steel cable, it is the organic wild card in an otherwise ordered water feature creating memorable visual interest. In such a confined space, the inclusion of all these different surfaces (soft, hard, natural and manmade materials) and the element of water mean that lights have a lot to play with. The indoor garden extends to a relaxed outdoor living room.*

soothing

sensual

tranquillity

lapping

sanctum

wellbeing

We don't need to promote the benefits of a pond or water feature in the outdoor space – Australians love 'em! Beautiful to look at, soothing to listen to, refreshing to the touch: they are second to none for creating an atmosphere of tranquillity and calm. There are many fine products on the market so you can install one yourself or go for broke and invest in one of the stunning ready-made features or one-off pieces of water-art available in the more up-market nurseries.

Plants look great in water and even the most contemporary design will be enhanced by the addition of leaves or flowers floating on the surface. They are a natural water filter and some species even discourage mosquitoes. Always take care to plant in water of a suitable depth or else you might find your water plants drowning.

If you're looking at plants for pools connected to natural watercourses rather than a contained water feature, your selection process will have to be quite different. Water is a dangerously effective distributor of weedy plants and you certainly don't want a vigorous species taking over your garden or – worse still – getting out and choking nearby waterways, so be careful with your choice. Many of our worst weeds are water weeds.

Even the smallest garden might have a wet patch, but before you pave it over or drain it to stormwater, think about turning it into a bog garden. Now it might not be the sexiest answer to your gardening dreams, but a constantly wet spot is a great way of doing your bit for the environment by retaining any excess water on your property. And it can become a glorious feature in itself: just imagine the bold leaves of elephant's ear; the exotic flowers of Louisiana irises floating above upright strappy foliage; the elegance of arum lilies; or the delicacy of a water fern. Throw in various banksias, paperbarks, Carex, Isolepis, tea trees and other natives and you'll start believing it's a blessing to be bogged.

If you don't have a naturally damp garden bed but like the idea of lush clumps of giant taro in your garden then maybe you could create one. With a fair bit of spade-work, you can make a bed hold its water and there you have your own mini-bog. The next step up the scale would be to build your own artificial water garden, creating a balanced ecosystem where water is oxygenated, algae and mozzie larvae are under control, and plants and fish can live happily and healthily. Not surprisingly this is a much more involved undertaking (water proofing, filters and pumps, specialist planting baskets and soil media) so you'll probably need professional help. There are many specialist aquatic nurseries around.

386

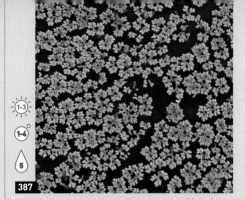

387

388

Acorus gramineus **JAPANESE RUSH** Although architectural as a single clump, this looks good massed like the turf of a water garden. 'Ogon' has golden variegation while 'Variegatus' has a white stripe. 'Pusillus' has green, weeping leaves. The leaves of *A. calamus* are aromatic. **0.25 m x 0.15 m**

Azolla spp. **FAIRY MOSS** Floating ferns native to just about everywhere because they multiply and spread so quickly. Better used in water features rather than ponds so it can be admired for its fine detail and kept under control. **0.01 m x indefinite**

Colocasia esculenta **TARO** Handsome as a specimen but easier to use as a filler as it will spread itself anyway. 'Black Magic' is the one with deep all-purple leaves. 'Fontanesii' is dark green with purple veins and stalks. **1.8m x 1.8m**

389

390

391

Cyperus papyrus **PAPYRUS** Historically important as Moses' bulrushes and ancient Egyptian source of paper. Now a sculptural element in modern gardens. Will grow in water or out but take precautions to prevent it getting into any waterways. **4m x 2m**

Cyperus prolifer **DWARF PAPYRUS** An accent or filler for tropical, Mediterranean and Asian designs on a smaller scale than the other *Cyperus*. Not as widely used as other species but as much caution should be taken in planting this one to avoid unwanted spread. **0.5m x 0.3m**

Iris Louisiana Hybrids **LOUISIANA IRIS** Although very effective mass planted and quick-clumping, take advantage of this perennial's erect habit for an accent in moist garden beds or water. Choose height and colour to suit tropical, Asian or Mediterranean design. **1m x 0.5m**

392

393

394

Juncus usitatus **TUSSOCK RUSH** Such an adaptable grassy native that it can grow in shallow water and tolerate drought conditions. A vertical accent as an individual on a small scale. Mass clumps together for a textural, tussocky effect when the scale is larger. **1m x 1.5m**

Pontederia cordata **PICKEREL WEED** Strong-growing heart-shaped leaves but dies back in winter. Grows in shallow water or boggy soil. Flower spikes appear over a long period from summer. 'Alba' is white flowering. Suits tropical, Asian and Mediterranean styles. **0.75 m x 0.5m**

Pratia pedunculata **MATTED PRATIA** A ground-hugging native that likes constant moisture and can happily grow at the water's edge of a pond. Blue or white flowers appear mostly through spring and summer. Also available is 'Pink Stars'. 'Country Park' has deep blue flowers. **0.05 m x 1m**

395

396

397

Thalia dealbata **WATER CANNA** Large leaves, each welded to a thin stem with a red collar, are more like and related to ctenanthes, only for water or boggy soils. An accent or filler for tropical and Asian themes. Violet and grey flowers from summer. **2m x 0.75 m**

Typha spp. **CUMBUNGI** Quick to colonise a watercourse and even the native species, *T. domingensis* and *T. orientalis*, should be used where they will be contained. Leaves die down in winter. Mediterranean, Asian or tropical effect. Entry to WA prohibited and restricted in Tasmania. **2m x 5m**

Zantedeschia aethiopica **ARUM LILY** Grows in shallow water or ordinary garden beds. Evergreen where moisture is constant but can be aggressive. Works in tropical, Mediterranean and Asian designs. 'Childsiana' is smaller. Flower spathe is pink in 'Marshmallow' while 'Green Goddess' is green and white. **1.5m x 1m**

Other plant options for water
FILLER 318-*Cyperus involucratus*

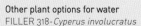

This garden has it all: a cacophony of plants and materials that blend in perfect harmony – it took out the award for Best Construction and an Award for Excellence at the World Garden Competition in Japan. Based on an amphitheatre, it is filled with complementary shapes, colours and textures with the soothing element of water spills over the space culminating in a still, restful pool.

Round timber islands dot the liquid surface like the shells of giant ancient turtles providing access from lawn to deck. This shell shape is repeated on a larger scale when the sweeping timber deck suddenly splits and rears up to display a lush bed of native violets like a tantalising glimpse into another realm.

The gabion wall is used to both retain and to give a sculptural effect. Mass plantings define and delight with beds of a spiky red Cordylin australis cultivar and flaming stands of Anigozanthos. The implacable Xanthorrhoea loom like sturdy Roman pillars and giant yukkas add their distinctive green spears. To the rear, tall groupings of Cordyline australis act as screens.

MATERIALS & PRODUCTS

During the last decade or so, a gradual revolution has been occurring in our backyards. Australians have begun to fully embrace the idea that every outdoor space has the potential to be a beautiful, functional garden – from a wild mess of scrubland to an urban concrete box.

Along with the shift in attitude has come a whole new way of thinking about what you can put in the garden. These days the rule is . . . well, there simply are no rules. Any material imaginable, as long as it withstands the elements, can be a part of the hard scape and the more bizarre the substance, the more interesting the result. Furniture and accessories personalise your space. Think about what suits the style of your garden, and what you would like to live with. This hardware is as much a part of your garden as the plants.

In this section, we cover as many materials and products for outdoor spaces as possible: from the traditional like timber, bricks, stone, cement, wire and tiles to the more innovative like river stones, ceramics, stainless-steel, polished stone, recycled timber – you name it, anything goes!

So how do you go about making your choices? I have an image in my head that I return to time and again when I need some help with decision making. I saw it several years ago, when I was travelling – a long, geometrical stainless-steel vase cradling an arrangement of orange tulips on a corner table by a window. That's the secret, I thought, that strong, simple object has made us focus our attention on the soft organic texture and natural lines of the tulip. If it had been in an even slightly more ornate vessel, it would not have made anything near the same impact and I would have looked straight past it

. . . I apply the same theory to a landscape, leaning towards materials that are simple and clean with an uncomplicated form that complements rather than competes with the featured item or plant.

So, how does this section work? Have a browse through the pages, organised into categories according to function, check out the product number, and then look up the directory at the back, starting on page 191 to find out who the supplier is. In most cases, a quick visit to the company's website will tell you where to find it near you.

So don't be afraid to try something new and unusual. Experimenting with the materials that frame the garden, define the areas for different activities, and elevate the landscape and featured plants, is often where the real excitement and creativity comes in.

The materials and products shown in this section have been chosen to both inspire you and to introduce you to the suppliers on PATIO's files. You'll discover materials and product ranges that you never knew existed and, apart from anything else, you'll get thousands of ideas for designing your own space.

Once you have found something that appeals to you and you'd like to know more about it, use the product number to find the supplier details at the back of the book. A phone call or a visit to the company's website will give you the nearest retailer, the recommended retail price and more product information than space allows us to give here. We've made sure that the details listed are enough to identify the product when you contact the supplier.

THE CAPTION TELLS YOU WHAT THE PRODUCT IS CALLED. USE THE SUPPLIER NUMBER TO LOOK UP THE DETAILS OF THE DISTRIBUTOR IN THE MATERIALS & PRODUCTS: SUPPLIERS SECTION STARTING ON PAGE 191.

THE PRODUCT NUMBER LINKS TO THE CAPTION ON THE SAME PAGE.

406 Feilf stone: Yarra
Supplier #241

407 Greenstone water feature & Lavastone stools: Clio Supplier #240

408 20x20mm copper mosaic tile
Supplier #180

409 Noosa hedge wall infill used as a breezeway Supplier #219

410 'Cobblestone' close up
Supplier #250

411 Wildstone 'Cobblestone' blocks
Supplier #250

412 Basalt blue bookleaf walling
Supplier #204

413 Wildstone garden settings: wall and pillars Supplier #250

oasis

privacy

enclosing

outlining

cocooning

refuge

WALLS

When security and privacy are priorities – and if you live in the city, that's pretty much a given – the garden wall is going to figure strongly in your overall design. You may be wanting to dress up or rebuild an existing fence line or to start completely from scratch. Either way, there's plenty to look at when it comes to selecting the material you'll eventually work with.

Inside and outside, walls define and provide the backdrop to the spaces we do our living in, so we need to think carefully about what we wish to achieve within in those spaces. Do you want it to be an intimate refuge for relaxation or will you need lots of room and built-in bench seating for entertaining a crowd? This will dictate where to position the walls and what materials to use.

A solid wall of brick or stone will score high points for privacy, security and noise-filtration. Timber also makes a solid wall if it's well-constructed. When capped top and bottom, a simple treated-pine paling fence is a far more sturdy barrier. And don't for a moment think that these traditional choices have to be boring.

There are so many marvellous ways to make your wall more interesting. It can be done in the design and construction of the wall. Turn and angle timber slats and palings in different ways. Lay bricks in patterns or with gaps, or set the wall out in a flowing shape.

Another option is to have a completely plain, structural wall and dress it up with something more attractive. There are all sorts of stone, bamboo and timber cladding to turn a wall into a feature. And of course the most straightforward makeup for an old brick wall is to slap on one of the many types of render and a good coat of paint (see 'Paint' starting on page 125).

Then there are the not-so-obvious choices like glass, resin, bamboo, brushwood and metal. Or go one step further and think about combining materials – that's when things really start to get interesting. A fine example of this can be seen in the 'gabion' walls shown on pages 86 and 87 where stiff, vertical wire 'cages' are braced by timber struts and filled with river stones making a strong, secure and flexible boundary that is an attractive focal point in itself.

If your yard is big enough you might want to divide it into several different spaces with a wall or more lightweight screens and partitions. Reed or bamboo screens are wonderful for creating new spaces – and diffusing sunlight when used overhead – while allowing the breezes through.

Wall-building is a terrific design opportunity. Think about interrupting the wall surface with narrow gaps to let in light and air, or larger windows that frame a view of what's on the other side. And shelves or niches will allow you to add a candle, a potted accent plant or a small sculpture to break up a dull expanse.

398

399

400

401

402

403

404

405

398 Cracked marble cladding in grey
Supplier #240

399 Matrix wide feature wall
Supplier #185

400 Forged wall: Pewter
Supplier #185

401 Matrix thin feature wall
Supplier #185

402 Wistow dry stack walling stone
Supplier #251

403 Aniseed granite water wall
Supplier #204

404 Sandstone bookleaf wall
Supplier #204

405 Wistow builders bookleaf walling stone
Supplier #251

406

407

408

409

410

411

412

413

406 Feilf stone: Yarra
Supplier #241

407 Greenstone water feature & Lavastone
stools: Clio Supplier #240

408 20x20mm copper mosaic tile
Supplier #180

409 Noosa hedge wall infill used as a
breezeway Supplier #219

410 'Cobblestone' close up
Supplier #250

411 Wildstone 'Cobblestone' blocks
Supplier #250

412 Basalt blue bookleaf walling
Supplier #204

413 Wildstone garden settings: wall and
pillars Supplier #250

414 Split face white marble cladding
Supplier #240

415 Wildstone entrance blocks
Supplier #250

416 Jasper bluestone bookleaf walling stone
Supplier #204

417 Natural stacked charcoal bookleaf wall
cladding Supplier #239

418 Chiselled strata stacked stone: modular
walling panel 610x152mm Supplier #239

419 Sandstone split strips
Supplier #204

420 Sandstone bookleaf walling
Supplier #204

421 Raised planter clad with stacked stone
Supplier #239

422 Yellow/beige wall cladding
Supplier #239

423 Roman brick range: Apricot blend
Supplier #192

424 Hawthorne Black in slimmer Roman
brick Supplier #192

425 Wildstone gate post blocks
Supplier #250

426 Colorbond steel slat gates & gables
Supplier #243

427 Roman brick in customised Seville blend
Supplier #192

428 Ochre MonaroStone (stain and graffiti
resistant) feature wall Supplier #229

429 MonaroStone in shades of grey
Supplier #229

430

431

432

433

434

435

430 Step treads: A combination of grey granite Norblock and MonaroStone Supplier #229

431 High wall clad in grey MonaroStone Supplier #229

432 Grey Granite Pavers – exfoliated surface finish Supplier #247

433 Contemporary Quartzstone pillars, wall blocks and coping Supplier #237

434 Large format reconstituted sandstone paving, wall blocks and wall capping Supplier #237

435 Stainless steel slat panels Supplier #243

436 Sandstone bookleaf wall Supplier #204

437 Noosa Hedge panel breaks up rendered block wall Supplier #219

436

437

438 Ironwood sleepers
Supplier #233

439 30mm brush fencing 30x1800x3000mm
Supplier #212

440 Ironwood outdoor treated pine
Supplier #233

441 Pencil picket gate
Supplier #219

442 Teak 2x1m trellis screens
Supplier #239

443 Boardwalk deck & screen
Supplier #238

444 Turpentine feature wall & seat
Supplier #183

445 45x22mm rough sawn screen board
Supplier #238

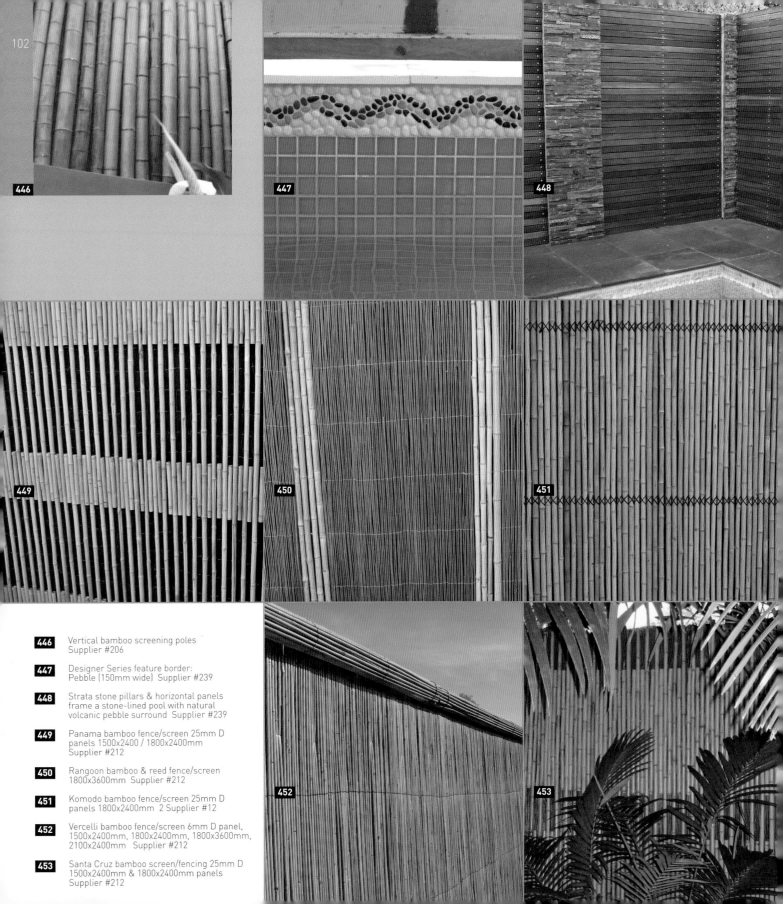

446 Vertical bamboo screening poles
Supplier #206

447 Designer Series feature border:
Pebble (150mm wide) Supplier #239

448 Strata stone pillars & horizontal panels
frame a stone-lined pool with natural
volcanic pebble surround Supplier #239

449 Panama bamboo fence/screen 25mm D
panels 1500x2400 / 1800x2400mm
Supplier #212

450 Rangoon bamboo & reed fence/screen
1800x3600mm Supplier #212

451 Komodo bamboo fence/screen 25mm D
panels 1800x2400mm 2 Supplier #12

452 Vercelli bamboo fence/screen 6mm D panel,
1500x2400mm, 1800x2400mm, 1800x3600mm,
2100x2400mm   Supplier #212

453 Santa Cruz bamboo screen/fencing 25mm D
1500x2400mm & 1800x2400mm panels
Supplier #212

454 Woven bamboo ply in multiple weave designs: 1200x2400mm, 1200x1800mm (thickness 2, 4 or 6mm) Supplier #212

455 Natureed screening
Supplier #206

456 NatureShade screening
Supplier #217

457 Ledge stone: Avoca
Supplier #241

458 Stacked stone: Murchison
Supplier #241

459 Contemporary Quartzstone pillar
Supplier #237

460 Large format reconstituted sandstone paving, wall blocks, capping and pond
Supplier #237

461 Arbour marble tiles
Supplier #188

This stark rooftop garden needed the suggestion of rooms without blocking any part of the breathtaking 360-degree cityscape. The solution was to create the idea of walls by erecting timber cubes that act as giant frames for the surrounding view – an effective way of focussing the eye towards stunning vistas. Galvanised iron tubs contain hardy plants that will grow into natural wind-breaks and a climbing bougainvillea scrambles across the timber frame, dissolving the rigid lines.

grounded
foundation
stability
pattern
undulating
base

Pavers are far and away the most popular option when it comes to outdoor floors, and why not? They come in a huge range of shapes and sizes and are made of anything from clay to concrete to reconstituted stone. Different elements can be added to the mixture for colour and texture and the surface treated to produce great finishes like sawn, polished, flamed, honed, split faced, bush hammered and picked. Keep in mind a space looks bigger with a larger format paver and consider the spaces between the pavers; from none at all with butt-jointing, to a joint large enough to allow herbs or scented 'floor' plants to poke through. Pavers can also be laid in patterns or with inlays of other materials, tying in the floor covering with other materials used in the garden or even in the house.

For small areas or as a highlight material, tiles are a great way to interrupt a large, monotonous expanse. Vitrified tiles are a ceramic tile baked at a very high temperature to produce a very hard, even surface and work particularly well outdoors. Multi-coloured mosaic is an age-old method of bringing an artistic touch to your garden and let's not forget about gravels. All sorts of wonderful colour and texture combinations can result from this simple and extremely cost-effective option (just two twenty kilogram bags covers a full square metre).

Make sure there's adequate drainage of your hard surfaces and that the run-off feeds into other areas of the garden so no rainfall is wasted. This makes good sense not only for your water bill, but for the environment in general. And take a good hard look at the permeable material options (pavers with drainage holes are available) as these help provide moisture to the green covers and mulches by allowing water to infiltrate to the soil beneath.

Timber decks make a really good firm, clean surface that lets rain trickle through the spaces between into the ground beneath where it would have ended up naturally. And think beyond the conventional deck where the timber is restricted to straight lines. Why not bend the wood to follow an organic line or sweep the edge of a deck around to mirror the natural curve of a path? Clever innovations are happening all the time, like the use of timber off-cuts with a plastic structure so they can interlock into any pattern.

Like the wall, using combinations of materials works really well. Think of large slabs of stone sunk in a sea of pebbles or a pattern of bricks linked by a mortar of fine gravel or an arrangement of stepping stones fringed with living groundcover.

Plot the areas that will have to endure a high level of foot activity and make sure the material you use is as durable as possible. And remember, if there's going to be lots of building going on, leave the floor to last so as to avoid damage from all the heavy equipment and humans tramping through.

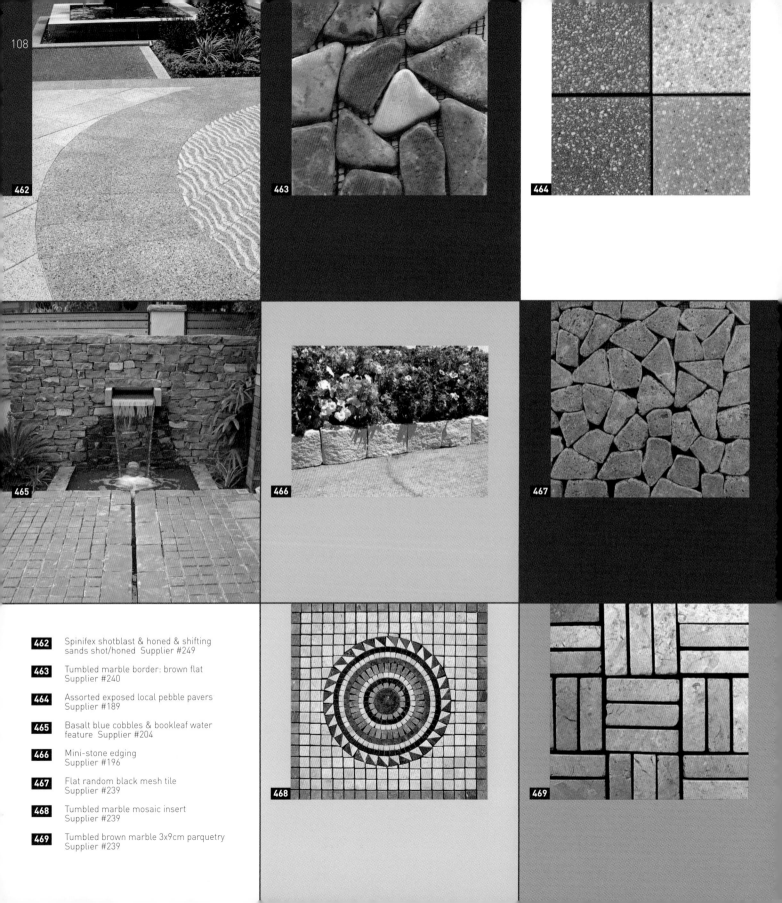

462

463

464

465

466

467

462 Spinifex shotblast & honed & shifting sands shot/honed Supplier #249

463 Tumbled marble border: brown flat Supplier #240

464 Assorted exposed local pebble pavers Supplier #189

465 Basalt blue cobbles & bookleaf water feature Supplier #204

466 Mini-stone edging Supplier #196

467 Flat random black mesh tile Supplier #239

468 Tumbled marble mosaic insert Supplier #239

469 Tumbled brown marble 3x9cm parquetry Supplier #239

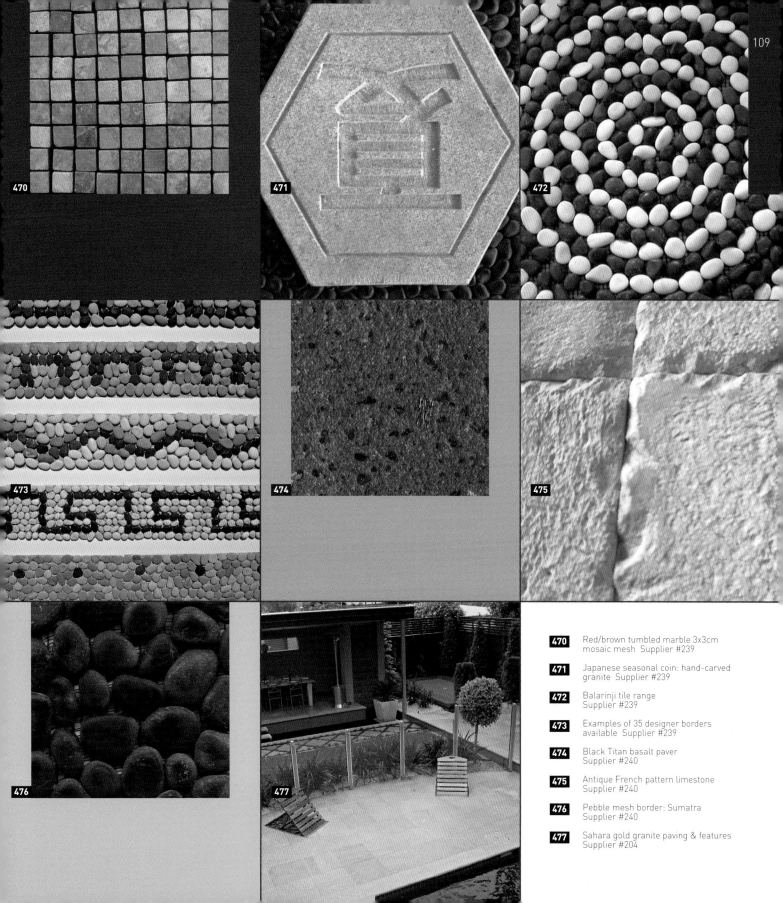

470

471

472

473

474

475

476

477

470 Red/brown tumbled marble 3x3cm mosaic mesh Supplier #239

471 Japanese seasonal coin: hand-carved granite Supplier #239

472 Balarinji tile range Supplier #239

473 Examples of 35 designer borders available Supplier #239

474 Black Titan basalt paver Supplier #240

475 Antique French pattern limestone Supplier #240

476 Pebble mesh border: Sumatra Supplier #240

477 Sahara gold granite paving & features Supplier #204

478 Sandblasted basalt pavers
Supplier #204

479 Classic terracotta tiles in sandstone
Supplier #192

480 Mahogany 50mm clay paver/Pilbara
border Supplier #218

481 Light yellow setts
Supplier #204

482 Basalt blue bookleaf walling & random
basalt paving Supplier #204

483 Coal Creek paver
Supplier #189

484 Aniseed granite strips
Supplier #204

485 Indo flat yellow pebbles 40–70mm
Supplier #194

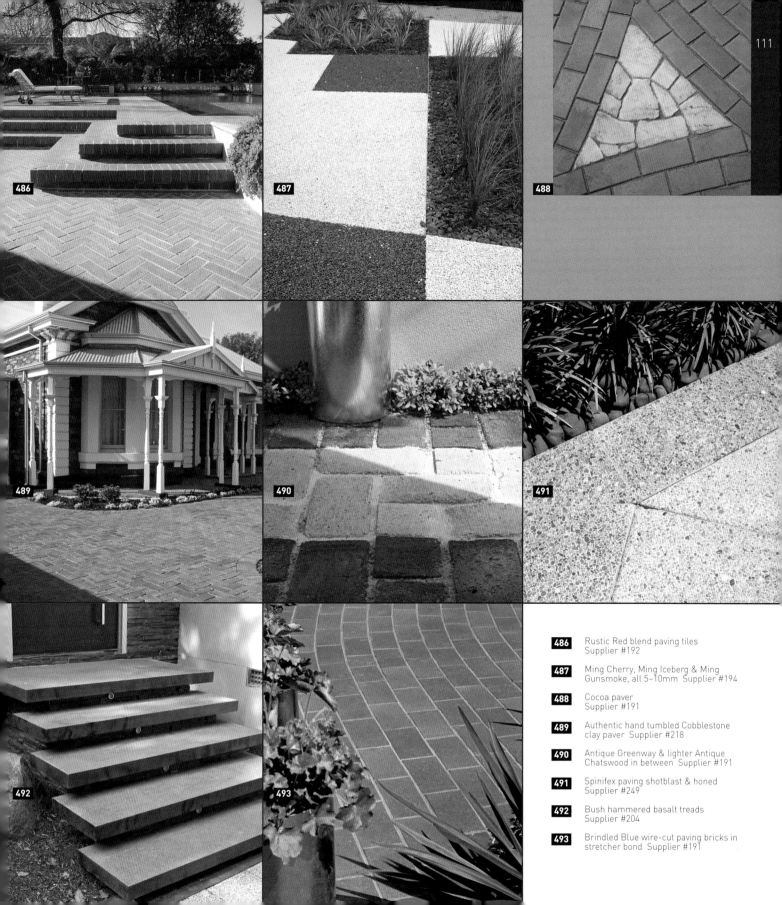

486 Rustic Red blend paving tiles
Supplier #192

487 Ming Cherry, Ming Iceberg & Ming
Gunsmoke, all 5–10mm Supplier #194

488 Cocoa paver
Supplier #191

489 Authentic hand tumbled Cobblestone
clay paver Supplier #218

490 Antique Greenway & lighter Antique
Chatswood in between Supplier #191

491 Spinifex paving shotblast & honed
Supplier #249

492 Bush hammered basalt treads
Supplier #204

493 Brindled Blue wire-cut paving bricks in
stretcher bond Supplier #191

112

494

495

496

497

498

499

500

501

494 Wistow bluestone pool & patio pavers 30–50mm thick Supplier #251

495 Hawthorne Black rustic paving from the Roman range Supplier #192

496 Antique Chatswood paver in basketweave Supplier #191

497 Carrarastone Tucana tile 330x330mm Supplier #199

498 Coachman Landau tile 300x300mm Supplier #199

499 Carrarastone Rococo tile 330x330mm Supplier #199

500 Dromana earth paver with fine exposure finish Supplier #189

501 Boulevard gold tile 400x400mm Supplier #199

502 Coal Creek paver
Supplier #189

503 Naturals Yulara tile 300x300mm
Supplier #199

504 Elegance Sequoia tile 330x330, 330x165,
165x165mm Supplier #199

505 Elegance Aquila tile 330x330, 330x165,
165x165mm Supplier #199

506 Wistow bluestone driveway pavers
50–75mm thick Supplier #251

507 Stonetek Sandstone tile 330x330mm
Supplier #199

508 Balarinji concept: bush hammered white
limestone with black volcanic diagonals
Balarinji billabong border Supplier #239

509 In situ poured natural limestone pool
surround & bullnose coping
Supplier #222

510

511

512

513

514

515

510 In situ poured natural limestone pool surround & bullnose coping Supplier #222

511 In situ poured natural limestone entrance & bullnose coping Supplier #222

512 Norblock in grey granite for paving, step treads & column trims Supplier #229

513 Crazy paving in natural basalt Supplier #239

514 In situ poured natural limestone driveway Supplier #222

515 Black Volcanic paver with Aubergine pebble insert Supplier #239

516 Peach pebble 25mm & tumbled grey pebble 20–40mm Supplier #232

517 Decking stain: Jarrah on treated pine Supplier #201

516

517

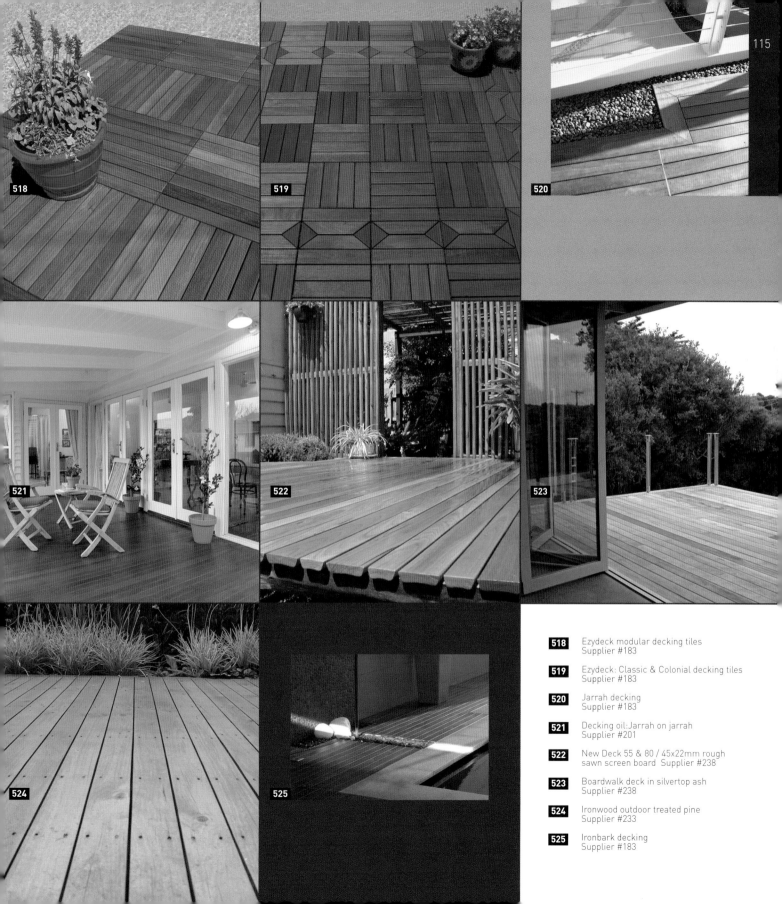

518 Ezydeck modular decking tiles
Supplier #183

519 Ezydeck: Classic & Colonial decking tiles
Supplier #183

520 Jarrah decking
Supplier #183

521 Decking oil:Jarrah on jarrah
Supplier #201

522 New Deck 55 & 80 / 45x22mm rough
sawn screen board Supplier #238

523 Boardwalk deck in silvertop ash
Supplier #238

524 Ironwood outdoor treated pine
Supplier #233

525 Ironbark decking
Supplier #183

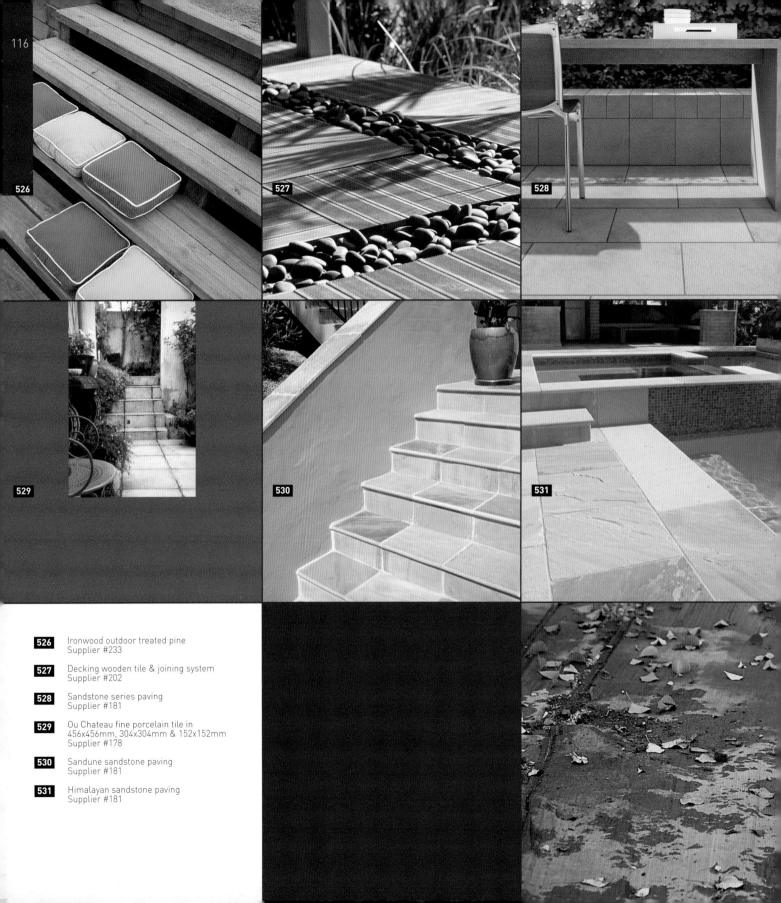

526

527

528

529

530

531

526 Ironwood outdoor treated pine
Supplier #233

527 Decking wooden tile & joining system
Supplier #202

528 Sandstone series paving
Supplier #181

529 Ou Chateau fine porcelain tile in
456x456mm, 304x304mm & 152x152mm
Supplier #178

530 Sandune sandstone paving
Supplier #181

531 Himalayan sandstone paving
Supplier #181

No longer just a functional
necessity, the material that floors
your outdoor room can be any one of
a thousand tactile, multi-textured
surfaces that can either dominate or
merely complement the space.

protection

seclusion

shade

airy

skyline

covering

OVERHEAD

Good garden design is all about extracting maximum value from the space. Any single distraction or disturbance you can eliminate from the equation will be an advantage, so blocking the view from tall neighbouring structures is a big plus. If that doesn't convince you, think of the added benefits in providing shade from the harmful effects of the sun, increasing your level of privacy, protecting your more valuable objects from the weather, and injecting a stronger sense of intimacy for that cosy closed-in feeling.

For all-year-round protection that still allows a degree of natural light, glass, perspex and the see-through corrugated plastic products will keep you dry and your more delicate plants frost-free. Sail cloths look great with their sharp lines and undulating curves, but their properties vary. Some aren't waterproof and others aren't sunproof so match the cloth to your requirements.

Less hardy and protective but far more natural-looking are the organic alternatives like bamboo blinds or sheets of reed. A timber trellis may not give much coverage on its own, but train a leafy climber across the grid and you have a perfect marriage of plant and structure.

If you decide to cut out all direct sun, the old corrugated iron roof has made a welcome return to contemporary design. Available in a rainbow of colours, it will last for many years and is still a great shelter under which to sit out a rain storm. Thatched roofs aren't cheap but don't get as hot underneath. They too have a long life and age beautifully, not to mention the slightly exotic element they bring to a garden.

532 MakMax CS32 architectural umbrella
Supplier #245

533 Natureed cladding for pergola
Supplier #206

534 Solid palm fibre roof cladding
Supplier #206

535 NatureShade rotates for shade through
360° Supplier #217

536 5m octagonal standard kit with standard
Cape Reed thatch Supplier #179

537 Natureed canopy
Supplier #206

538 NatureShade shades a pool & eating area
Supplier #217

539 Natureed overhead shade
Supplier #206

540 Vertiroll retractable tensioned vertical screen Supplier #211

541 Unicom drop arm awning and Laguna folding arm awning Supplier #211

542 Vertiroll retractable tensioned vertical screen Supplier #211

543 Vertiroll blue vertical blind reducing glare & wind Supplier #211

544 Laguna folding arm awning Supplier #211

545 Straight cut Cape Reed thatching Supplier #179

546 Natureed overhead shade & bamboo screen Supplier #206

547 Unicom drop arm awning Supplier #211

548 4.4m round on 4 Permarod Posts standard kit with standard Cape Reed thatching Supplier #179

549 5m square custom made unit with 60° pitch Supplier #179

550 Natureed canopy Supplier #206

551 Solid membrane sail over first floor – Fabric Ferrari 502 Supplier #197

552 4.5m2 custom built Bar Shelter with off set angle of 60° Supplier #179

553 Sails over paved area overlooking water – Fabric Ferrari Soltis Supplier #197

Right. This small courtyard garden is used all year round by a young family so sturdy overhead protection was a must to keep out the wind and weather. Privacy from neighbouring buildings was also an issue so this broad sail was deliberately chosen for its opaque screening properties. Harmful UV-rays are kept at bay while still allowing natural light and warmth to penetrate below.

It's hard to imagine that only minutes before these photographs were taken, the garden was awash with toys, games and other assorted kiddie paraphernalia. Although compact, there's loads of storage tucked away in the voids of timber seating so only minimal effort is required to transform a child's playground into a sophisticated adult zone. Clever storage ideas and built-in furniture means it's easy to maintain the integrity of the original design and serve everyone's needs at the same time.

mood

calm

dimension

harmony

ambience

palette

In any garden, landscape or building exterior we can be faced with fences, walls, partitions or boundaries that seem daunting, constricting or just plain ugly. Luckily, a simple splash of paint over the top can sometimes be the solution.

Rendering and bagging the surface first can add to the masking job. Various render products have been developed to be water-repellent, water-vapour permeable, weather-resistant or to withstand mechanical stress. These days lots of different ingredients have been thrown into the mix like cement, graded quartz sand, crushed limestone, polymer-modified cement binders, plasticisers, coloured acrylic, synthetic resin and silicon resin, to name but a few. And you haven't even considered colour, texture and pattern yet. Float, trowel or patterned finish?

With or without render, the preparation you do before painting will make a big difference to the final look of the job. As tempting as it is to rush in, it's always better in the long run to put the investment of time and labour into a solid, appropriate foundation for your paint. Then all you have to worry about is getting the right paint for masonry, timber or metal, deciding on the right texture and sheen and the little problem of choosing a good colour. The choice of colours and paint effects can be absolutely daunting.

And that doesn't take into account the host of other solutions to disguise those eyesores. You can dress up a dull surface with cladding – not the faux-brick horrors of days gone by – but stacked stones like sandstone, slate, granite, bluestone and schist or lashed bamboo and reed sheets, for example. Mosaic tiles are also an effective and popular finish. With so many colours, sizes and designs available today you can quite easily create your very own personalised mural. Or you could get in a professional to finish almost any surface with a metal coating.

On the other hand, maybe the look you need is no finish at all. Many of the best elements of a garden lie in the beauty of the raw materials like the patterns in stone, the grain of wood, the oxide in pavers and the rich ochre hues of terracotta clay. Contemporary designs are drawing more and more from these natural features, so look before you leap because the best solution might already be right there in front of you.

Take inspiration from the following pages and remember that most hardware stores have a paint department. Your local one will probably offer options that don't appear here but which are still excellent solutions. Decide what look you want and seek advice from the sales staff about how to achieve the effect.

554

555

556

557

558

554 Kalk, colours 60/80 & 60/05: Limepaint on garden feature wall Supplier #186

555 Solagard Stone Finish, wall Hydrotherapy, pot: Rigolet Supplier #254

556 Über, colour 44/25: Limepaint for previously painted surfaces Supplier #186

557 Kalk, colour 44/35: painted on old rendered wall Supplier #186

558 Kalk, colour 60/80 & 60/05: colours painted simultaneously Supplier #186

559 Kalk, colour 104/96 Supplier #186

560 Interno lime wash Supplier #235

559

560

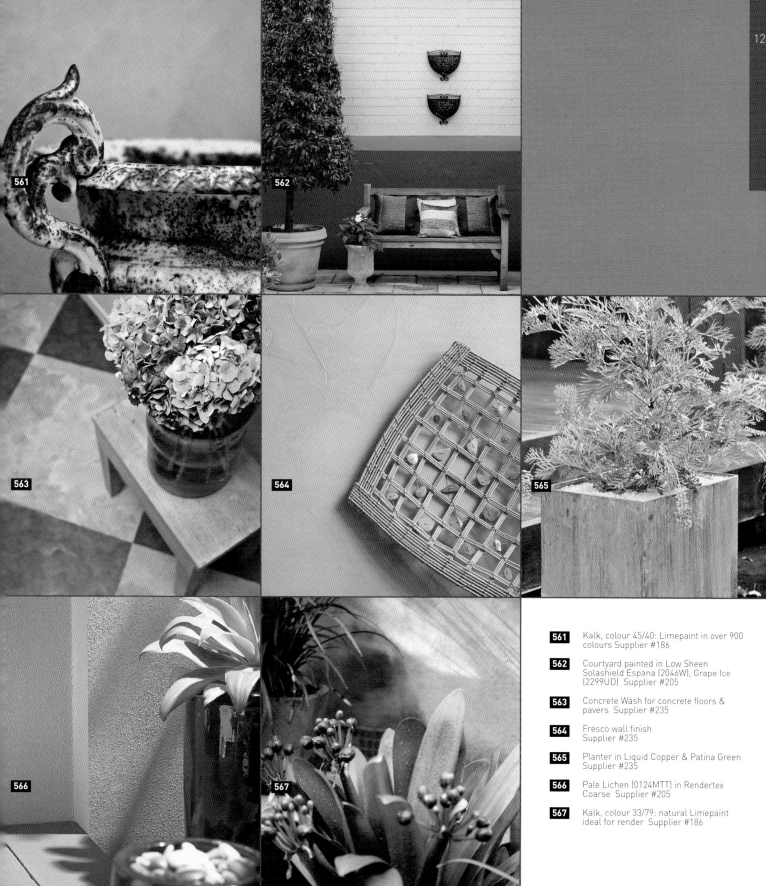

561 Kalk, colour 45/40: Limepaint in over 900 colours Supplier #186

562 Courtyard painted in Low Sheen Solashield Espana (2046W), Grape Ice (2299UD) Supplier #205

563 Concrete Wash for concrete floors & pavers Supplier #235

564 Fresco wall finish Supplier #235

565 Planter in Liquid Copper & Patina Green Supplier #235

566 Pale Lichen (0124MTT) in Rendertex Coarse Supplier #205

567 Kalk, colour 33/79: natural Limepaint ideal for render Supplier #186

568 Kalk, colour 36/34: Limepaint ideal for render Supplier #186

569 Stone Paint (fine) Supplier #235

570 Kalk, Limepaint Colour 20/66: Kalk requires no undercoat Supplier #186

571 Kalk, colour 110/50: natural paint for fresh render Supplier #186

572 Kalk, colour 110/80: cheers up an old shed Supplier #186

573 Potwash: available in over 400 colours Supplier #186

574 Weathershield exterior low sheen, furniture, battens & planter boxes: Sandslip, pergola frame, deck surround, paling fence & wall: Designer Plum Supplier #253

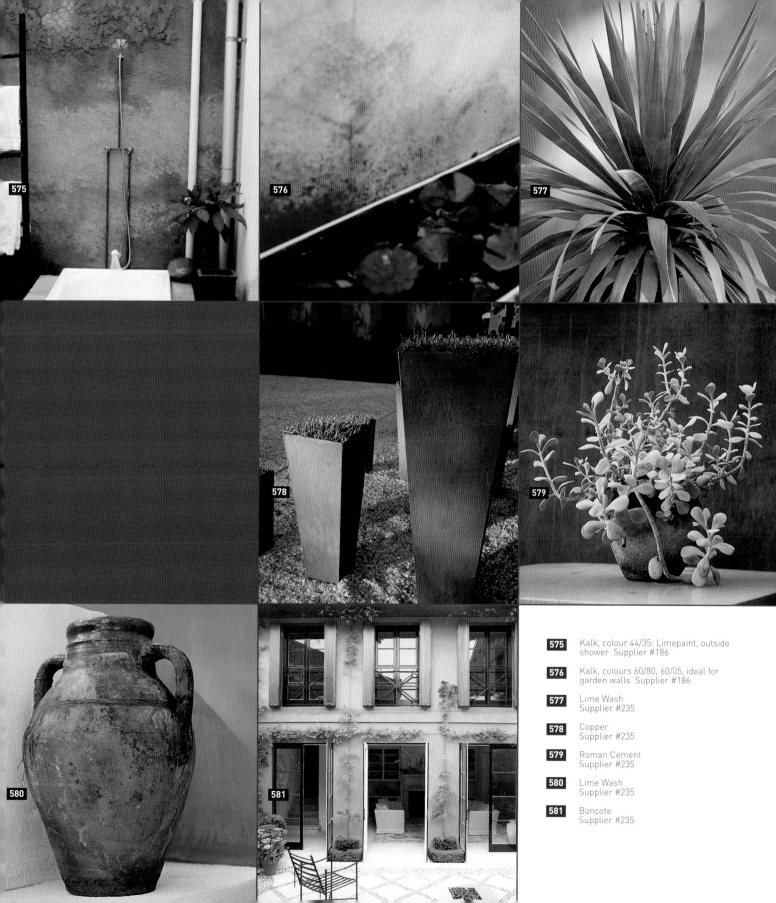

575 Kalk, colour 44/35: Limepaint, outside shower Supplier #186

576 Kalk, colours 60/80, 60/05, ideal for garden walls Supplier #186

577 Lime Wash
Supplier #235

578 Copper
Supplier #235

579 Roman Cement
Supplier #235

580 Lime Wash
Supplier #235

581 Boncote
Supplier #235

Weathering steel (a steel/copper alloy) is the star material here. Its surface oxidises just like ordinary steel but this particular rust forms such a dense crust that oxygen is excluded from the metal underneath so there's no deeper rusting.

The sculpture was made from recycled 'Austen' steel (representing over 500,000 recycled cans) and was chosen specifically for the way its burnished coppery tones reflect the colours of the Australian landscape. But it's the soaring silhouette of the main structure, echoed in so many of the surrounding cactus shapes and ultimately - decisively – in that famous Sydney icon looming in the background, that makes this such a breathtaking scene.

Strategic lighting achieves an even more dramatic effect at night time, throwing fabulous shadows onto the metal, turning one section into an almost lunar landscape and thousands of tiny cactus prickles into golden auras. Although built on a monumental scale, there are still plenty of ideas to take away from this awe-inspiring garden and adapt to your own outdoor space.

peace

translucence

romance

glow

atmosphere

haven

LIGHTING

It's no exaggeration to say that a garden isn't really finished without some form of lighting. First and foremost, if you can't properly access your outdoor room at night, you're depriving yourself of many potential hours of peace, calm and enjoyment. When your days are busy – even frantic – with work, family and domestic tasks, this is often the only time when you can recharge the batteries, and what better place to do it than the one area of your home with the least distractions.

Of course there are compelling practical reasons, too. Lighting pathways, stairs and entrances is a must for safety and a sensor spotlight at the front will double as a deterrent for any unwelcome guests. Your entertainment area will extend its opening hours considerably with an inviting wash of light, and if you are lucky enough to have a pool or spa, an evening dip in glowing surrounds with a canopy of stars above is surely one of the great pleasures in life.

On a pure design level, lights create instant atmosphere, dictating the mood of the evening, whether it be warm and romantic or vibrant and invigorating. A well-positioned spot will draw the eye to an architectural plant and a graduated beam of gold will silhouette a handsome tree. Gazebos and pergolas turn into cosy outdoor havens with the addition of a few twinkling lanterns. And water features can look their very best with light gleaming on the water's surface, picking up the texture and movement of its flow and highlighting little splashes.

New innovations in decorative lighting are more accessible and affordable in the home garden than ever before. Illuminators with stencils throw wild patterns on a wall and rotating colour wheels bathe their surrounds in ever-changing hues. Truly dazzling effects can be achieved with fibre optic or LED lights, building seemingly solid columns and sculptures of light. Then again, simple solutions are sometimes the best: a strategically placed row of torches or lanterns, glowing candle in niches and fragrant incense burners merely require a good location and a box of matches.

Presentation of the light fixture should be taken into account. Just like all the other garden elements it must make its own unique statement and should be treated as an integral part of your design. An ornate, cast iron lamp is a decorative feature which will work well in a Federation setting, but if your garden is Balinese or has a tropical theme, bamboo torch lamps are the more appropriate choice. Oil lamps are especially fine for atmosphere with their twinkling naked flames, but take care with positioning – the changeable conditions of the Australian climate (sudden gusts of wind and tinder-dry foliage) must be respected all year round.

Put some effort into finding attractive, durable, good quality fittings that harmonise with the theme of the design and execute their function properly.

582

583

584

585

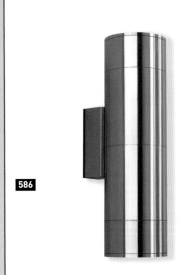

586

587

582 Vedi/LS563LED: Marine grade stainless steel, LED, path lighting Supplier #221

583 Hunza Pond Supplier #207

584 Hunza Pillar Supplier #207

585 Hunza Deck Lite Supplier #207

586 Eterna/LS521A: marine grade stainless steel, wall mount outdoor lighting Supplier #221

587 LS363: Marine grade stainless steel, recessed up-lighting Supplier #221

588 Via/LS553LED-8: Marine grade stainless steel, LED, path lighting Supplier #221

589 Hunza Mouse Supplier #207

588

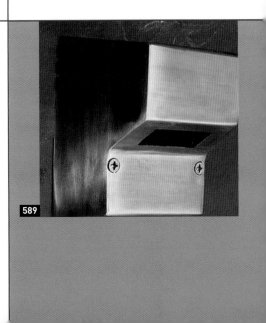

589

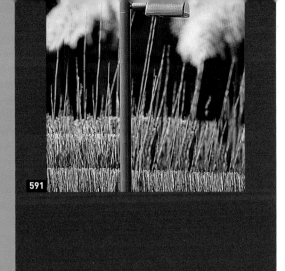

590 Hunza Cockpit Lite
Supplier #207

591 Hunza Border Lite
Supplier #207

592 Hunza Tier Lite
Supplier #207

593 Balinese Hut Lights (W3)
Supplier #225

594 Acacia/LS101A: adjustable, wall mount
copper outdoor lighting Supplier #221

595 Hunza Spike Spot adjustable
Supplier #207

596 Hunza Wall Spot
Supplier #207

597 Melia/LS151A: recessed, wall mount
copper outdoor lighting Supplier #221

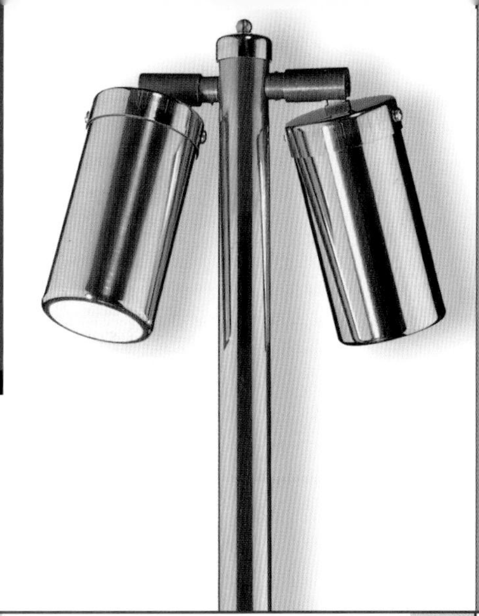

598

599

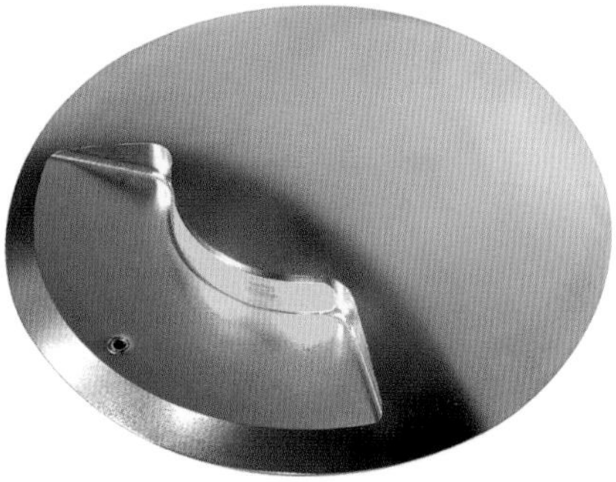

600

601

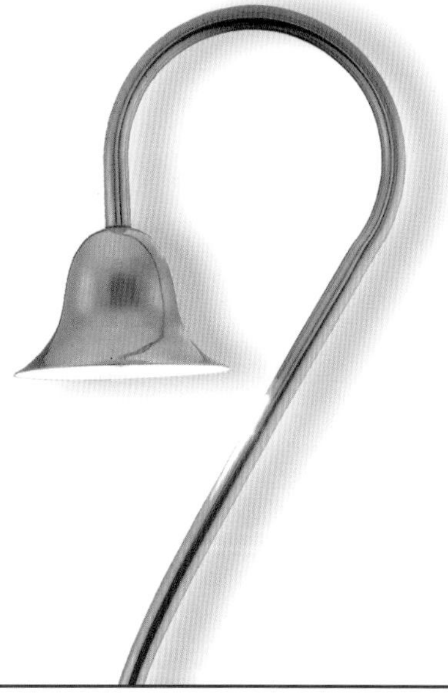

602

603

598 Grevillea/LS192A: Fixed spike, ground mount copper outdoor lighting Supplier #221

599 Hunza Twin Pole Lite Supplier #207

600 Via/LS553LED-1: marine grade stainless steel, LED, path lighting Supplier #221

601 Balitza/LS482: marine grade stainless steel bollard lighting Supplier #221

602 Wattle/LS222: fixed spike, ground mount copper outdoor lighting Supplier #221

603 The Blue Room Lights (L3S) Supplier #225

604 Boulevard/LS371A: brass, wall mount outdoor lighting Supplier #221

605 Hunza Euro Spot Supplier #207

604

605

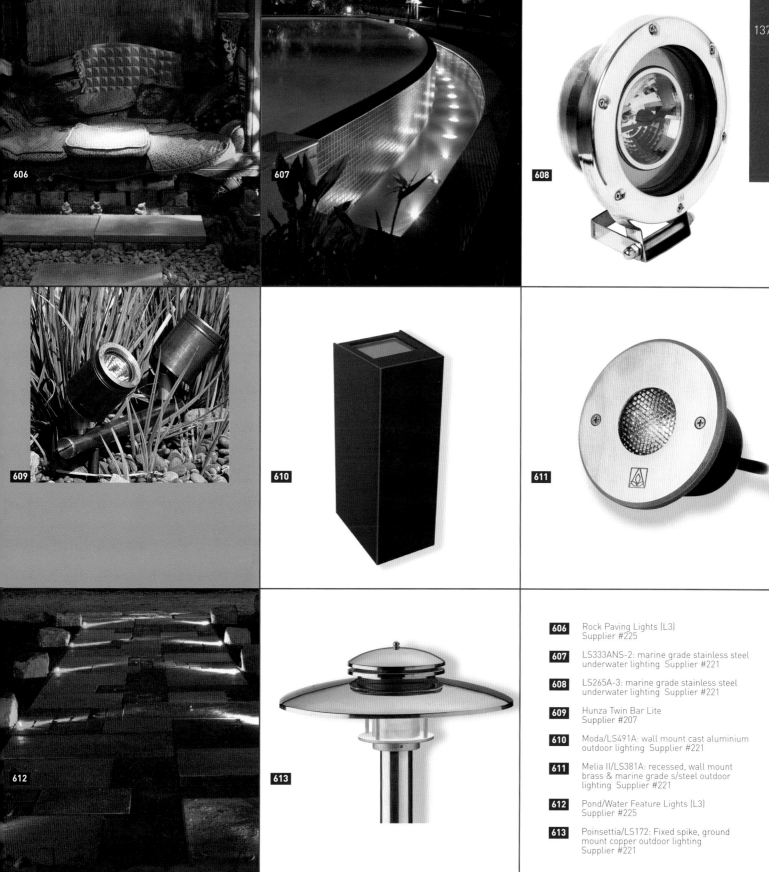

606 Rock Paving Lights (L3)
Supplier #225

607 LS333ANS-2: marine grade stainless steel
underwater lighting Supplier #221

608 LS265A-3: marine grade stainless steel
underwater lighting Supplier #221

609 Hunza Twin Bar Lite
Supplier #207

610 Moda/LS491A: wall mount cast aluminium
outdoor lighting Supplier #221

611 Melia II/LS381: recessed, wall mount
brass & marine grade s/steel outdoor
lighting Supplier #221

612 Pond/Water Feature Lights (L3)
Supplier #225

613 Poinsettia/LS172: Fixed spike, ground
mount copper outdoor lighting
Supplier #221

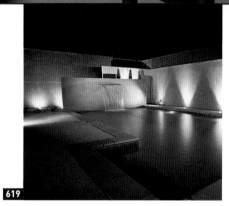

614 Mesh garden spikes
Supplier #230

615 Quartz lantern
Supplier #230

616 Taman metal hurricane
Supplier #230

617 Peeping pods: vitreous china lanterns
bob on fine stainless steel springs
Supplier #242

618 Panorama Newport
Supplier #248

619 Wall washed using in-ground up-lights
c/w cool touch lenses & stainless steel
spot light accenting Supplier #203

620 Panorama: Long Reef
Supplier #248

621 The Kipp Family: post top, wall & bollard
Supplier #220

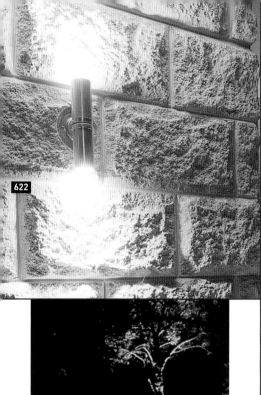

622

623

624

625

626

627

628

629

622 Panorama: Long Reef
Supplier #248

623 Grass trees silhouetted in fog using
M2520 stake-mounted lights with non-
standard frosted lenses Supplier #203

624 Stainless steel wall spots combine with
M2520 accent lights reflecting light off
walls & foliage Supplier #203

625 Pharo
Supplier #220

626 Morph
Supplier #220

627 Brass M2500 underwater lights c/w
M1500 base accenting water feature
Supplier #203

628 Simple up-lighting with Piccolo (M2600)
sub-miniature accent lights hidden
among plants Supplier #203

629 Panorama: Manly Supplier #248

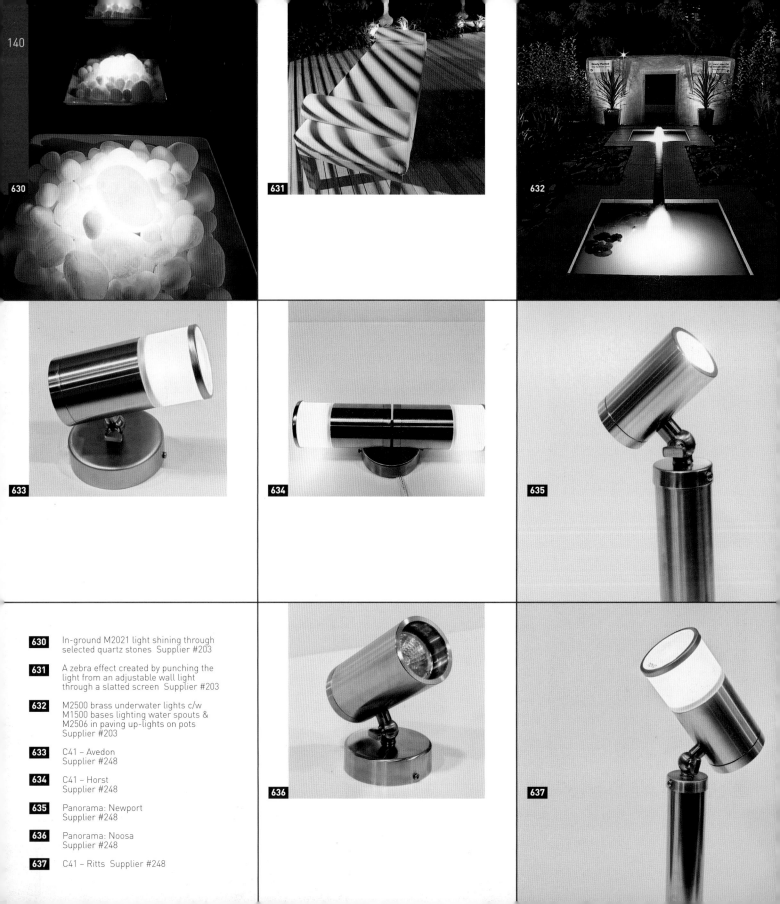

630

631

632

633

634

635

630 In-ground M2021 light shining through selected quartz stones Supplier #203

631 A zebra effect created by punching the light from an adjustable wall light through a slatted screen Supplier #203

632 M2500 brass underwater lights c/w M1500 bases lighting water spouts & M2506 in paving up-lights on pots Supplier #203

633 C41 – Avedon Supplier #248

634 C41 – Horst Supplier #248

635 Panorama: Newport Supplier #248

636 Panorama: Noosa Supplier #248

637 C41 – Ritts Supplier #248

636

637

Larger than your average backyard, but the emphasis in this public display is still very much on day-to-day activities like cooking, bathing, dining and lounging around. Here, the lighting plan needs to effectively illuminate all activity areas without killing atmosphere. The rear wall is the key. Backlit with a warm golden wash that picks out the honey tones of the onyx tiles and turns the paler squares into reflectors, it's a broad glowing screen that impacts on all corners. Lots of built-in timber furniture means a crowd can be easily accommodated, but there's no risk of a small gathering feeling lost in the space as the subtle effect of rooms within rooms achieved by light screens, minor level shifts and discreet dividers do their work. See pages 42 and 43 for other views of this outdoor space.

comfort
shape
architecture

style
structure
reclining

Furniture is integral to the function of the room as well as being a feature and ornament, so never treat it as an afterthought. The presentation and quality of an item of furniture can make or break the look of your space so when you're budgeting, be prepared to pay for a good quality piece.

Outdoor furniture is a booming business these days and there's lots to choose from. The three big things to keep in mind when you're shopping is strength, durability and style. Make sure the coating or finish can withstand all weathers and 'test-drive' chairs and couches for comfort as you would for their indoor equivalents.

But don't limit yourself in terms of the places you shop. Lots of contemporary indoor furniture is made with hardy weather-resistant materials like ironwork, stainless steel, cane and treated timber. And if a piece isn't suited to outdoor conditions, why not explore the possibility of a tough coating or finish to equip an ordinary indoor object for exterior circumstances?

If you decide to custom-build, take full advantage of the options open to you such as added lumbar support for comfort, storage space in the voids of bench-seating, and foldaway facilities for tables, lounges etc. Using a combination of organic and inorganic materials gives a pleasing result,

with the much tried and tested marriage of timber and stainless-steel right up there among the most flexible and appealing.

Last but definitely not least, using recycled materials to build your own furniture is not only clever and creative, but another great way you can contribute towards saving the planet. Wreckers yards, garage sales and home demolitions can yield a host of surprising treasures. Found objects can be wonderful to work with if you want to build your own furniture. Hunks of driftwood, used tyres and bits of old machinery, for example, can be transformed into tables, chairs, benches, platforms ... whatever!

638 Gunghult rocking chair: clear lacquered rattan on a steel frame Supplier #208

639 Tarquin chair
Supplier #184

640 Memphis rocker
Supplier #184

641 Klackbo easy chair: lacquered oak veneer frame & washable slip-cover in green or red Supplier #208

642 Metal-coated table with stainless steel X legs Supplier #210

643 Glass chaise amongst the gum trees Supplier #247

644 Dedon Panama beach chair
Supplier #195

645 Ninix storage box
Supplier #231

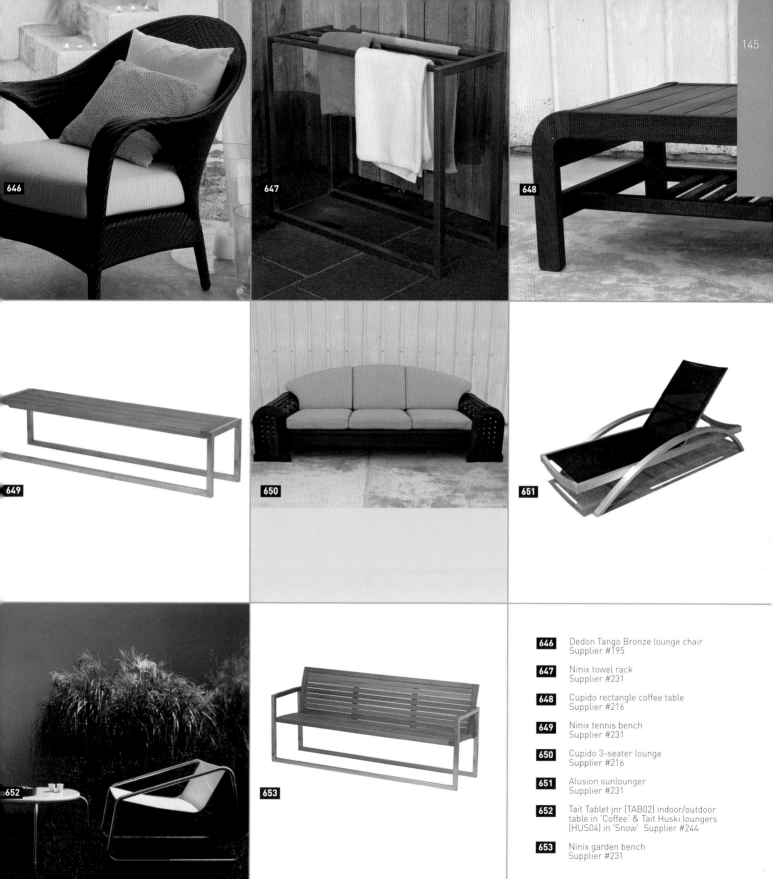

646 Dedon Tango Bronze lounge chair
Supplier #195

647 Ninix towel rack
Supplier #231

648 Cupido rectangle coffee table
Supplier #216

649 Ninix tennis bench
Supplier #231

650 Cupido 3-seater lounge
Supplier #216

651 Alusion sunlounger
Supplier #231

652 Tait Tablet jnr (TAB02) indoor/outdoor
table in 'Coffee' & Tait Huski loungers
(HUS04) in 'Snow' Supplier #244

653 Ninix garden bench
Supplier #231

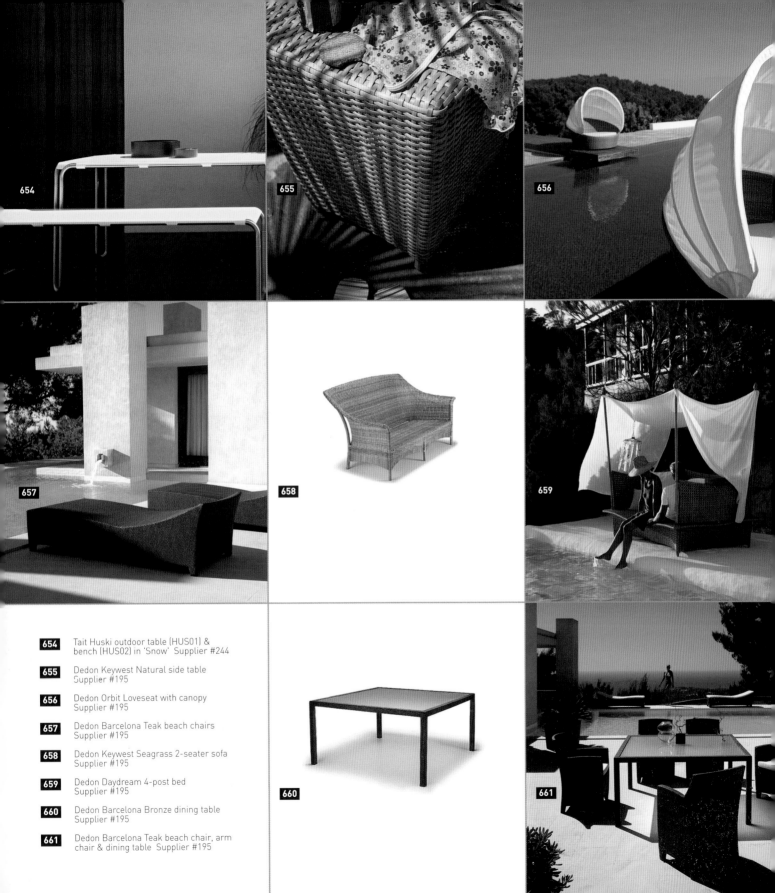

654 Tait Huski outdoor table (HUS01) &
bench (HUS02) in 'Snow' Supplier #244

655 Dedon Keywest Natural side table
Supplier #195

656 Dedon Orbit Loveseat with canopy
Supplier #195

657 Dedon Barcelona Teak beach chairs
Supplier #195

658 Dedon Keywest Seagrass 2-seater sofa
Supplier #195

659 Dedon Daydream 4-post bed
Supplier #195

660 Dedon Barcelona Bronze dining table
Supplier #195

661 Dedon Barcelona Teak beach chair, arm
chair & dining table Supplier #195

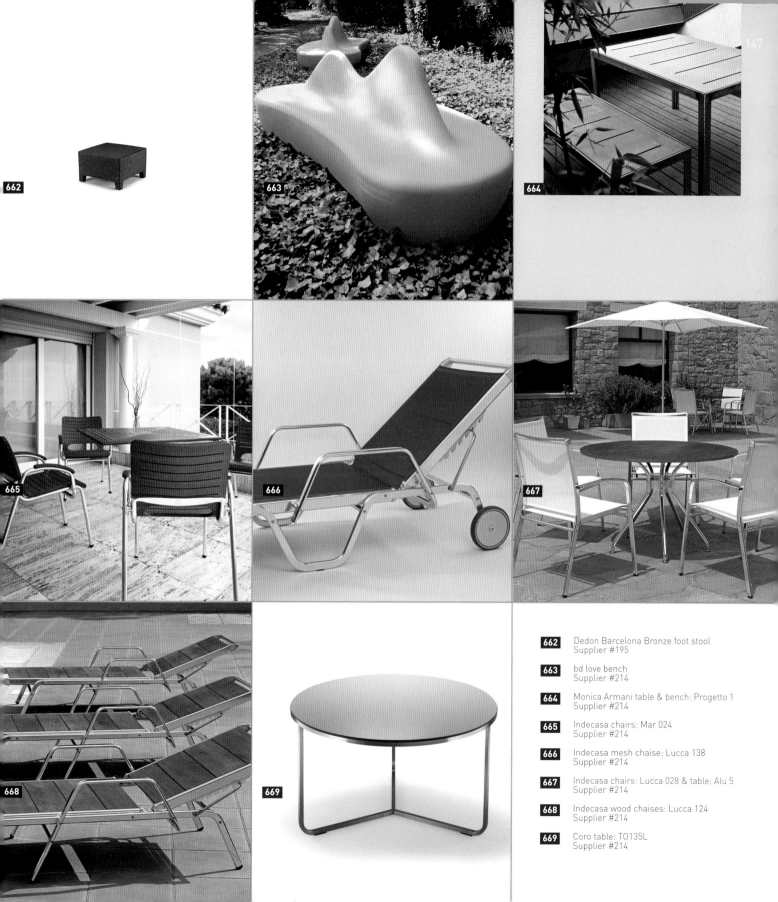

662 Dedon Barcelona Bronze foot stool
Supplier #195

663 bd love bench
Supplier #214

664 Monica Armani table & bench: Progetto 1
Supplier #214

665 Indecasa chairs: Mar 024
Supplier #214

666 Indecasa mesh chaise: Lucca 138
Supplier #214

667 Indecasa chairs: Lucca 028 & table: Alu 5
Supplier #214

668 Indecasa wood chaises: Lucca 124
Supplier #214

669 Coro table: TO135L
Supplier #214

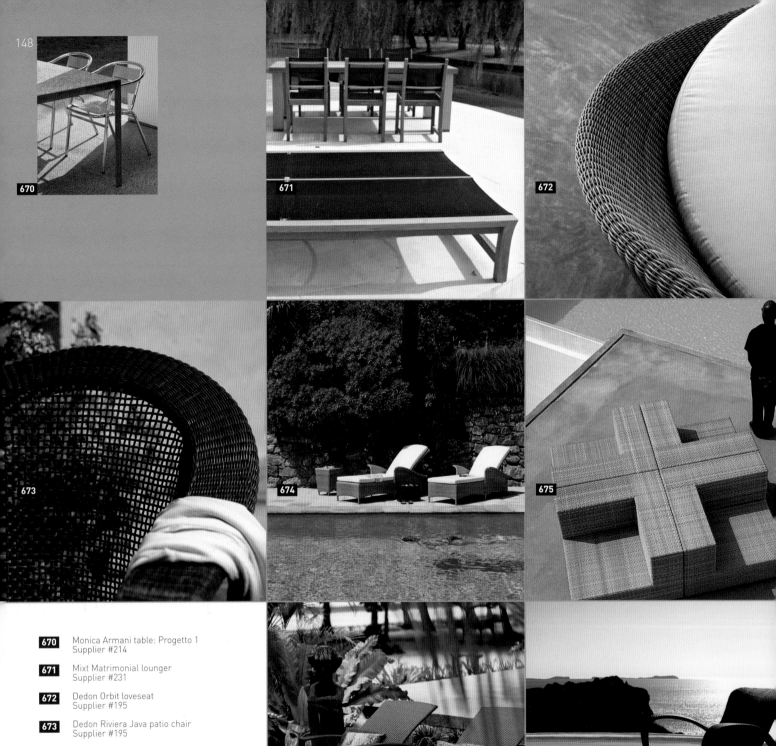

670

671

672

673

674

675

670 Monica Armani table: Progetto 1
Supplier #214

671 Mixt Matrimonial lounger
Supplier #231

672 Dedon Orbit loveseat
Supplier #195

673 Dedon Riviera Java patio chair
Supplier #195

674 Dedon Keywest Natural side table &
beach chairs Supplier #195

675 Dedon lounge corner modules
Supplier #195

676 Dedon Panama beach chairs
Supplier #195

677 Dedon Tango Teak beach chair
Supplier #195

676

677

678

679

680

681

682

683

684

685

678   Dedon lounge corner & centre modules
Supplier #195

679   Ninix mailbox
Supplier #231

680   Mobile SwingShare
Supplier #217

681   Coro stacking chair: S01
Supplier #214

682   Tait Huski outdoor setting: chair
(HUS03), table (HUS01) & bench (HUS02)
in 'Snow' Supplier #244

683   Stanton 5-piece setting
Supplier #182

684   Coro armchair: P02
Supplier #214

685   Join outdoor deck table: stainless steel
frame, top with Casuarina slats
Supplier #180

686

687

688

689

690

691

686 Dedon lounge (left, right, centre & corner modules) & coffee table Supplier #195

687 Curtis extension table with Matilda folding chairs Supplier #182

688 Cream Alfresco timber & granite setting Supplier #182

689 Sellex chairs: Irina Supplier #214

690 Dedon Riviera Natural 2-Seater, dining table & patio chair Supplier #195

691 Cupido lounge chair Supplier #216

692 Dedon Tango Teak side table/coffee/ lounge chair & 2-seater Supplier #195

693 Monica Armani table & bench: Progetto 1 Supplier #214

692

693

694

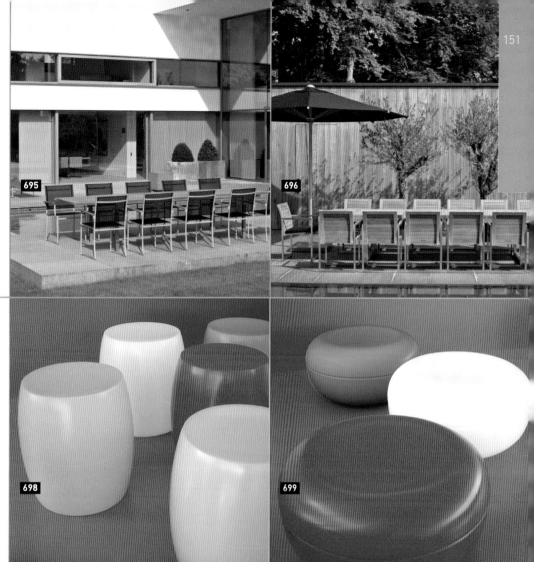

695

696

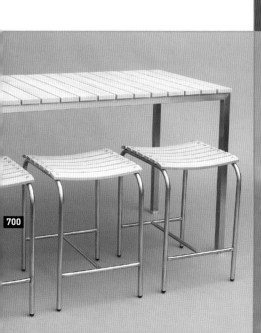

697

698

699

700

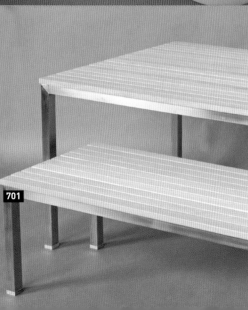

701

694 Dedon Daydream bed XXL
Supplier #195

695 Flexi outdoor setting
Supplier #231

696 Ninix extension setting
Supplier #231

697 IKEA PS VÅGÖ plastic stackable easy
chair & foot stool in black or orange
Supplier #208

698 Bongo: Rotomoulded polyethylene
stool/side table/decorative bubble
Supplier #215

699 Pod: Rotomoulded polyethylene lounging
bubble stool/side table Supplier #215

700 White beech & stainless bar table & bar
stools Supplier #234

701 White beech & stainless lengthwise slat
table & bench Supplier #234

702 White beech & brushed aluminium double sun lounge

703 White beech paddle pop chair

704 White beech & stainless chair

705 White beech & aluminium sun lounge

This garden is a superb living space – casual, relaxed and very sophisticated – with the stunning central dynamic of a vast crystal clear swimming pool. Choosing the right furniture was crucial here as the generous proportions and panoramic views mean every element has to stand up and be counted.

Timber and cane more than meets the requirements. Not only is wood repeated elsewhere in pillars, fences and screens, but also in the surrounding bushland so the theme is reinforced indoors, outdoors and beyond the property itself. The inherent warmth of these natural materials is offset by pale cotton fabric covering armchairs and ottomans. Thai silk cushions provide muted shades of fuchsia, violet, aqua and lime and swaying palm trees promote a relaxed holiday atmosphere.

702 White beech & brushed aluminium double sun lounge Supplier #234

703 White beech paddle pop chair Supplier #234

704 White beech & stainless chair Supplier #234

705 White beech & aluminium sun lounge Supplier #234

706 10-seat concrete panel table Supplier #223

form

drama
expression

pleasure
inspiration
creation

ORNAMENTS & ACCESSORIES

When you think about it, so much of what we do in the home and garden is about art: arranging forms, colours, sounds and movement to produce something that is purely for pleasure.

Every element in the garden, including the functional fixtures, can be seen as an object of art – pots and planters, weather vanes, barbecues, bowls, water features, wind chimes, fountains and bird baths.

Art can be embedded within existing elements of the garden: a pattern in the paving, a mosaic or a mural. The paint or render that finishes a wall can be an artistic statement and the same goes for those plants clipped, hedged and topiaried into all sorts of shapes to create eye-catching compositions.

But then there are the purely decorative items which may be the truest forms of art in the garden: the statues, free-standing and relief sculptures, urns, totem poles and wood carvings. As with all art, these elements are a matter of individual taste and personal expression, but there are a few things to keep in mind before you commit.

First, choose these objects to suit the style of your garden: too many eclectic pieces wind up looking cluttered and confused. Be disciplined about sticking with one design scheme such as terracotta pots in a Tuscan garden, smiling Buddhas in a Balinese garden, and classical urns in a formal garden. It's the overall design that makes a garden Japanese, not just whacking in the odd granite lantern.

If you need some ideas to get the creative ball rolling, better garden centres have a range of outdoor sculptures, ornamental ponds and water features. Other places you might find useful to browse through include interior design showrooms, homeware shops, furniture importers, second-hand markets and if you're really serious, art galleries.

Lastly, take some time to site you're ornaments carefully. Make sure it's protected from the elements if it's on the fragile side and that it commands the attention it deserves.

There are so many ways to get decorative touches into your yard, the main challenge is to identify and embrace what really expresses you as creator and caretaker.

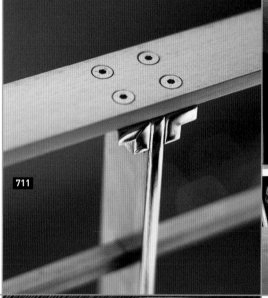

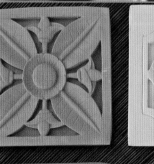

707 Home oven
Supplier #187

708 Wood burning brazier: painted wrought
iron 77 H x 50cm D (top) Supplier #180

709 nani marquina jute rug: De Yute
Supplier #214

710 Coro BBQ 02
Supplier #214

711 Balcony balustrade: Allen key 'T-section'
mechanical fixing system Supplier #180

712 Woodfired oven with mosaic
Supplier #226

713 Sandstone & ivory hanging wall/fence
tiles 300x300mm, multiple colours
available Supplier #212

714 Family limestone sculpture
Supplier #213

715 Sandstone Easter Island head 1200x500x300mm, multiple colours available Supplier #212

716 Sandstone sitting Buddha, 550 or 900mm, multiple colours available Supplier #212

717 Balinese wall hanging: hand-carved sandstone wall-hangings or feature pieces Supplier #239

718 Wall plaque with embossed design of frolicking cherubs: terracotta with white wash finish (V-7508-390) Supplier #198

719 Reproduction Cambodian, Khmer-style figure: green/black finish 480 H x 180mm W (V-N29-155) Supplier #198

720 Terracotta candle hut, 450 or 900mm Supplier #212

721 Female seated: abstract hand-carved white granite sculpture Supplier #247

722 Bronze sculpture Supplier #185

723 Nova limestone sculpture
Supplier #213

724 Black baroong hanging tile water feature
450x450mm, multiple colours available
Supplier #212

725 Luxor Sphinx
Supplier #252

726 Aztec Queen
Supplier #224

727 Egyptian wall plaque
Supplier #224

728 Wall plaque embossed with Griffin &
Cornucopia: distressed cream painted
finish (V-7508-376) Supplier #198

729 Buddha head
Supplier #224

730 Cast stone gate piers with decorative
large ball finials Supplier #190

731 Cast stone garden folly
Supplier #190

732 Sandstone Bali print head
400x200x200mm Supplier #212

733 Reproduction Cambodian, Khmer-style
wall plaque: green/black finish 320 H x
260mm W (V-3018-155) Supplier #198

734 Sandstone Pagoda, multiple colours &
sizes available Supplier #212

735 Antique stone grinder
Supplier #228

736 Black granite helix fountain 80cm H
Supplier #247

737 Black granite millstone fountain 45cm D
Supplier #247

738 Zen Bachi Japanese hand-carved coin bowl
Supplier #247

739

740

741

742

743

744

739 Hand-carved black granite fountain (model New 4) Supplier #247

740 60cm D grey granite hand-carved spiral fountain Supplier #247

741 90cm D blossom granite Sagatsugi bowl with 45cm D black orange peel sphere Supplier #247

742 Tall square with ball fountain Supplier #193

743 Sandstone frangipani bird bath 900 H x 600mm D, multiple colours available Supplier #212

744 Spiral egg 50cm H: hand-carved blossom granite Supplier #247

745 Tapered square stone fountain Supplier #228

746 Bali water planters Supplier #228

745

746

747

748

749

750

751

752

753

754

747 Trough fountain with bronze tap
Supplier #252

748 Round form sculpture
Supplier #213

749 Rectangle fountain 80cm H: machine &
hand-carved black granite Supplier #247

750 Buddha in kneeling position: green/black
finish 580 H x 520 W x 530mm D (V-044-
155) Supplier #198

751 Black granite wave striped fountain
80cm H Supplier #247

752 Copper water bowl
Supplier #242

753 White rocks: hand-thrown earthenware
rocks for seating or sculpture
Supplier #242

754 Rusted hand-forged iron rose climber
Supplier #210

755

756

757

758

759

760

755	Hydra tic-tac-toe Supplier #230
756	Verona wall panel Supplier #230
757	Steel Effects: zinc galvanised planter transformed into a water feature Supplier #236
758	Crucible urns Supplier #252
759	Tropicanna wall panel 1800 x 800mm Supplier #246
760	Amphora keil Supplier #252
761	Glass water feature Supplier #227
762	Woodfired oven in an indoor-outdoor room Supplier #226

761

762

More substantial pots, like this ornate Balinese bowl, make fine water features, too. A small single jet of water keeps the surface moving to keep mozzies away. The dove-grey stone blends with nearby pavers and over time patches of moss will appear, gently ageing the surface. A delicate frangipani design carved around the rim fits in well with the lush growth, reinforcing the tropical theme of this cool, restful oasis.

feature

ornamentation

innovation

texture

decoration

flourish

POTS & PLANTERS

Pots and planters are finally getting the attention they deserve in the average Australian garden. People have begun to realise that not only do they house your precious plants, they are also ornamental statements either enhancing the theme of the space or acting as a standout feature in themselves. Just remember that different plants require different micro-climates so you must find the right position for the pot and its plant just as you would if the plant were going directly in the ground.

As long as a container has sufficient drainage and root space, it could be any shape, size or colour that will work with your design. Metal is a wonderful, contemporary substance to work with. Copper ages beautifully, with a fine green patina emerging over time. Marine grade aluminium is highly malleable and withstands the harsh Australian elements with ease, as does stainless steel.

Galvanised iron also works well, but make sure the welds or folds are galvanised (or sealed) too, otherwise they can rust and compromise the strength of the vessel.

Terracotta is a classic for that more traditional look and reconstituted stone is becoming very popular as it can be moulded into all sorts of shapes and sizes. Make sure the interiors of these products are sealed in some way as the extremely porous properties of sand and cement will draw the moisture away from the soil and your plant at a dramatic rate. Fine Asian ceramic, porcelain and marble pots are extremely elegant and look great both inside and outside the house. When you buy, make sure the manufacturers have punched holes in the base that are large enough for ample drainage.

Trusty plastic pots tend to look temporary and insubstantial on their own so use them to protect the inside of other containers like old wine barrels (direct contact with moist soil will rot the wood over time) and the more collectable rustic pieces like steel buckets, laundry tubs and even old butter churns.

Hanging baskets are always a favourite for cascading varieties.

If you don't have much garden bed space, a custom-built planter will do the business. A long trough of ornamental grasses can bring a natural softness to an inner-city balcony without taking up too much of your entertainment space.

Don't forget that pots and planters don't have the same reservoir of ground moisture that plants in garden beds can drink from, so it will be more important to set up appropriate irrigation or take the responsibility to be vigilant in watering your potted plants.

763

764

765

766

767

768

763 Flower cups: hand-thrown in pigmented porcelain Supplier #242

764 Shoreline pots: in chalk, flint & peat Supplier #242

765 Screw pots: in white, sand & matt black Supplier #242

766 Cast stone majestic Bowral urns Supplier #190

767 Glazed and unglazed antique feature pots in rustic hues Supplier #239

768 Ninix planter Supplier #231

769 Striped Tulip urn Supplier #228

770 Red Table Feature Supplier #200

769

770

771 Cast iron urns
Supplier #228

772 Empire box squares
Supplier #228

773 Small 'Union' planter blonde plywood
Supplier #200

774 Medium 'Manhattan' planter stainless
steel & blonde plywood
Supplier #200

775 5 piece set of galvanised steel bonsai
planters(A-748-5-096): large & small
avail Supplier #198

776 Sandstone urn on pedestal
Supplier #228

777 Empire Tall Cones
Supplier #228

778 Copper bowl: plaster base with metal
finish Supplier #185

779 Dedon accessories in planters High/Low in XXL, XL, Teak or Bronze
Supplier #195

780 Palm planters
Supplier #228

781 Custom made Sahara Gold granite pot
Supplier #204

782 Tread Plate Large Trough 900 L x 400 W x 375 H Supplier #209

783 Petites: brightens both indoor and outdoor settings Supplier #236

784 Copper: crafted from pure copper will not rust Supplier #236

785 Casanova Collection: handmade Italian pots coloured with dyes Supplier #236

786 SANDVITA glazed earthenware plant pot
Supplier #208

THE RULES OF ENGAGEMENT

Just like meeting the in-laws for the first time, there are certain unspoken rules that should be observed with the people you deal with as you enter the planning, construction and purchasing stages of garden-making.

When an architect or designer is involved in the planning, be wary of the mighty concept. Ideas and intellectual property are extremely valuable commodities in this game, so always show respect for the work, even if it is not to your taste. When a professional has suggested an array of concepts for your project, think through the design before forming any position. Every idea – however off-the-mark you may think it is – is a valid contribution that deserves attention. To a certain extent, every designer or architect puts themselves out on a limb in the initial stages as they pitch their concepts – it's always a big call selling your ideas to a client (be it a company or an individual). If you are the client, remember that the 'pitch' is part of an on-going process. Ideas will continue to develop and grow with time. Before you commission any consultants, find out what the fee structure is, how and when the work will be presented, and what exactly you can expect for your hard-earned dollars.

If by chance the results aren't your cup of tea, honesty is always the best policy. Clear up any residual fee and search for a new set of ideas, but remember, you must expect to pay for the concepts even if you don't end up using them.

A consultant will usually be able to give you a fairly accurate estimate on construction costs based on the initial concept. However, it's difficult to obtain a fixed quote until full, accurate construction drawings have been completed. Only then can the amount of required materials and labour be measured precisely and a quote settled. Our advice is never to go with one quote. Shop it around to at least a couple of licensed contractors before you make your final decision.

When you're looking for a contractor – or a landscape architect or designer, horticulturalist, tree surgeon or maintenance team – it's always good to have a recommendation and to be armed with as much information as possible. epresentative bodies of industry professionals like the Australian Institute of Landscape Architects or your local state landscape contractors' association can help. You'll find information about the nature of the work done by those professionals, particular specialities of members and codes of practice on their websites (see pages 194 and 195).

When you finally meet with a consultant, be clear about how much they charge, familiarise yourself with as many examples of their past work as you can, check they are insured for the work they propose to do, and always have the contract in writing before the work starts.

If you plan to design a garden yourself, I cannot urge strongly enough that you get some professional advice before building starts. (Most consultants will propose an hourly rate to help you on your way.) No matter how foolproof your plans may seem, you'd be amazed at the things that can go wrong. I would never attempt to repair my washing machine – that's what experts are for – and so it goes for the outdoor room.

Getting the right people to do the right jobs (astute planning, sound construction and ongoing care) is the best insurance you can possibly buy.

It's been said before, but make sure you do your homework with the local council. There are many council restrictions and laws to abide by when constructing a garden, and the rules vary slightly depending on where you live.

One of the most important rules of engagement is that you need to respect the relationship between wholesalers, retailers and customers. Before you use the supplier section, please read page 171 so that you can fully appreciate how much goes into bringing the plants, materials and products in this book to you.

HOW TO USE THE SUPPLIER SECTION

The wonderful network of wholesale–retail–customer exists in every industry, so that the product you need can be sourced in the most effective way, arriving in your hot little hands quickly and in mint condition. Wholesalers (generally) do business only with other registered businesses in the industry. They leave the retail side of things to the retailers, whose business it is to keep you – the customer – satisfied. Retailers are there to help you and their business depends on the service they provide. So, respect what wholesalers do (please don't try to sneak in the backdoor), and make the retail side of things work for you.

Remember that many of the plants we have included will be available at your local nursery even though they are not listed here. And if they don't have the plant you're after, we've included wholesale nurseries so you can let your local people know where to source it, if they're willing. We've listed the manufacturers or distributors of products and materials, rather than the retailers, because they are best placed to give you up-to-date retailers of their products. Nine times out of ten, you just need to check the manufacturer's website. The Internet has made accessing products a breeze!

Look for the mail order symbol or the e-commerce symbol to see at a glance which wholesalers, manufacturers or distributors also deal with domestic customers.

Remember that retailers can provide you with lots of information about the product you are buying, so don't hesitate to seek their advice. Whether they're selling you a plant or a product, a good retailer will be able to tell you what you need to know about its care and how to get the most out of your investment.

Plants

This is the plant number. It connects to the picture and horticultural notes that appear on page 19.

048 PLUM PINE **NSW:** 002, 008, 011, 013, 016, 017, 019, 021, 024, 027, 029, 031, 032, 037, 042, 048, 050, 051, 052, 053, 054, 055, 056, 057, 060, 061, 067, 071, 072 **NT:** 074 **QLD:** 086, 097, 098 **SA:** 113, 119 **TAS:** 125 **VIC:** 143, 161 **WA:** 171, 172, 175

049 PURPLE LEAFED PLUM **NSW:** 002, 008, 011,

State by state, these numbers refer to a supplier whose contact details can be found in the Plants: Suppliers section starting on page 184.

118	Heyne's Wholesale Nursery	W	wholesale@heyne.com.au	P:08 8280 8088 F:08 8280 6322	Lot 5 Bolivar Rd Burton SA 5110	Environmentally aware wholesale production nursery
119	Newman's Nursery & Topiary Tea House	R	garden@newmansnursery.com.au www.newmansnursery.com.au	P:08 8264 2661 F:08 8396 2124	PO Box 10 Tea Tree Gully SA 5097	Camellia specialists, old-fashioned service & advice
120	The Plant People SA	W R	phil@goglobaltrading.com	P:08 8389 1393 F:08 8389 1398	PO Box 110 Gumeracha SA 5233	One of the largest ranges of any mobile nursery

Materials & products

This is the product number. It connects to the picture on page 134.

587 LS363: Marine grade stainless steel, recessed up-lighting Supplier #221

588 Via/LS553LED-8: Marine grade stainless steel, LED, path lighting Supplier #221

589 Hunza Mouse Supplier #207

The supplier number refers to the manufacturer or distributor whose contact details can be found in the Materials & Products: Suppliers section starting on page 191. Phone or visit the website to find the nearest retailer.

221	Lumascape Lighting	PHC	sales@lumascape.com.au www.lumascape.com.au	P:07 3286 2299 F:07 3286 6599	38–44 Enterprise St Cleveland QLD 4163	Australian made, corrosion resistant outdoor & underwater lighting
222	Lumeah Limestone		lumeah@lumeah.com.au www.lumeah.com.au	P:08 9204 1400 F:08 9204 1044	1/7 Guthrie St Osborne Park WA 6017	Hand crafted, insitu poured, reconstituted natural limestone
223	Made in Concrete		info@madeinconcrete.com www.madeinconcrete.com	P:03 9391 3317 F:03 9391 3001	6 Ramsay St Spotswood VIC 3015	Beautiful contemporary concrete products for home and garden use

PLANT DIRECTORY

001 FIR NSW: 037, 046, 048, 049, 069, 070, 071, 072 SA: 113, 116, 117, 119 TAS: 125, 126, 127, 128, 129 VIC: 143, 149, 150, 154, 159, 161, 162, 164

002 COOTAMUNDRA WATTLE NSW: 009, 015, 016, 017, 019, 024, 027, 029, 035, 037, 042, 044, 046, 047, 048, 049, 050, 051, 052, 053, 054, 055, 056, 057, 058, 059, 061, 067, 069, 071, 072 QLD: 085, 086, 097 SA: 113, 115, 116, 117, 118, 119, 120, 124 TAS: 125, 126, 127, 128, 129 VIC: 145, 146, 148, 149, 150, 153, 155, 159, 161, 162, 163 WA: 171, 172, 175

003 COASTAL MYALL NSW: 020, 024, 031, 042, 047, 048, 050, 051, 052, 053, 054, 055, 056, 057, 067, 071, 072 SA: 116, 117 VIC: 145, 148, 153, 161

004 CEDAR WATTLE NSW: 015, 017, 020, 024, 029, 031, 032, 035, 037, 042, 046, 047, 048, 050, 051, 052, 053, 054, 055, 056, 057, 060, 067, 069, 071, 072 QLD: 086 SA: 113, 116, 117 TAS: 129 VIC: 145, 146, 148, 153, 161, 162 WA: 172, 175

005 JAPANESE MAPLE NSW: 002, 008, 011, 014, 015, 016, 019, 021, 024, 027, 029, 032, 037, 044, 046, 047, 048, 049, 059, 064, 069, 070, 071, 072 QLD: 107 SA: 113, 115, 116, 117, 118, 119, 124 TAS: 125, 126, 127, 128, 129 VIC: 137, 143, 145, 146, 149, 150, 153, 154, 159, 161, 162, 164, 166 WA: 171, 173, 175

006 SYDNEY RED GUM NSW: 002, 011, 015, 016, 017, 020, 024, 031, 037, 042, 046, 047, 048, 050, 051, 052, 053, 054, 055, 056, 057, 058, 060, 067, 071, 072 QLD: 079, 086, 097 SA: 113, 116, 117, 118, 119 TAS: 125 VIC: 145, 146, 148, 149, 150, 153, 154, 155, 159, 161, 162, 164 WA: 171, 172, 173, 175

007 BUNYA BUNYA NSW: 016, 021, 029, 042, 048, 050, 051, 052, 053, 054, 055, 056, 057, 060, 071, 072 NT: 074 QLD: 079, 086, 107 SA: 113 TAS: 125, 128, 129 VIC: 137, 143, 146, 149, 161

008 NORFOLK ISLAND PINE NSW: 002, 016, 017, 021, 029, 037, 042, 048, 050, 051, 052, 053, 054, 055, 056, 057, 060, 071, 072 QLD: 079, 086, 098, 103, 107, 112 SA: 113, 115, 119, 124 TAS: 125, 128 VIC: 138, 143, 145, 146, 149, 150, 153, 154, 161, 162 WA: 171, 173, 175

009 STRAWBERRY TREE NSW: 002, 013, 016, 017, 019, 024, 027, 037, 044, 048, 059, 069, 070, 071, 072 SA: 113, 115, 116, 117, 119, 124 TAS: 125, 126, 127, 128, 129 VIC: 137, 145, 146, 149, 153, 154, 159, 161, 162, 164, 166 WA: 171, 172, 173

010 ALEXANDRA PALM NSW: 002, 011, 016, 017, 021, 024, 027, 029, 031, 037, 041, 042, 047, 048, 059, 060, 071, 072 NT: 074 QLD: 079, 080, 085, 086, 089, 090, 094, 098, 099, 107, 110 SA: 113, 115, 116, 117, 119, 124 TAS: 125, 128, 129 VIC: 139, 146, 149, 150, 159, 161 WA: 171, 175, 177

011 COAST BANKSIA NSW: 002, 008, 009, 011, 016, 017, 020, 021, 024, 027, 029, 031, 032, 035, 037, 040, 042, 047, 048, 050, 051, 052, 053, 054, 055, 056, 057, 059, 060, 061, 067, 069, 071, 072 QLD: 079, 085, 086, 097, 098 SA: 113, 115, 116, 117, 118, 120, 124 TAS: 125, 126, 127, 128, 129 VIC: 145, 146, 148, 149, 150, 153, 154, 155, 158, 159, 161, 162, 163, 164 WA: 171, 172

012 ORCHID TREE NSW: 002, 011, 016, 019, 021, 024, 027, 029, 037, 042, 048, 071, 072 NT: 074 SA: 116, 117, 121, 124 TAS: 125 VIC: 146, 162 WA: 171, 173

013 SILVER BIRCH NSW: 002, 015, 016, 017, 019, 024, 027, 029, 032, 046, 047, 048, 049, 059, 064, 069, 070, 071, 072 QLD: 079, 085, 107 SA: 113, 114, 115, 116, 117, 118, 124 TAS: 125, 126, 127, 128, 129 VIC: 144, 146, 149, 150, 154, 159, 161, 162, 164, 166 WA: 171, 173, 175, 177

014 ILLAWARRA FLAME TREE NSW: 002, 017, 020, 021, 024, 029, 031, 032, 037, 042, 046, 048, 059, 060, 061, 071, 072 NT: 074 QLD: 079, 084, 085, 086, 090, 094, 097, 098, 112 SA: 115, 116, 117, 124 TAS: 125 VIC: 145, 146, 149, 150, 153, 155, 161, 162, 164 WA: 171, 172, 173, 175

015 QLD BOTTLE TREE NSW: 002, 020, 022, 029, 035, 037, 040, 042, 048, 058, 071, 072 QLD: 079, 086, 097, 106, 107, 109 SA: 116, 117 TAS: 125 VIC: 139, 146, 149, 150, 152, 155, 161, 162

016 IVORY CURL FLOWER NSW: 002, 011, 016, 019, 021, 024, 027, 029, 031, 032, 037, 040, 042, 044, 047, 048, 050, 051, 052, 053, 054, 055, 056, 057, 059, 060, 061, 064, 071, 072 QLD: 079, 080, 085, 086, 090, 093, 097, 098 SA: 116, 117 VIC: 150 WA: 175

017 WEEPING BOTTLEBRUSH NSW: 002, 011, 016, 017, 020, 021, 024, 027, 029, 031, 032, 033, 035, 037, 040, 042, 044, 046, 047, 048, 050, 051, 052, 053, 054, 055, 056, 057, 058, 059, 060, 061, 067, 069, 071, 072 NT: 074 QLD: 079, 085, 086, 090, 094, 097, 098 SA: 113, 115, 116, 117, 118, 120 TAS: 125, 126, 127, 128, 129 VIC: 134, 145, 146, 148, 149, 150, 151, 153, 154, 155, 159, 161, 162, 164 WA: 171, 172, 173, 175

018 CAPE CHESTNUT NSW: 002, 008, 011, 019, 021, 024, 027, 029, 032, 037, 044, 048, 059, 069, 071, 072 QLD: 107 SA: 115, 124 TAS: 125 VIC: 146, 149, 150, 159, 161, 162, 164 WA: 173, 175

019 BLACK BEAN NSW: 002, 016, 021, 024, 029, 037, 040, 042, 048, 050, 051, 052, 053, 054, 055, 056, 057, 060, 071, 072 NT: 074 QLD: 079, 080, 085, 086, 094 TAS: 125 VIC: 149, 150 WA: 173

020 CITRUS NSW: 002, 008, 016, 021, 024, 027, 029, 032, 037, 042, 044, 046, 047, 048, 059, 069, 071, 072 QLD: 079, 085, 086 SA: 113, 114, 115, 116, 117, 119, 124 TAS: 125, 126, 127, 128, 129 VIC: 144, 146, 149, 150, 154, 159, 161, 162 WA: 171, 173, 175, 177

021 BLUEBERRY ASH NSW: 002, 008, 011, 016, 017, 019, 021, 024, 027, 029, 031, 032, 037, 040, 042, 044, 045, 046, 047, 048, 050, 051, 052, 053, 054, 055, 056, 057, 059, 060, 061, 071, 072 QLD: 079, 085, 086, 093, 098, 103 VIC: 146, 149, 150, 161, 162, 166 WA: 173, 175

022 LEMON SCENTED GUM NSW: 002, 011, 015, 017, 020, 021, 024, 027, 029, 031, 032, 035, 037, 042, 046, 048, 050, 051, 052, 053, 054, 055, 056, 057, 058, 060, 061, 067, 069, 071, 072 QLD: 079, 080, 085, 086, 097 SA: 113, 115, 116, 117, 118, 119, 120, 124 TAS: 125, 126, 128, 129 VIC: 134, 145, 146, 148, 149, 150, 153, 154, 155, 158, 159, 161, 162, 163, 164 WA: 171, 172, 175

023 RED FLOWERED GUM NSW: 002, 015, 021, 024, 027, 029, 031, 032, 035, 037, 040, 042, 046, 048, 050, 051, 052, 053, 054, 055, 056, 057, 058, 059, 060, 067, 071, 072 QLD: 085, 086, 097 SA: 115, 116, 117, 118, 120, 124 TAS: 125, 126, 127, 129 VIC: 145, 146, 149, 150, 151, 153, 154, 155, 158, 159, 161, 162, 163, 164 WA: 171, 172, 173, 175, 177

024 SCRIBBLY GUM NSW: 002, 011, 015, 017, 020, 024, 027, 029, 031, 032, 042, 046, 047, 048, 050, 051, 052, 053, 054, 055, 056, 057, 060, 061, 067, 069, 071, 072 VIC: 146, 148, 150, 155, 161

025 SPOTTED GUM NSW: 002, 011, 015, 017, 020, 024, 027, 029, 031, 032, 035, 042, 046, 047, 048, 050, 051, 052, 053, 054, 055, 056, 057, 058, 060, 067, 071, 072 QLD: 086, 097 SA: 113, 115, 116, 117, 118, 124 TAS: 125, 126 VIC: 145, 146, 148, 149, 150, 153, 154, 155, 158, 161, 162, 164 WA: 171, 172, 173, 175

026 MUGGA IRON BARK NSW: 002, 015, 017, 020, 024, 027, 029, 031, 032, 035, 042, 046, 047, 048, 050, 051, 052, 053, 054, 055, 056, 057, 060, 061, 067, 069, 071, 072 QLD: 086 SA: 113, 115, 116, 117, 118, 120, 124 TAS: 125, 128, 129 VIC: 145, 146, 149, 150, 153, 154, 155, 161, 162, 163, 164 WA: 171, 172, 173, 175

027 CLARET ASH NSW: 002, 013, 015, 016, 017, 019, 024, 027, 029, 032, 046, 047, 048, 059, 069, 070, 071, 072 QLD: 079 SA: 113, 114, 115, 116, 117, 119, 124 TAS: 125, 126, 127, 128, 129 VIC: 146, 149, 150, 154, 159, 161, 162 WA: 171, 173, 175, 177

028 GOLDEN ASH NSW: 002, 011, 013, 015, 016, 017, 019, 024, 027, 029, 032, 046, 047, 048, 059, 069, 070, 071, 072 SA: 113, 115, 116, 117, 118, 119, 124 TAS: 125, 126, 127, 128, 129 VIC: 146, 149, 150, 154, 159, 161, 162, 164 WA: 171, 173, 175, 177

029 MAIDENHAIR TREE NSW: 002, 008, 013, 014, 015, 016, 019, 021, 024, 027, 029, 032, 037, 042, 044, 046, 047, 048, 069, 070, 071, 072 QLD: 079 SA: 113, 115, 116, 117, 118, 119, 124 TAS: 125, 126, 127, 128, 129 VIC: 137, 143, 146, 149, 150, 161, 162, 164, 166 WA: 171, 172, 173, 175

030 GOLDEN HONEY LOCUST NSW: 002, 008, 011, 013, 015, 016, 017, 024, 027, 029, 032, 037, 046, 047, 048, 069, 070, 071, 072 QLD: 079 SA: 113, 115, 116, 117, 118, 119, 124 TAS: 125, 126, 127, 128, 129 VIC: 137, 146, 149, 150, 154, 159, 161, 162, 164, 166 WA: 173, 175

031 GORDONIA NSW: 002, 008, 011, 013, 016, 017, 019, 021, 024, 027, 029, 032, 037, 043, 044, 046, 047, 048, 064, 069, 071, 072 QLD: 078, 079, 085, 094, 107 SA: 113, 120 TAS: 125, 126, 127, 128, 129 VIC: 143, 146, 149, 150, 151, 159, 161, 162, 164, 166 WA: 175

032 JACARANDA NSW: 002, 008, 011, 013, 016, 017, 019, 021, 024, 027, 029, 032, 037, 042, 044, 046, 047, 048, 050, 051, 052, 053, 054, 055, 056, 057, 059, 061, 064, 066, 071, 072 NT: 074 QLD: 079, 080, 085, 095, 098, 107, 112 SA: 113, 115, 116, 117, 118, 120, 124 TAS: 125, 126, 127, 128, 129 VIC: 145, 146, 149, 150, 151, 153, 154, 161, 162, 164 WA: 171, 172, 173, 175, 177

033 CREPE MYRTLE NSW: 002, 008, 013, 015, 016, 017, 019, 021, 024, 027, 029, 032, 037, 042, 044, 046, 047, 048, 069, 070, 071, 072 NT: 074 QLD: 079, 080, 085, 086, 095, 103 SA: 113, 115, 116, 117, 118, 119, 124 TAS: 125, 127, 128, 129 VIC: 146, 149, 150, 159, 161, 162, 163, 164, 166 WA: 171, 175

034 TULIP TREE NSW: 002, 011, 015, 016, 019, 024, 027, 029, 032, 046, 047, 048, 069, 070, 071, 072 QLD: 107 SA: 113, 115, 116, 117 TAS: 125, 126, 127, 128, 129 VIC: 144, 146, 149, 154, 159, 161, 162, 166

035 MACADAMIA NSW: 002, 021, 024, 027, 029, 032, 037, 042, 046, 048, 060, 071, 072 QLD: 079, 085, 086 SA: 113, 115, 116, 117, 119, 124 TAS: 125 VIC: 146, 149, 159, 162 WA: 171, 175

036 YULAN MAGNOLIA NSW: 014, 016, 019, 021, 024, 027, 029, 037, 046, 048, 059, 069, 070, 071, 072 QLD: 107 SA: 113, 119 TAS: 125, 128 VIC: 143, 146, 149, 161

037 BULL BAY MAGNOLIA NSW: 002, 011, 013, 015, 017, 019, 021, 024, 027, 029, 032, 037, 042, 044, 046, 047, 048, 064, 069, 070, 071, 072 QLD: 085, 093, 094, 107 SA: 116, 117, 119, 124 TAS: 125, 126, 127, 128, 129 VIC: 143, 146, 149, 150, 159, 161, 162, 164 WA: 171, 173, 175

038 MAGNOLIA NSW: 002, 008, 011, 013, 014, 015, 016, 017, 019, 021, 024, 027, 029, 032, 037, 044, 046, 047, 048, 059, 069, 070, 071, 072 QLD: 107 SA: 115, 116, 117, 119 TAS: 125, 126, 127, 128, 129 VIC: 143, 146, 149, 150, 151, 159, 161, 162, 164, 166, 169 WA: 173

039 JAPANESE FLOWERING CRABAPPLE NSW: 002, 008, 011, 015, 016, 017, 019, 024, 027, 029, 032, 037, 044, 046, 047, 048, 059, 069, 070, 071, 072 SA: 113, 114, 115, 116, 117, 118, 119 TAS: 125, 126, 127, 128, 129 VIC: 137, 146, 149, 150, 159, 161, 162, 164, 166 WA: 171, 173

040 BROAD LEAFED PAPER BARK NSW: 002, 011, 016, 017, 020, 021, 024, 027, 029, 031, 037, 042, 046, 047, 048, 060, 061, 067, 069, 071, 072 QLD: 085, 086, 094, 097, 098 SA: 113, 119 TAS: 125, 129 VIC: 146, 148, 161, 162 WA: 171, 172, 173, 175

041 WHITE CEDAR NSW: 002, 011, 013, 015, 017, 019, 020, 024, 027, 029, 031, 032, 037, 039, 042, 047, 048, 049, 050, 051, 052, 053, 054, 055, 056, 057, 060, 067, 069, 070, 071, 072 QLD: 085, 086 SA: 113, 116, 117, 118, 124 TAS: 125, 126, 129 VIC: 134, 145, 146, 149, 150, 153, 154, 159, 161, 162, 164 WA: 171, 173, 175

042 MEDLAR NSW: 048, 070, 071, 072 SA: 113, 115 TAS: 125, 126, 128, 129 VIC: 137, 146, 161, 162

043 OLIVE NSW: 008, 013, 016, 021, 024, 027, 029, 032, 037, 044, 046, 048, 059, 069, 070, 071, 072 QLD: 079, 085, 094 SA: 114, 115, 122, 124 TAS: 125, 126, 127, 128, 129 VIC: 146, 149, 150, 154, 159, 161, 162 WA: 171, 173, 175, 177

044 PERSIAN IRONWOOD NSW: 012, 048, 069, 070, 071 TAS: 125, 126, 127, 128, 129 VIC: 137, 144, 149, 161, 162, 166 WA: 173, 175

045 SWEET PITTOSPORUM NSW: 002, 021, 024, 027, 029, 032, 037, 042, 048, 050, 051, 052, 053, 054, 055, 056, 057, 059, 067, 069, 071, 072 QLD: 085, 086, 097, 107 SA: 113, 115, 116, 117, 119, 120 TAS: 125, 126, 127, 129 VIC: 145, 146, 149, 150, 153, 162 WA: 171, 172, 175

046 WHITE FRANGIPANI NSW: 002, 013, 021, 024, 027, 029, 032, 037, 042, 046, 048, 071, 072 NT: 074, 075 QLD: 079, 080, 085, 094, 098, 099, 112 SA: 115, 116, 117 TAS: 126 VIC: 139, 146, 149, 150, 159, 161, 162 WA: 171, 175, 177

047 FRANGIPANI NSW: 002, 013, 016, 017, 021, 024, 027, 029, 032, 037, 042, 044, 046, 047, 048, 059, 071, 072 NT: 074, 075 QLD: 079, 080, 085, 088, 099, 103, 112 SA: 113, 115, 116, 117, 124 TAS: 125, 126, 129 VIC: 139, 146, 149, 150, 159, 161, 162 WA: 171, 175, 176, 177

048 PLUM PINE NSW: 002, 008, 011, 013, 016, 017, 019, 021, 024, 027, 029, 031, 032, 037, 042, 048, 050, 051, 052, 053, 054, 055, 056, 057, 060, 061, 067, 071, 072 NT: 074 QLD: 086, 097, 098 SA: 113, 119 TAS: 125 VIC: 143, 161 WA: 171, 172, 175

049 PURPLE LEAFED PLUM NSW: 002, 008, 011, 015, 017, 024, 027, 029, 032, 037, 044, 046, 047, 048, 050, 051, 052, 053, 054, 055, 056, 057, 059, 069, 070, 071, 072 SA: 113, 115, 116, 117, 118, 119, 124 TAS: 125, 126, 127, 128, 129 VIC: 137, 146, 149, 150, 154, 159, 161, 162 WA: 171, 173, 175

050 CAPITAL CALLERY PEAR NSW: 002, 015, 016, 017, 024, 027, 029, 032, 044, 046, 048, 069, 070, 071, 072 SA: 113, 114, 115, 116, 117, 118, 119, 124 TAS: 125, 126, 127, 128, 129 VIC: 146, 149, 150, 159, 161, 162, 164 WA: 173, 175

051 GOLDEN ROBINIA NSW: 002, 008, 011, 013, 014, 016, 017, 019, 024, 027, 029, 032, 037, 044, 046, 047, 048, 059, 069, 070, 071, 072 QLD: 107 SA: 113, 115, 116, 117, 118, 119, 124 TAS: 125, 126, 127, 128, 129 VIC: 146, 149, 150, 154, 159, 161, 162, 164 WA: 171, 173, 175

052 CHINESE TALLOW TREE NSW: 002, 008, 011, 013, 014, 015, 016, 017, 019, 024, 027, 029, 032, 037, 039, 044, 046, 047, 048, 049, 069, 070, 071, 072 SA: 113, 115, 116, 117, 118, 119, 124 TAS: 125, 126 VIC: 146, 149, 150, 159, 161, 162 WA: 171, 172, 173, 175, 176, 177

053 QLD UMBRELLA TREE NSW: 002, 024, 027, 029, 032, 037, 043, 048, 071, 072 NT: 074 QLD: 079, 080, 085, 112 SA: 113, 115, 116, 117, 119, 122, 124 TAS: 125, 126 VIC: 139, 146, 149, 150, 159, 161, 162 WA: 175

054 PEPPER TREE NSW: 002, 006, 008, 011, 013, 015, 017, 019, 024, 027, 029, 032, 035, 037, 042, 044, 046, 047, 048, 050, 051, 052, 053, 054, 055, 056, 057, 059, 069, 070, 071, 072 QLD: 079 SA: 113, 115, 116, 117, 118, 119, 120, 124 TAS: 125, 126, 127, 128, 129 VIC: 134, 137, 144, 145, 146, 149, 150, 153, 154, 159, 161, 162, 164 WA: 172, 173

055 AFRICAN TULIP TREE NSW: 002, 019, 021, 024, 037, 042, 048, 071, 072 NT: 074 SA: 113 VIC: 146 WA: 175

056 QLD FIREWHEEL TREE NSW: 002, 011, 013, 016, 019, 021, 024, 027, 029, 031, 032, 037, 040, 042, 046, 047, 048, 050, 051, 052, 053, 054, 055, 056, 057, 060, 061, 071, 072 NT: 074 QLD: 079, 080, 085, 086 TAS: 125 VIC: 146, 149, 150, 161, 162 WA: 171, 173

057 ALSTONVILLE TIBOUCHINA NSW: 002, 006, 008, 011, 016, 017, 019, 021, 024, 027, 029, 032, 037, 044, 046, 047, 048, 059, 061, 071, 072 QLD: 078, 079, 080, 085, 094, 098, 107 TAS: 125 VIC: 146, 149, 150, 161, 162

058 WATER GUM NSW: 002, 011, 013, 015, 016, 017, 020, 021, 024, 027, 029, 031, 032, 037, 042, 046, 047, 048, 059, 060, 061, 064, 070, 071, 072 QLD: 085, 098 SA: 116, 117 TAS: 125 VIC: 145, 146, 149, 150, 153, 159, 161, 162, 164

059 CHINESE WEEPING ELM NSW: 002, 008, 011, 013, 016, 017, 024, 027, 029, 032, 037, 044, 046, 047, 048, 059, 069, 070, 071, 072 SA: 113, 115, 116, 117, 118, 124 TAS: 125, 126, 127, 128, 129 VIC: 145, 146, 149, 150, 153, 154, 159, 161, 162, 164 WA: 171, 173, 175

060 COTTON PALM NSW: 002, 016, 017, 021, 024, 029, 032, 037, 042, 048, 071, 072 NT: 074 QLD: 079, 085 SA: 113, 115, 119, 124 TAS: 125, 128, 129 VIC: 139, 146, 149, 150, 161 WA: 171

061 GLOSSY ABELIA NSW: 002, 006, 009, 011, 014, 016, 017, 019, 020, 024, 026, 027, 029, 032, 037, 044, 046, 047, 048, 049, 059, 061, 069, 071, 072 QLD: 079, 080, 085, 107 SA: 113, 115, 116, 117, 118, 119, 120, 124 TAS: 125, 126, 127, 128, 129 VIC: 134, 137, 140, 145, 146, 149, 150, 153, 154, 159, 161, 162 WA: 171, 172, 175

062 HAIRY WATTLE NSW: 012, 020, 024, 035, 042, 046, 050, 051, 052, 053, 054, 055, 056, 057, 058, 060, 067, 071, 072 TAS: 125 VIC: 146, 148, 149, 155, 161, 162 WA: 172

063 PINEAPPLE GUAVA NSW: 008, 019, 024, 027, 029, 032, 037, 046, 048, 059, 071, 072 QLD: 079 SA: 113, 116, 117, 120, 124 TAS: 125, 126, 128, 129 VIC: 145, 149, 150, 153, 159, 161 WA: 171, 175

064 CREEK LILLYPILLY NSW: 002, 006, 008, 011, 013, 014, 016, 020, 021, 024, 027, 029, 031, 032, 037, 042, 044, 046, 047, 048, 050, 051, 052, 053, 054, 055, 056, 057, 059, 060, 061, 067, 071, 072 QLD: 080, 085, 094, 097, 098, 107 SA: 113, 115, 116, 117, 118, 119, 120 TAS: 125, 126, 127, 128, 129 VIC: 145, 146, 148, 149, 150, 153, 155, 159, 161, 162, 164 WA: 171, 172, 173, 175

065 WINTER SWEET NSW: 037, 071, 072 TAS: 126 VIC: 146, 150, 161 WA: 175

066 SHELL GINGER NSW: 002, 008, 011, 021, 024, 027, 029, 037, 042, 048, 071, 072 QLD: 079, 080, 081, 085, 094, 099, 103, 105, 107 TAS: 125, 129 VIC: 139, 146, 149 WA: 171, 176

067 ANISEED MYRTLE NSW: 011, 020, 021, 029, 031, 037, 042, 048, 060, 071, 072 QLD: 080, 085, 086, 097 SA: 116, 117 TAS: 125 VIC: 146, 149, 161 WA: 175

068 LEMON SCENTED MYRTLE NSW: 002, 008, 011, 016, 017, 020, 021, 024, 027, 029, 031, 032, 033, 035, 037, 042, 046, 047, 048, 059, 060, 061, 063, 069, 071, 072 QLD: 079, 080, 085, 086, 090, 093, 097, 098, 105 SA: 115, 116, 117, 119 TAS: 125 VIC: 146, 149, 150, 155, 159, 161, 162 WA: 172

069 HEDGE BAMBOO NSW: 002, 014, 021, 024, 027, 029, 032, 036, 037, 042, 048, 059, 071, 072 NT: 074 QLD: 076, 077, 078, 079, 085, 099 SA: 116, 117, 124 TAS: 125, 126 VIC: 146, 149, 150, 161, 164 WA: 175, 176

070 HEATH BANKSIA NSW: 002, 008, 009, 011, 012, 016, 017, 020, 021, 024, 027, 029, 031, 032, 035, 037, 040, 042, 047, 048, 050, 051, 052, 053, 054, 055, 056, 057, 058, 059, 060, 061, 067, 069, 071, 072 QLD: 079, 085, 086, 097 SA: 113, 115, 116, 117, 118, 120, 124 TAS: 125, 126, 127, 128, 129 VIC: 134, 145, 146, 148, 149, 150, 153, 154, 155, 158, 159, 161, 162, 163 WA: 172, 175

071 POWDERPUFF TREE NSW: 002, 016, 021, 024, 027, 029, 037, 042, 044, 048, 071, 072 NT: 074 QLD: 079, 085, 094, 098 TAS: 125

072 SASANQUA CAMELLIA NSW: 002, 008, 011, 012, 013, 014, 015, 016, 017, 019, 021, 024, 027, 029, 032, 037, 043, 044, 045, 046, 047, 048, 049, 059, 064, 069, 070, 071, 072 QLD: 079, 090, 093, 103, 107 SA: 113, 114, 115, 116, 117, 119, 120, 124 TAS: 125, 126, 127, 128, 129 VIC: 140, 146, 149, 150, 151, 154, 159, 161, 162, 166, 169 WA: 171, 173, 175, 177

073 JAPANESE PLUM YEW NSW: 002, 008, 037, 069, 071, 072 SA: 116, 117 TAS: 125, 126, 128, 129 VIC: 146, 150, 161

074 NSW CHRISTMAS BUSH NSW: 002, 006, 008, 011, 016, 017, 019, 021, 024, 027, 029, 031, 032, 033, 037, 040, 042, 044, 046, 047, 048, 050, 051, 052, 053, 054, 055, 056, 057, 060, 061, 067, 069, 071, 072 QLD: 079, 085, 086, 097, 107 SA: 115, 116, 117, 119 TAS: 125, 126, 128, 129 VIC: 146, 149, 150, 159, 161, 162, 164, 166 WA: 172

075 MEDITERRANEAN FAN PALM NSW: 002, 011, 016, 021, 024, 037, 042, 046, 048, 071, 072 NT: 074 QLD: 079, 085, 099 SA: 115, 116, 117, 119, 124 TAS: 125, 128, 129 VIC: 139, 146, 149, 150, 161, 162

076 LOOKING GLASS PLANT NSW: 002, 006, 008, 014, 021, 024, 026, 027, 029, 032, 037, 046, 048, 069, 071, 072 QLD: 079 SA: 113, 115, 116, 117, 119, 120, 124 TAS: 125, 127, 128 VIC: 145, 146, 149, 150, 153, 161, 168 WA: 171, 172, 175, 176

077 ARIZONA CYPRESS NSW: 002, 014, 024, 026, 027, 029, 037, 046, 048, 069, 070, 071, 072 QLD: 107 SA: 113, 116, 117, 118, 119, 120, 124 TAS: 125, 126, 128, 129 VIC: 143, 145, 146, 149, 150, 153, 159, 161, 162 WA: 175

078 LEYLAND CYPRESS NSW: 002, 008, 011, 013, 015, 017, 019, 024, 026, 027, 029, 032, 037, 044, 046, 047, 048, 049, 059, 066, 067, 069, 070, 071, 072 QLD: 085, 107 SA: 113, 114, 115, 116, 117, 118, 119, 120, 124 TAS: 125, 126, 127, 128, 129 VIC: 143, 145, 149, 150, 153, 154, 159, 161, 162, 164 WA: 171, 172, 175

079 GOLDEN CANE PALM NSW: 002, 017, 021, 027, 037, 042, 047, 048, 071, 072 QLD: 079, 080, 089, 093, 094, 098, 099, 110 WA: 171, 175

080 POINSETTIA NSW: 016, 021, 024, 027, 029, 037, 042, 046, 048, 072 NT: 074 QLD: 079, 082, 085, 094 SA: 114, 115, 119 TAS: 125, 126, 128 VIC: 146, 149, 159, 161 WA: 171

081 WEEPING FIG NSW: 002, 016, 017, 021, 024, 027, 029, 032, 037, 039, 044, 046, 048, 050, 051, 052, 053, 054, 055, 056, 057, 059, 063, 069, 071, 072 NT: 074 QLD: 079, 085, 086, 094, 095, 097, 103, 112 SA: 113, 115, 116, 117, 119, 124 TAS: 125, 126, 127, 128, 129 VIC: 139, 146, 149, 150, 159, 161, 162 WA: 171, 173, 175, 176, 177

082 MOONLIGHT GREVILLEA NSW: 002, 008, 011, 016, 017, 019, 021, 024, 027, 029, 031, 032, 033, 035, 037, 040, 042, 044, 046, 047, 048, 050, 051, 052, 053, 054, 055, 056, 057, 059, 060, 061, 063, 069, 071, 072 QLD: 079, 085, 086, 097, 098, 107 SA: 115, 116, 117, 118, 119, 124 TAS: 125, 128 VIC: 146, 149, 150, 154, 155, 161, 162 WA: 171, 172, 175

083 GIANT RHUBARB NSW: 003, 008, 019, 027, 032, 037, 048, 068, 069, 071, 072 SA: 113, 116, 117, 119 TAS: 125, 126, 128, 129 VIC: 144, 146, 149, 161, 162

084 HIBISCUS NSW: 002, 011, 016, 017, 021, 024, 027, 029, 037, 042, 046, 047, 048, 049, 069, 071, 072 NT: 074 QLD: 079, 094 SA: 115, 116, 117, 118, 124 TAS: 125, 126, 127, 129 VIC: 146, 149, 150, 159, 161 WA: 171, 175, 176

085 COTTONWOOD NSW: 002, 021, 024, 029, 037, 042, 048, 071, 072 NT: 074 QLD: 079, 080, 085, 086 SA: 113 VIC: 150 WA: 171, 172, 173, 175, 177

086 SPARTAN JUNIPER NSW: 002, 008, 011, 013, 014, 016, 017, 019, 024, 026, 027, 029, 032, 037, 044, 046, 047, 048, 063, 064, 069, 070, 071, 072 QLD: 079, 085, 093, 107 SA: 113, 114, 115, 116, 117, 118, 119, 120, 124 TAS: 125, 126, 128, 129 VIC: 134, 143, 145, 146, 149, 150, 151, 153, 154, 159, 161, 162, 164 WA: 176

087 BAY LAUREL NSW: 002, 006, 008, 011, 014, 016, 019, 021, 024, 026, 027, 029, 032, 037, 039, 042, 044, 046, 047, 048, 059, 066, 070, 071, 072 QLD: 079, 085 SA: 113, 114, 115, 116, 117, 118, 120, 124 TAS: 125, 126, 127, 128, 129 VIC: 137, 144, 145, 146, 149, 150, 153, 154, 159, 161, 162, 164, 166 WA: 171, 172, 174, 175

088 TEMU NSW: 002, 008, 009, 019, 024, 032, 037, 046, 048, 069, 071, 072 SA: 113, 116, 117, 120 TAS: 125, 126, 127, 128, 129, 131 VIC: 134, 140, 144, 145, 146, 149, 150, 151, 153, 154, 159, 161, 162, 166 WA: 175

089 BRAZILIAN RED CLOAK NSW: 008, 021, 037, 042, 048, 071 QLD: 078, 080, 085, 094 VIC: 146

090 KERMADEC POHUTUKAWA NSW: 002, 013, 016, 024, 026, 027, 029, 037, 042, 046, 048, 059, 071, 072 QLD: 085 SA: 115, 116, 117, 118, 119 TAS: 125, 126, 127, 128, 129 VIC: 145, 146, 150, 153, 161, 164 WA: 171

091 PORT WINE MAGNOLIA NSW: 002, 008, 011, 013, 016, 017, 019, 021, 024, 026, 027, 029, 032, 033, 037, 042, 044, 046, 047, 048, 059, 064, 069, 071, 072 NT: 074 QLD: 078, 079, 085, 090, 093, 094, 098, 107 SA: 115, 116, 117, 119, 120, 124 TAS: 125, 126, 127, 128, 129 VIC: 137, 140, 145, 146, 149, 150, 151, 153, 159, 161, 162, 164, 169 WA: 171, 172, 173, 175, 176

092 MURRAYA NSW: 002, 006, 008, 011, 013, 014, 016, 017, 019, 021, 024, 026, 027, 029, 032, 033, 037, 042, 044, 045, 046, 047, 048, 059, 061, 063, 064, 066, 069, 071, 072 NT: 074 QLD: 078, 079, 080, 085, 090, 093, 094, 095, 097, 098, 103, 107, 108 SA: 115, 116, 117, 119, 120, 124 TAS: 125, 128, 129 VIC: 145, 146, 149, 150, 151, 153, 154, 159, 161, 162 WA: 171, 172, 175

093 SACRED BAMBOO NSW: 002, 011, 013, 016, 017, 019, 021, 024, 027, 029, 032, 037, 042, 044, 046, 047, 048, 050, 051, 052, 053, 054, 055, 056, 057, 059, 069, 071, 072 QLD: 078, 079, 085, 098, 099, 107 SA: 113, 115, 116, 117, 118, 119, 124 TAS: 125, 126, 127, 128, 129 VIC: 134, 137, 140, 145, 146, 149, 150, 151, 153, 154, 159, 161, 162 WA: 171, 172, 175, 176, 177

094 OLEANDER NSW: 002, 006, 008, 011, 016, 019, 021, 024, 027, 029, 032, 037, 044, 046, 047, 048, 059, 069, 071, 072 QLD: 079, 085, 098 SA: 113, 115, 116, 117, 118, 119, 120, 124 TAS: 125, 126, 127, 128, 129 VIC: 145, 146, 149, 150, 153, 159, 161, 162 WA: 171, 172, 175, 176, 177

095 PINE-LEAFED GEEBUNG NSW: 002, 008, 024, 027, 029, 032, 037, 040, 042, 048, 050, 051, 052, 053, 054, 055, 056, 057, 060, 071, 072 TAS: 125, 129 VIC: 146, 150, 161, 162 WA: 175

096 SMALL LEAFED PHOTINIA NSW: 002, 006, 011, 013, 016, 017, 019, 021, 024, 026, 027, 029, 032, 033, 037, 043, 046, 047, 048, 059, 061, 067, 069, 070, 071, 072 QLD: 085, 107 SA: 113, 115, 116, 117, 119 TAS: 125, 126, 127, 128, 129 VIC: 134, 140, 145, 146, 149, 150, 153, 159, 161, 162, 164, 166

097 BLACK BAMBOO NSW: 002, 021, 024, 029, 036, 037, 048, 071, 072 QLD: 076, 079, 085 SA: 124 TAS: 125, 128 VIC: 146, 149, 161, 162, 164 WA: 171

098 PITTOSPORUM NSW: 002, 009, 011, 015, 016, 019, 024, 027, 032, 037, 042, 044, 046, 048, 069, 070, 071, 072 QLD: 079, 107 SA: 113, 114, 116, 117, 118, 119 TAS: 125, 126, 128, 129 VIC: 140, 145, 146, 149, 150, 153, 154, 159, 161, 162, 164 WA: 172, 175

099 PLUMBAGO NSW: 002, 006, 008, 016, 017, 019, 021, 024, 025, 027, 029, 032, 037, 044, 046, 047, 048, 059, 069, 071, 072 QLD: 078, 079, 080, 085, 103, 107 SA: 113, 114, 115, 116, 117, 118, 119, 120, 124 TAS: 125, 126, 127, 128, 129 VIC: 134, 145, 146, 149, 150, 153, 154, 159, 160, 162, 168 WA: 171, 172, 175, 176

100 POMEGRANATE NSW: 008, 024, 027, 029, 037, 046, 048, 069, 071, 072 SA: 113, 115, 116, 117, 124 TAS: 125, 126, 127, 128, 129 VIC: 137, 146, 149, 150, 154, 159, 161, 162 WA: 171, 175

101 LADY PALM NSW: 002, 013, 017, 021, 022, 024, 027, 029, 032, 037, 042, 044, 046, 048, 059, 071, 072 QLD: 079, 084, 085, 089, 094, 099, 103, 109 SA: 113, 114, 116, 117, 124 TAS: 125 VIC: 146, 149, 150, 159, 161, 162 WA: 171, 175

102 RHODODENDRON NSW: 002, 012, 016, 019, 024, 027, 029, 032, 044, 046, 048, 059, 069, 070, 071, 072 QLD: 079, 085 SA: 113, 119 TAS: 125, 126, 127, 128, 129 VIC: 143, 146, 149, 150, 159, 161, 162, 166

103 MINIATURE UMBRELLA TREE NSW: 002, 016, 024, 029, 032, 037, 042, 046, 048, 063, 071, 072 NT: 074 QLD: 079, 080, 085, 094, 103 SA: 113, 115, 116, 117, 119, 124 TAS: 125, 126, 129 VIC: 139, 146, 149, 150, 159, 161, 162 WA: 171, 172, 175, 176

104 GIANT BIRD OF PARADISE NSW: 002, 011, 016, 017, 021, 024, 027, 029, 032, 037, 042, 044, 046, 048, 059, 071, 072 NT: 074 QLD: 079, 080, 081, 085, 092, 094, 099, 103 SA: 115, 116, 117, 119, 124 TAS: 125, 126, 127, 128 VIC: 139, 145, 146, 149, 150, 153, 159, 161, 162 WA: 171, 175, 177

105 SCRUB CHERRY NSW: 002, 008, 011, 013, 014, 016, 017, 019, 021, 024, 026, 027, 029, 031, 032, 033, 037, 039, 042, 043, 044, 046, 047, 048, 050, 051, 052, 053, 054, 055, 056, 057, 059, 060, 061, 063, 064, 069, 071, 072 NT: 074 QLD: 079, 080, 085, 086, 087, 093, 094, 097, 098, 099 SA: 113, 114, 115, 116, 117, 118, 119, 120, 124 TAS: 125, 126, 127, 128, 129 VIC: 145, 146, 148, 149, 150, 151, 153, 154, 159, 161, 162, 164 WA: 171, 172, 175

106 RIBERRY NSW: 002, 008, 011, 013, 016, 017, 019, 021, 024, 026, 027, 029, 031, 032, 033, 037, 039, 040, 042, 044, 045, 046, 047, 048, 050, 051, 052, 053, 054, 055, 056, 057, 059, 060, 061, 063, 064, 069, 071, 072 NT: 074 QLD: 078, 079, 080, 085, 086, 093, 094, 095, 097, 098 SA: 113, 115, 116, 117, 119 TAS: 125, 126, 128, 129 VIC: 146, 148, 149, 150, 159, 161, 162 WA: 172, 175, 177

107 YELLOW OLEANDER NSW: 048

108 WESTERN RED CEDAR NSW: 002, 014, 016, 019, 024, 026, 029, 048, 069, 070, 071, 072 SA: 113, 115 TAS: 125, 126, 128 VIC: 143, 145, 146, 149, 150, 153, 161, 162, 164 WA: 175

109 SWEET VIBURNUM NSW: 002, 006, 008, 011, 014, 016, 017, 019, 021, 024, 026, 027, 029, 032, 037, 042, 044, 046, 047, 048, 061, 063, 064, 069, 070, 071, 072 QLD: 079, 085, 100, 107 SA: 115, 116, 117, 118, 119 TAS: 125, 126, 127, 128 VIC: 145, 146, 149, 150, 153, 154, 159, 161, 162, 164, 166 WA: 171, 172, 175

110 LAURISTINUS NSW: 002, 006, 008, 009, 011, 013, 014, 016, 017, 019, 021, 024, 026, 027, 029, 032, 037, 042, 044, 046, 047, 048, 049, 059, 061, 069, 070, 071, 072 QLD: 079, 107 SA: 113, 114, 115, 116, 117, 118, 119, 120, 124 TAS: 125, 126, 127, 128, 129 VIC: 134, 137, 140, 145, 146, 149, 150, 151, 153, 154, 159, 161, 162, 164, 166 WA: 171, 172, 175, 176

111 WEEPING LILLYPILLY NSW: 002, 011, 013, 016, 017, 021, 024, 027, 029, 031, 032, 033, 037, 042, 046, 047, 048, 060, 061, 070, 071, 072 QLD: 079, 080, 085, 086, 090, 093, 094, 095, 098 SA: 113, 115, 116, 117 TAS: 125, 126, 128 VIC: 139, 145, 146, 149, 150, 153, 159, 161, 162, 164 WA: 171, 173, 175, 177

112 BOWER WATTLE NSW: 009, 024, 027, 035, 042, 046, 048, 058, 059, 071, 072 QLD: 079 SA: 113, 115, 116, 117, 119 TAS: 125, 127, 128, 129 VIC: 146, 149, 150, 159, 160, 161, 162, 163 WA: 171, 172, 173, 175

113 SMALL LEAFED LILLYPILLY NSW: 002, 008, 011, 013, 016, 017, 019, 020, 021, 024, 027, 029, 031, 032, 033, 037, 040, 042, 044, 046, 047, 048, 050, 051, 052, 053, 054, 055, 056, 057, 059, 060, 061, 063, 067, 071, 072 QLD: 080, 085, 090, 093, 094, 097, 107 SA: 113, 115, 116, 117, 119, 120 TAS: 125, 126, 127, 128, 129 VIC: 139, 145, 146, 148, 149, 150, 153, 155, 159, 161, 162, 164 WA: 171, 172, 175, 177

114 AECHMEA BROMELIAD NSW: 007, 010, 016, 021, 024, 027, 029, 037, 039, 042, 046, 048, 071, 072 QLD: 080, 084, 085, 089, 094, 099, 107, 112 SA: 113, 115, 116, 117, 124 TAS: 125, 126, 128 VIC: 139, 141, 142, 146, 149, 150, 159, 161, 162 WA: 171, 175

115 AFTER DARK AGONIS NSW: 002, 016, 024, 027, 029, 032, 037, 042, 044, 046, 048, 050, 051, 052, 053, 054, 055, 056, 057, 059, 060, 071, 072 QLD: 079 SA: 115, 119, 124 TAS: 125, 126, 128, 129 VIC: 146, 149, 150, 159, 161, 162 WA: 171, 173

116 CANDELABRA ALOE NSW: 002, 014, 024, 037, 042, 048, 071, 072 QLD: 079 SA: 116, 117, 118 TAS: 125, 126 VIC: 141, 142, 146, 149, 150, 152, 161, 162 WA: 171, 175

117 JOY WEED NSW: 002, 008, 011, 014, 016, 017, 021, 024, 027, 037, 042, 044, 048, 059, 069, 071, 072 NT: 074 QLD: 080, 094 SA: 116, 117 TAS: 125 VIC: 146 WA: 171, 172, 175

118 FLAMINGO FLOWER NSW: 002, 016, 021, 024, 027, 029, 037, 042, 044, 046, 048, 059, 071, 072 NT: 074 QLD: 079, 081, 085, 094, 099, 103, 110 SA: 113, 115, 116, 117, 119, 124 TAS: 125, 126, 128 VIC: 139, 146, 149, 150, 159, 161 WA: 171, 177

119 POWIS CASTLE WORMWOOD NSW: 002, 008, 016, 021, 024, 025, 027, 037, 038, 044, 047, 048, 069, 071, 072 SA: 115, 116, 117 TAS: 125, 126, 129 VIC: 134, 137, 144, 145, 150, 153, 161, 162 WA: 171, 175, 176

120 RENGA LILY NSW: 008, 009, 011, 017, 024, 027, 032, 037, 042, 044, 048, 059, 071, 072 QLD: 085, 103, 107 SA: 113, 122 TAS: 125, 127, 128 VIC: 140, 144, 145, 146, 149, 150, 153, 159, 161, 162, 168 WA: 172

121 CAST IRON PLANT NSW: 002, 011, 016, 017, 021, 024, 027, 029, 037, 039, 042, 044, 048, 059, 069, 071, 072 QLD: 079, 080, 085, 103 SA: 113, 115, 116, 117, 119, 124 TAS: 125, 126, 128, 129 VIC: 137, 146, 149, 150, 159, 161, 162 WA: 171, 175, 176, 177

122 GOLD DUST PLANT NSW: 002, 008, 017, 024, 026, 027, 029, 032, 037, 042, 044, 047, 048, 049, 059, 069, 071, 072 SA: 113, 115, 116, 117, 119, 120, 124 TAS: 125, 126, 127, 128, 129 VIC: 137, 145, 146, 149, 150, 151, 153, 159, 161, 162, 166 WA: 171, 175, 176

123 HAIRPIN BANKSIA NSW: 002, 009, 011, 012, 016, 017, 020, 021, 024, 027, 029, 031, 032, 035, 037, 040, 042, 046, 047, 048, 050, 051, 052, 053, 054, 055, 056, 057, 058, 059, 060, 061, 064, 067, 069, 071, 072 QLD: 079, 085, 086, 097, 098 SA: 115, 116, 117, 120, 124 TAS: 125, 126, 127, 128, 129 VIC: 145, 146, 149, 150, 153, 154, 155, 158, 159, 161, 162, 163 WA: 172

124 JAPANESE BARBERRY NSW: 002, 008, 014, 016, 019, 024, 026, 027, 032, 037, 044, 046, 047, 048, 049, 069, 071, 072 QLD: 085, 101 SA: 113, 115, 116, 117, 118, 124 TAS: 125, 126, 127, 128, 129 VIC: 137, 145, 146, 149, 150, 153, 159, 161, 162 WA: 175

125 YESTERDAY TODAY TOMORROW NSW: 002, 006, 008, 017, 021, 024, 026, 027, 029, 032, 037, 042, 046, 047, 048, 059, 071, 072 QLD: 078, 079, 080, 085, 094, 098, 107 SA: 113, 115, 116, 117, 120 TAS: 126, 128, 129 VIC: 146, 149, 150, 159, 161, 162 WA: 171, 172, 175, 177

126 SOUTH AFRICAN POMEGRANATE NSW:048, 071, 072 VIC: 146

127 **DUTCH BOX** NSW: 002, 008, 011, 016, 017, 019, 020, 021, 024, 026, 027, 029, 032, 037, 042, 045, 046, 047, 048, 049, 059, 066, 069, 070, 071, 072 QLD: 079, 107, 108 SA: 113, 114, 115, 116, 117, 119, 120 TAS: 125, 126, 127, 128, 129, 130 VIC: 134, 138, 140, 143, 144, 145, 146, 149, 150, 151, 153, 154, 159, 161, 162, 166, 169 WA: 172, 175

128 **LITTLE JOHN BOTTLEBRUSH** NSW: 002, 006, 008, 011, 017, 021, 024, 027, 029, 031, 032, 035, 037, 042, 044, 046, 047, 048, 050, 051, 052, 053, 054, 055, 056, 057, 058, 059, 060, 061, 069, 071, 072 QLD: 078, 079, 085, 086, 090, 097, 098 SA: 113, 115, 116, 117, 118, 120, 124 TAS: 125, 126, 127, 128, 129 VIC: 134, 145, 146, 149, 150, 153, 154, 155, 159, 161, 162, 163 WA: 171, 172, 175, 176

129 **FLOWERING QUINCE** NSW: 008, 016, 019, 024, 027, 029, 032, 037, 044, 048, 049, 069, 071, 072 SA: 113, 115, 116, 117, 119, 120, 124 TAS: 125, 126, 128 VIC: 137, 144, 146, 149, 150, 159, 161, 162, 166 WA: 172, 175

130 **MEXICAN ORANGE BLOSSOM** NSW: 002, 006, 008, 009, 016, 019, 024, 027, 029, 032, 037, 042, 044, 047, 048, 059, 069, 071, 072 SA: 113, 115, 116, 117, 118, 119, 120, 124 TAS: 125, 126, 127, 128, 129 VIC: 134, 137, 138, 140, 144, 145, 146, 149, 150, 151, 153, 154, 159, 161, 162, 166, 168 WA: 171, 172, 175

131 **HEART-LEAFED FLAME PEA** NSW: 002, 009, 027, 031, 032, 035, 037, 040, 042, 046, 048, 060, 061, 071, 072 SA: 115, 116, 117, 120 TAS: 125, 129 VIC: 146, 149, 150, 159, 162 WA: 171, 172, 175, 176

132 **CROTON** NSW: 002, 016, 021, 024, 029, 037, 041, 046, 048, 071, 072 QLD: 079, 080, 082, 084, 085, 094, 099, 102, 103 SA: 116, 117, 119, 124 TAS: 125, 126, 128 VIC: 139, 146, 149, 150, 159, 162 WA: 171, 176, 177

133 **DIOSMA** NSW: 002, 006, 009, 016, 017, 019, 020, 021, 024, 029, 032, 037, 042, 044, 046, 047, 048, 049, 050, 051, 052, 053, 054, 055, 056, 057, 059, 069, 071, 072 QLD: 079, 107 SA: 113, 115, 116, 117, 118, 119, 120, 124 TAS: 125, 126, 127, 128, 129 VIC: 140, 145, 146, 149, 150, 151, 153, 154, 159, 161, 162, 169 WA: 171, 172, 175, 176, 177

134 **WHITE CORREA** NSW: 002, 017, 024, 027, 032, 040, 042, 048, 058, 059, 060, 061, 067, 069, 071, 072 SA: 116, 117, 118, 120, 124 TAS: 125, 126, 127, 128, 129 VIC: 145, 146, 149, 150, 153, 154, 155, 158, 159, 161, 162 WA: 171, 175

135 **JADE PLANT** NSW: 002, 008, 014, 016, 021, 024, 025, 027, 028, 029, 032, 037, 039, 044, 048, 071, 072 QLD: 079, 085, 107, 112 SA: 113, 115, 116, 117, 124 TAS: 125, 126, 128, 129, 130 VIC: 134, 137, 141, 142, 145, 146, 149, 150, 153, 159, 161, 162, 168 WA: 171, 175, 177

136 **MEXICAN HEATHER** NSW: 002, 016, 021, 024, 025, 027, 029, 037, 042, 044, 047, 048, 069, 071, 072 NT: 074 QLD: 079, 080, 094 SA: 116, 117, 118, 119, 120, 124 TAS: 125, 126, 127, 129 VIC: 134, 145, 149, 150, 153, 159, 161, 162 WA: 171, 175, 176

137 **YELLOW PEACOCK FLOWER** NSW: 001, 002, 006, 008, 011, 016, 019, 021, 024, 027, 029, 030, 032, 033, 037, 039, 042, 044, 046, 047, 048, 050, 051, 052, 053, 054, 055, 056, 057, 061, 063, 069, 071, 072 QLD: 078, 079, 080, 085, 094, 098, 100 SA: 113, 114, 115, 116, 117, 118, 119, 120, 124 TAS: 125, 126, 127, 128, 129 VIC: 134, 137, 140, 144, 145, 146, 149, 150, 153, 154, 159, 160, 161, 162 WA: 171, 172, 175, 176

138 **PURPLE STICKY HOP BUSH** NSW: 002, 009, 011, 017, 019, 021, 024, 027, 029, 031, 032, 037, 042, 048, 050, 051, 052, 053, 054, 055, 056, 057, 058, 061, 067, 069, 071, 072 QLD: 086, 097 SA: 113, 115, 116, 117, 118, 120, 124 TAS: 125, 127, 128, 129 VIC: 134, 145, 146, 149, 150, 151, 153, 154, 155, 158, 159, 161, 162 WA: 171, 172, 175

139 **PIGEON BERRY** NSW: 002, 006, 008, 011, 016, 017, 019, 024, 027, 029, 033, 037, 042, 044, 046, 047, 048, 061, 066, 071, 072 NT: 074 QLD: 079, 094, 098, 100, 103 SA: 115, 116, 117, 119, 120, 124 TAS: 125 VIC: 146, 149, 150 WA: 171, 172, 175

140 **PRIDE OF MADEIRA** NSW: 002, 008, 011, 014, 016, 017, 019, 024, 027, 029, 032, 037, 042, 044, 048, 059, 069, 071, 072 QLD: 079, 085, 107 SA: 114, 115, 116, 117, 119, 123, 124 TAS: 125, 126, 127, 128, 129, 130 VIC: 134, 145, 146, 149, 150, 153, 154, 161, 162, 168 WA: 171, 172, 175, 176

141 **ESCALLONIA** NSW: 002, 008, 009, 011, 014, 016, 017, 019, 021, 024, 026, 027, 029, 032, 037, 044, 046, 047, 048, 049, 059, 063, 069, 071, 072 QLD: 079, 103 SA: 113, 114, 116, 117, 118, 119, 120, 124 TAS: 125, 126, 127, 128, 129 VIC: 134, 140, 145, 146, 149, 150, 153, 154, 159, 160, 161, 162, 166, 168 WA: 171, 172, 175

142 **CROWN OF THORNS** NSW: 027, 028, 037, 042, 046, 048, 071, 072 QLD: 079, 085 TAS: 125, 128 VIC: 145, 146, 153 WA: 171

143 **BRIGHT EYES** NSW: 002, 016, 021, 024, 027, 037, 046, 048, 049, 069, 071, 072 SA: 113, 115, 116, 117, 119, 120, 124 TAS: 125, 126, 127, 128, 129 VIC: 134, 140, 145, 146, 149, 153, 154, 161, 162 WA: 171, 172, 175, 177

144 **FATSIA** NSW: 002, 011, 016, 017, 024, 027, 029, 037, 042, 048, 071, 072 QLD: 079 SA: 113, 115, 116, 117, 119, 120, 124 TAS: 125, 126 VIC: 146, 149, 150, 159, 161, 162 WA: 171, 175, 176

145 **GARDENIA** NSW: 002, 006, 008, 011, 013, 014, 016, 019, 021, 024, 026, 027, 029, 032, 037, 042, 044, 045, 046, 047, 048, 059, 063, 069, 071, 072 NT: 074 QLD: 078, 079, 093, 094, 098, 099, 107, 112 SA: 113, 114, 115, 116, 117, 119, 120, 124 TAS: 125, 126, 127, 128, 129 VIC: 139, 145, 146, 149, 150, 153, 159, 161, 162 WA: 171, 172, 175, 176, 177

146 **WIRI MIST HEBE** NSW: 002, 009, 014, 016, 017, 021, 024, 027, 029, 037, 042, 044, 046, 048, 059, 069, 071, 072 QLD: 085 SA: 113, 115, 116, 117, 119, 120, 124 TAS: 125, 127, 128, 129 VIC: 145, 146, 149, 150, 153, 161, 162 WA: 171, 172, 175

147 **DAY LILY** NSW: 002, 004, 008, 011, 012, 016, 019, 021, 024, 025, 027, 029, 030, 032, 037, 039, 042, 046, 047, 048, 069, 071, 072 QLD: 079, 080, 096, 100, 103 SA: 115, 116, 117, 120, 121, 124 TAS: 125, 126, 127, 128, 129, 130 VIC: 136, 138, 145, 146, 149, 150, 153, 159, 160, 161, 162, 165 WA: 171, 175

148 **HYDRANGEA** NSW: 002, 006, 008, 011, 016, 017, 019, 021, 024, 027, 029, 032, 037, 043, 044, 046, 047, 048, 059, 069, 071, 072 QLD: 079, 085, 098, 103, 107 SA: 113, 114, 115, 116, 117, 119, 120, 124 TAS: 125, 126, 127, 128, 129 VIC: 137, 140, 143, 145, 146, 149, 150, 153, 154, 159, 161, 162, 168 WA: 171, 175, 176, 177

149 **BEEFSTEAK PLANT** NSW: 002, 008, 011, 014, 024, 027, 037, 042, 048, 059, 071, 072 QLD: 079 TAS: 125, 126, 129 VIC: 146, 149 WA: 171, 175

150 **ROSE CONEFLOWER** NSW: 002, 016, 024, 027, 029, 031, 035, 040, 042, 048, 050, 051, 052, 053, 054, 055, 056, 057, 058, 061, 071, 072 SA: 115, 116, 117, 119, 120 TAS: 125 VIC: 146, 149, 154, 161, 162 WA: 172, 175

151 **JUNGLE FLAME** NSW: 002, 016, 017, 021, 024, 027, 029, 037, 042, 044, 048, 059, 071, 072 NT: 074 QLD: 079, 080, 094, 103 SA: 116, 117 TAS: 125 VIC: 146, 149, 150, 159, 161, 162 WA: 171, 175

152 **ITALIAN LAVENDER** NSW: 002, 006, 008, 016, 017, 019, 021, 024, 025, 027, 029, 032, 037, 042, 043, 044, 046, 048, 059, 069, 071, 072 QLD: 079, 085, 100, 107 SA: 113, 114, 115, 116, 117, 119, 120, 124 TAS: 125, 126, 127, 128, 129 VIC: 134, 137, 138, 140, 144, 145, 146, 149, 150, 153, 154, 159, 160, 161, 162 WA: 171, 172, 175

153 **LEUCADENDRON** NSW: 002, 009, 016, 021, 024, 027, 029, 032, 037, 042, 044, 048, 050, 051, 052, 053, 054, 055, 056, 057, 071, 072 QLD: 079, 098 SA: 113, 119, 120, 124 TAS: 125, 126, 127, 128, 129 VIC: 132, 138, 146, 149, 150, 151, 154, 159, 161, 162 WA: 171, 175

154 **SILVER CUSHION BUSH** NSW: 002, 006, 008, 009, 016, 024, 027, 029, 032, 037, 042, 048, 060, 071, 072 QLD: 079 SA: 113, 115, 116, 117, 118, 120, 124 TAS: 125, 126, 127, 128, 129 VIC: 134, 144, 145, 146, 149, 150, 153, 154, 155, 159, 161, 162, 168 WA: 171, 175, 176

155 **LILY TURF** NSW: 001, 002, 006, 008, 011, 014, 016, 017, 019, 021, 024, 025, 027, 029, 032, 037, 039, 042, 044, 045, 046, 047, 048, 059, 066, 069, 071, 072 NT: 074 QLD: 078, 079, 080, 085, 090, 094, 098, 099, 103, 110 SA: 113, 114, 116, 117, 118, 119, 120, 124 TAS: 125, 126, 127, 128, 129 VIC: 134, 137, 145, 146, 149, 150, 153, 154, 159, 161, 162 WA: 171, 172, 175, 176

156 BOX LEAFED HONEYSUCKLE NSW: 002, 008, 016, 017, 020, 024, 027, 029, 037, 042, 043, 044, 046, 047, 048, 059, 066, 069, 071, 072 QLD: 079, 107 SA: 113, 115, 116, 117, 118, 119, 120, 124 TAS: 125, 126, 127, 128, 129 VIC: 134, 138, 140, 145, 146, 149, 150, 153, 154, 159, 160, 161, 162 WA: 171, 175

157 LOPHOMYRTUS NSW: 006, 014, 016, 024, 027, 029, 048, 069, 071, 072 SA: 113, 115 TAS: 125, 126, 127, 128, 129 VIC: 132, 140, 145, 146, 150, 153, 159, 160, 162

158 CHINESE FRINGE FLOWER NSW: 002, 006, 008, 014, 016, 019, 021, 024, 027, 029, 032, 037, 042, 046, 048, 061, 069, 071, 072 QLD: 078, 079, 085, 094 SA: 113, 115, 119 TAS: 125, 126, 128, 129 VIC: 137, 140, 146, 149, 150, 151, 159, 160, 161, 162, 166

159 WEEVIL LILY NSW: 011, 021, 037, 048, 071, 072 QLD: 094

160 MYRTLE NSW: 002, 024, 029, 032, 037, 048, 069, 071, 072 QLD: 085, 105 SA: 113, 115, 116, 117, 118, 119 TAS: 125, 126, 127, 128, 129 VIC: 137, 144, 145, 146, 149, 150, 151, 153, 161, 162 WA: 171, 172, 175

161 DWARF SACRED BAMBOO NSW: 002, 006, 011, 014, 017, 019, 021, 024, 026, 027, 029, 032, 037, 042, 044, 046, 047, 048, 049, 059, 061, 069, 071, 072 QLD: 078, 079, 085, 099, 103, 107 SA: 113, 114, 115, 116, 117, 118, 119, 120, 124 TAS: 125, 126, 127, 128, 129 VIC: 138, 140, 143, 146, 149, 150, 151, 154, 159, 161, 162, 166 WA: 171, 175

162 FIRESPIKE NSW: 008, 011, 016 SA: 119

163 ZONAL GERANIUM NSW: 021, 024, 027, 032, 037, 044, 046, 048, 069, 071, 072 SA: 115, 116, 117, 119, 124 TAS: 125, 126, 129 VIC: 146, 149, 150, 159, 161, 162 WA: 171, 172

164 XANADU PHILODENDRON NSW: 002, 008, 011, 017, 021, 024, 027, 029, 032, 037, 042, 044, 046, 048, 059, 063, 069, 071, 072 NT: 074 QLD: 079, 085, 090, 094, 098, 099, 102, 103, 107 SA: 113, 116, 117, 118, 119, 124 TAS: 125, 126, 128, 129 VIC: 139, 146, 149, 150, 159, 161, 162 WA: 171, 175, 176

165 JERUSALEM SAGE NSW: 008, 016, 038, 044, 048, 069, 071, 072 QLD: 098 SA: 116, 117 TAS: 126, 129 VIC: 137, 144, 149, 161, 162 WA: 172

166 MOUNTAIN FLAX NSW: 002, 008, 009, 011, 014, 016, 017, 019, 024, 027, 037, 042, 044, 048, 059, 064, 069, 071, 072 QLD: 078 SA: 113, 114, 116, 117, 118, 119 TAS: 125, 126, 127, 128, 129 VIC: 145, 146, 149, 150, 153, 159, 161, 162, 168

167 JAPANESE PIERIS NSW: 002, 011, 012, 016, 019, 024, 027, 029, 032, 037, 042, 044, 046, 047, 048, 069, 071, 072 SA: 113, 119 TAS: 125, 126, 127, 128, 129 VIC: 143, 145, 146, 149, 150, 153, 159, 160, 161, 162, 166 WA: 175

168 JAPANESE MOCK ORANGE NSW: 002, 011, 016, 017, 024, 027, 029, 037, 044, 047, 048, 069, 071 QLD: 097, 107 SA: 113, 114, 116, 117, 118, 119, 124 TAS: 125, 127 VIC: 146, 149, 150, 161, 162 WA: 171, 175

169 MINIATURE BAMBOO GRASS NSW: 027, 032, 036, 037, 048, 071 QLD: 078 VIC: 145, 149, 153 WA: 172

170 OLEANDER LEAFED PROTEA NSW: 002, 021, 024, 027, 029, 032, 037, 042, 046, 048, 050, 051, 052, 053, 054, 055, 056, 057, 059, 069, 071, 072 QLD: 079 SA: 113, 115, 119 TAS: 125, 126, 127, 128, 129 VIC: 132, 146, 149, 150, 159, 161, 162 WA: 172, 175

171 DWARF POMEGRANATE NSW: 008, 024, 029, 032, 037, 048, 069, 071, 072 SA: 113, 115, 116, 117, 124 TAS: 125, 126, 127, 128, 129 VIC: 146, 149, 150, 159, 161, 162 WA: 171

172 INDIAN HAWTHORN NSW: 002, 008, 011, 013, 016, 017, 019, 021, 024, 026, 027, 029, 032, 037, 042, 043, 044, 046, 048, 069, 071, 072 QLD: 078, 079, 085, 103 SA: 113, 114, 115, 116, 117, 118, 119, 120, 124 TAS: 125, 126, 127, 128, 129 VIC: 137, 146, 149, 154, 159, 161, 162 WA: 171, 172, 175

173 AZALEA NSW: 002, 016, 017, 019, 021, 024, 027, 029, 032, 037, 044, 046, 048, 059, 069, 071, 072 QLD: 085 SA: 113, 119, 124 TAS: 125, 126, 127, 128, 129 VIC: 133, 143, 146, 149, 150, 159, 161, 162, 166 WA: 171, 175, 177

174 RIBBED SAGE NSW: 002, 008, 027, 037, 042, 048, 065, 072 QLD: 079 SA: 114, 119, 120, 123 TAS: 125, 130 VIC: 134, 145, 146, 148, 149, 153, 161, 162 WA: 175

175 COTTON LAVENDER NSW: 002, 006, 008, 021, 024, 027, 029, 032, 037, 047, 048, 069, 071, 072 QLD: 079, 101 SA: 113, 115, 116, 117, 119, 120, 124 TAS: 125, 126, 129 VIC: 134, 137, 138, 144, 145, 149, 150, 153, 154, 161, 162 WA: 171, 174, 175

176 BIRD OF PARADISE NSW: 002, 011, 013, 016, 017, 019, 021, 024, 025, 027, 029, 032, 037, 042, 044, 046, 047, 048, 059, 071, 072 NT: 074 QLD: 078, 079, 080, 081, 085, 092, 093, 094, 099, 102, 103 SA: 113, 114, 115, 116, 117, 119, 120, 121, 124 TAS: 125, 126, 127, 128, 129 VIC: 134, 139, 145, 146, 149, 150, 153, 154, 159, 161, 162 WA: 171, 172, 175, 176, 177

177 BUSH GERMANDER NSW: 002, 008, 011, 016, 017, 019, 024, 027, 037, 044, 047, 048, 066, 069, 071, 072 SA: 113, 114, 116, 117 TAS: 125, 126, 127, 129 VIC: 137, 145, 149, 150, 153, 159, 160, 161, 162 WA: 175

178 JULES TIBOUCHINA NSW: 002, 006, 008, 011, 014, 016, 017, 021, 024, 027, 029, 032, 033, 037, 042, 044, 046, 047, 048, 059, 061, 066, 071, 072 QLD: 078, 079, 080, 085, 094, 098, 107 SA: 113, 114, 115, 116, 117, 119, 120, 124 TAS: 125, 127, 128, 129 VIC: 134, 146, 149, 150, 159, 161, 162 WA: 172, 175

179 SOCIETY GARLIC NSW: 002, 006, 008, 011, 016, 021, 024, 027, 032, 037, 038, 044, 046, 047, 048, 071, 072 QLD: 078, 079, 080, 085, 092, 094, 103, 105 SA: 113, 115, 116, 117, 120, 124 TAS: 125, 126, 127, 129 VIC: 134, 135, 146, 149, 150, 159, 160, 161, 162 WA: 175

180 COAST ROSEMARY NSW: 002, 008, 009, 011, 014, 016, 017, 019, 021, 024, 026, 027, 029, 031, 032, 033, 035, 037, 040, 042, 044, 046, 047, 048, 050, 051, 052, 053, 054, 055, 056, 057, 058, 059, 060, 061, 063, 067, 069, 071, 072 QLD: 079, 080, 085, 086, 098 SA: 113, 115, 116, 117, 118, 119, 120, 124 TAS: 125, 126, 127, 128, 129 VIC: 134, 138, 145, 146, 149, 150, 151, 153, 154, 155, 159, 161, 162, 163 WA: 171, 172, 175, 176

181 STORM FLOWER NSW: 001, 002, 003, 006, 008, 011, 017, 021, 024, 027, 032, 037, 039, 042, 044, 046, 047, 048, 068, 071, 072 NT: 074 QLD: 078, 085, 094, 098, 100 SA: 113, 119, 123 TAS: 125, 126, 129 VIC: 135, 136, 137, 138, 149 WA: 175

182 OVENS WATTLE NSW: 009, 012, 020, 024, 042, 060, 067, 071, 072 QLD: 079 SA: 113, 116, 117 TAS: 125, 126, 127, 128 VIC: 146, 159, 161

183 CARPET BUGLE WEED NSW: 006, 008, 011, 012, 014, 016, 017, 021, 024, 025, 027, 029, 032, 037, 038, 042, 044, 046, 047, 066, 069, 071, 072 QLD: 078, 079, 085 SA: 113, 115, 116, 117, 118, 119, 120, 123, 124 TAS: 125, 126, 127, 128, 129, 131 VIC: 134, 140, 145, 146, 149, 150, 153, 154, 159, 161, 162 WA: 171, 175

184 HEARTLEAF ICE PLANT NSW: 002, 024, 025, 037, 071, 072 QLD: 078 SA:124 TAS: 125, 127 VIC: 152 WA: 175

185 BIRTHDAY CANDLES BANKSIA NSW: 002, 008, 016, 024, 027, 029, 032, 037, 040, 042, 048, 050, 051, 052, 053, 054, 055, 056, 057, 059, 060, 064, 069, 071, 072 QLD: 079, 085, 101 SA: 113, 115, 116, 117, 124 TAS: 125, 126, 127, 128, 129 VIC: 146, 149, 150, 154, 155, 159, 161, 162 WA: 171, 172, 175

186 BERGENIA NSW: 002, 006, 008, 011, 016, 024, 025, 027, 032, 037, 038, 044, 048, 069, 071, 072 SA: 113, 115, 116, 117, 119, 120 TAS: 125, 126, 127, 128, 129, 130 VIC: 137, 144, 146, 149, 150, 154, 159, 161, 162, 166 WA: 175

187 SNOW IN SUMMER NSW: 002, 006, 008, 011, 016, 017, 020, 024, 025, 027, 029, 032, 037, 044, 046, 047, 048, 069, 071, 072 QLD: 107 SA: 113, 115, 116, 117, 118, 119, 120, 124 TAS: 125, 126, 127, 128, 129 VIC: 134, 137, 144, 145, 146, 149, 150, 153, 154, 159, 161 WA: 171, 172, 175, 176

188 YELLOW BUTTONS NSW: 002, 024, 025, 027, 031, 048, 058, 060, 071, 072 SA: 116, 117, 122 VIC: 145, 146, 149, 150, 153, 159, 161, 162

189 KANGAROO VINE NSW: 002, 011, 017, 020, 021, 024, 027, 037, 042, 047, 048, 071, 072 QLD: 079, 080, 085, 086, 097 SA: 115, 116, 117 TAS: 125, 126 VIC: 149, 150, 161 WA: 171, 175

190 GROUND MORNING GLORY NSW: 002, 006, 008, 011, 017, 024, 025, 027, 029, 032, 037, 042, 044, 046, 047, 048, 059, 066, 069, 071, 072 NT: 074 QLD: 079 SA: 113, 114, 115, 116, 117, 118, 119, 120, 124 TAS: 125, 126, 127, 128, 129 VIC: 134, 138, 140, 144, 145, 146, 149, 150, 153, 154, 159, 160, 161, 162, 168 WA: 171, 175

191 KIDNEY WEED NSW: 001, 002, 006, 008, 011, 017, 020, 021, 024, 025, 027, 032, 037, 042, 044, 046, 048, 060, 069, 071, 072 QLD: 079, 085 SA: 113, 115, 116, 117, 119, 120, 124 TAS: 125, 127, 128 VIC: 134, 144, 146, 149, 150, 159, 161, 162, 168 WA: 171, 172, 175

192 PRICKLY RASP FERN NSW: 002, 011, 016, 017, 024, 027, 032, 037, 042, 048, 060, 071, 072 QLD: 086 TAS: 129 VIC: 147, 150, 161, 162 WA: 171

193 MEXICAN SNOWBALL NSW: 002, 008, 009, 014, 016, 021, 024, 025, 027, 028, 029, 032, 037, 039, 042, 048, 059, 066, 069, 071, 072 QLD: 079, 085, 107, 109 SA: 114, 115, 116, 117, 118, 119, 121, 123, 124 TAS: 125, 126, 128, 129 VIC: 134, 137, 138, 141, 142, 144, 146, 149, 150, 152, 159, 161, 162 WA: 175

194 SEASIDE DAISY NSW: 002, 006, 008, 011, 016, 017, 021, 024, 025, 027, 029, 032, 037, 044, 046, 047, 048, 049, 059, 061, 069, 071, 072 QLD: 078, 079, 080, 085, 098, 100 SA: 114, 115, 116, 117, 118, 119, 120, 124 TAS: 125, 126, 127, 128, 129 VIC: 137, 138, 140, 144, 145, 146, 148, 149, 150, 153, 154, 159, 161, 162 WA: 171, 172, 175

195 BLUE DAZE NSW: 002, 006, 008, 011, 016, 017, 019, 021, 024, 027, 029, 033, 037, 044, 047, 048, 061, 063, 069, 071, 072 QLD: 079, 085, 094, 098, 107 SA: 115 TAS: 125 VIC: 145, 146, 149, 150, 153 WA: 171, 172, 175

196 TREASURE FLOWER NSW: 002, 006, 008, 011, 016, 017, 021, 024, 025, 027, 029, 032, 037, 042, 044, 046, 047, 048, 069, 071, 072 QLD: 078, 079, 085, 098, 103 SA: 113, 114, 115, 116, 117, 118, 119, 120, 124 TAS: 125, 126, 127, 128, 129 VIC: 134, 140, 145, 146, 149, 150, 153, 154, 159, 161, 162, 168 WA: 171, 172, 175, 176

197 MOTHER OF PEARL PLANT NSW: 002, 029, 037, 039, 048, 071, 072 TAS: 125 VIC: 137, 152

198 BRONZE RAMBLER GREVILLEA NSW: 002, 006, 009, 011, 012, 014, 016, 017, 021, 024, 027, 029, 031, 032, 033, 035, 037, 040, 042, 044, 046, 047, 048, 050, 051, 052, 053, 054, 055, 056, 057, 058, 059, 060, 061, 067, 069, 071, 072 QLD: 079, 085, 086, 097, 107 SA: 113, 115, 116, 117, 118, 119, 124 TAS: 125, 126, 127, 128, 129 VIC: 134, 145, 146, 149, 150, 151, 153, 154, 155, 161, 162, 163 WA: 172, 175

199 ENGLISH IVY NSW: 002, 006, 008, 016, 017, 021, 024, 027, 029, 037, 042, 044, 046, 048, 066, 071, 072 QLD: 079 SA: 115, 116, 117, 118, 119, 124 TAS: 125, 126, 129 VIC: 140, 146, 149, 159, 161 WA: 171, 175

200 SHORE JUNIPER NSW: 002, 006, 011, 016, 017, 021, 024, 026, 027, 029, 032, 037, 046, 047, 048, 061, 069, 071, 072 QLD: 078, 079, 085, 098, 107 SA: 113, 115, 116, 117, 118, 120, 124 TAS: 125, 126, 127, 128, 129 VIC: 134, 143, 145, 146, 149, 150, 151, 153, 154, 159, 161, 162 WA: 171, 172, 175

201 WAUKEGAN JUNIPER NSW: 002, 016, 017, 024, 026, 027, 047, 048, 069, 071, 072 QLD: 085, 107 SA: 115, 116, 117, 118, 124 TAS: 125, 126, 127, 128, 129 VIC: 143, 145, 146, 149, 150, 153, 161, 162 WA: 171, 172, 175

202 FLOWER DUST PLANT NSW: 002, 014, 016, 024, 027, 037, 042, 046, 048, 066, 071 QLD: 079, 085 SA: 121 TAS: 125, 128 VIC: 134, 139, 141, 142, 146, 149, 152, 159, 161 WA: 175, 177

203 DEAD NETTLE NSW: 002, 008, 016, 024, 025, 027, 029, 032, 037, 044, 048, 069, 071, 072 SA: 113, 116, 117, 119, 120 TAS: 125, 127, 129, 131 VIC: 134, 140, 145, 146, 149, 150, 153, 161, 162 WA: 175

204 ICE PLANT NSW: 002, 024, 025, 029, 032, 037, 046, 048, 071, 072 QLD: 079 SA: 115, 116, 117, 124 TAS: 125, 126, 128, 129 VIC: 134, 145, 146, 149, 152, 153, 155, 161, 162 WA: 171, 175

205 TRAILING LANTANA NSW: 002, 006, 011, 016, 017, 024, 025, 027, 029, 032, 037, 044, 047, 048, 059, 071, 072 NT: 074 SA: 113, 115, 116, 117, 118, 120, 124 TAS: 125, 126, 127, 128, 129 VIC: 134, 145, 146, 149, 150, 153, 159, 161, 162, 168 WA: 171, 172, 175, 176

206 PINCUSHION CACTUS NSW: 024, 027, 028, 037, 039, 048, 071, 072 SA: 116, 117, 121 TAS: 125, 126, 129 VIC: 141, 142, 146, 149, 162

207 APPLE MINT NSW: 008, 021, 024, 027, 029, 037, 048, 072 QLD: 079, 105 SA: 113, 115, 116, 117, 120 TAS: 125, 126, 129 VIC: 134, 146, 149, 150, 161, 162 WA: 174, 175

208 WATERLILY NSW: 002, 003, 004, 005, 016, 021, 023, 024, 027, 032, 037, 046, 048, 059, 068, 071, 072 QLD: 079, 080, 085, 111 SA: 113, 115, 116, 117, 124 TAS: 125, 126, 127, 129 VIC: 146, 149, 150, 159, 161, 162 WA: 171, 175

209 BLACK MONDO GRASS NSW: 002, 008, 011, 014, 016, 017, 021, 024, 025, 026, 027, 029, 032, 035, 037, 039, 042, 044, 046, 047, 048, 059, 069, 071, 072 QLD: 078, 079, 085, 099, 103, 107 SA: 113, 114, 115, 116, 117, 119, 121, 124 TAS: 125, 126, 127, 128, 129 VIC: 134, 138, 139, 144, 145, 146, 149, 150, 153, 154, 159, 161, 162 WA: 171, 175, 176

210 OREGANO NSW: 002, 008, 016, 021, 024, 025, 027, 029, 037, 038, 039, 044, 046, 048, 059, 071, 072 QLD: 079, 085, 105 SA: 113, 115, 116, 117, 120, 124 TAS: 125, 126, 127, 128, 129, 131 VIC: 134, 146, 149, 150, 154, 159, 160, 161, 162 WA: 171, 174, 175, 177

211 REINECKEA NSW: 002, 008, 011, 042, 048, 071, 072 QLD: 078 VIC: 145, 153 WA: 175

212 PEARLWORT NSW: 002, 016, 021, 024, 027, 029, 037, 044, 047, 048, 069, 072 QLD: 079 SA: 115, 119, 120 TAS: 125, 126, 127, 128, 129 VIC: 146, 149, 150, 159, 161, 162 WA: 171, 175

213 FAN FLOWER NSW: 002, 006, 008, 009, 011, 016, 020, 021, 024, 027, 029, 031, 032, 035, 037, 042, 047, 048, 050, 051, 052, 053, 054, 055, 056, 057, 058, 060, 061, 067, 069, 071, 072 QLD: 079, 085, 086 SA: 113, 115, 116, 117, 118, 119, 120, 124 TAS: 125, 126, 127, 129 VIC: 145, 146, 149, 150, 153, 154, 159, 161, 162, 168 WA: 170, 171, 172, 175

214 SCLERANTHUS NSW: 009, 024, 032, 042, 048, 059, 060, 067, 071, 072 QLD: 079 SA: 115, 116, 117, 119, 124 TAS: 125, 126, 127, 128, 129 VIC: 134, 143, 145, 149, 150, 153, 159, 161, 162

215 JELLY BEAN PLANT NSW: 002, 008, 012, 014, 021, 024, 025, 027, 028, 029, 032, 037, 039, 046, 048, 066, 069, 071, 072 QLD: 079, 085, 107 SA: 116, 117, 121, 123, 124 TAS: 125, 129 VIC: 134, 141, 142, 146, 152, 161, 162 WA: 175

216 HOUSELEEK NSW: 008, 014, 024, 025, 027, 028, 037, 039, 044, 048, 066, 071, 072 QLD: 085, 107 SA: 114, 115, 120, 121, 124 TAS: 125, 126, 129 VIC: 141, 142, 145, 146, 149, 152, 153, 154, 162 WA: 175

217 BLUE CHALK STICKS NSW: 002, 008, 024, 025, 027, 028, 029, 037, 039, 048, 072 QLD: 085 SA: 115, 116, 117, 119, 121 TAS: 125 VIC: 134, 141, 142, 144, 149, 152, 161 WA: 175

218 BABY'S TEARS NSW: 002, 006, 016, 021, 024, 025, 027, 029, 032, 037, 042, 048, 059, 071, 072 QLD: 082 SA: 113, 115, 116, 117, 119, 120, 124 TAS: 125, 126, 128 VIC: 146, 149, 150, 159, 161, 162 WA: 171

219 LAMBS' EARS NSW: 002, 006, 008, 011, 012, 016, 017, 024, 025, 027, 029, 032, 037, 038, 046, 047, 048, 059, 069, 071, 072 QLD: 079 SA: 113, 114, 115, 116, 117, 118, 119, 120, 124 TAS: 125, 126, 127, 128, 129, 131 VIC: 134, 137, 146, 148, 149, 150, 154, 159, 161, 162 WA: 171, 175

220 THYME NSW: 002, 008, 012, 016, 021, 024, 025, 027, 029, 032, 037, 046, 048, 059, 069, 071, 072 QLD: 079, 085, 105 SA: 113, 114, 115, 116, 117, 119, 120, 124 TAS: 125, 126, 127, 128, 129 VIC: 134, 145, 146, 149, 150, 153, 154, 159, 161, 162 WA: 171, 174, 175

221 PURPLE HEART NSW: 002, 008, 011, 014, 016, 017, 024, 027, 029, 032, 037, 048, 071, 072 NT: 074 QLD: 078, 080 SA: 113, 115, 116, 117, 122 TAS: 125, 126 VIC: 134, 146, 149 WA: 175

222 SILVER INCH PLANT NSW: 002, 024, 027, 029, 037, 048, 066, 071, 072 TAS: 125, 126 VIC: 146, 149, 162

223 LESSER PERIWINKLE NSW: 002, 006, 008, 011, 016, 017, 024, 027, 029, 037, 042, 044, 046, 048, 071, 072 QLD: 085 SA: 113, 116, 117, 119 TAS: 125, 128, 129 VIC: 137, 140, 146, 149, 161 WA: 171, 175

224 NATIVE VIOLET NSW: 002, 008, 011, 016, 017, 020, 021, 024, 025, 027, 029, 032, 037, 042, 044, 046, 047, 048, 059, 060, 067, 069, 071, 072 QLD: 078, 079, 085, 086, 097, 098 SA: 113, 115, 116, 117, 118, 119, 120, 124 TAS: 125, 126, 127, 128, 129 VIC: 137, 140, 145, 146, 149, 150, 153, 154, 158, 159, 161, 162 WA: 171, 172, 175

225 NORWAY GLOBE MAPLE NSW: 002, 024, 027, 029, 037, 044, 046, 048, 049, 069, 070, 071, 072 QLD: 107 SA: 113, 115, 119 TAS: 125, 126, 127, 128 VIC: 137, 146, 149, 150, 154, 159, 161, 162 WA: 175

226 IMPALA LILY NSW: 037, 048, 071, 072 QLD: 083, 084, 087 TAS: 125 VIC: 146

227 AEONIUM NSW: 008, 024, 025, 027, 028, 032, 037, 044, 048, 066, 071, 072 QLD: 085 SA: 116, 117, 121, 123, 124 TAS: 125, 130 VIC: 137, 144, 146, 152, 161, 162 WA: 175

228 CENTURY PLANT NSW: 002, 008, 016, 021, 024, 027, 028, 029, 037, 042, 046, 048, 071, 072 QLD: 079, 085 SA: 114, 116, 117, 119 TAS: 125, 126, 128, 129 VIC: 137, 141, 142, 146, 149, 150, 152, 159, 161 WA: 171, 175

229 AGAVE NSW: 002, 008, 011, 016, 017, 021, 024, 027, 028, 029, 032, 037, 042, 044, 045, 046, 048, 059, 066, 071 NT: 074 QLD: 079, 080, 084, 085, 089, 090, 094, 099, 107, 109 SA: 113, 114, 115, 116, 117, 118, 119, 124 TAS: 125, 126, 128, 129 VIC: 137, 139, 141, 142, 144, 145, 146, 149, 150, 153, 159, 161, 162, 168 WA: 171, 175, 177

230 PARRY'S AGAVE NSW: 016, 024, 028, 029, 037, 046, 048, 071 QLD: 079, 084, 089, 107 SA: 114, 116, 117 TAS: 125 VIC: 139, 141, 142, 146, 149, 150, 154, 161, 162

231 ALLUAUDIA NSW: 028, 037, 048, 072 TAS: 125

232 CUNJEVOI NSW: 003, 004, 008, 011, 021, 024, 027, 030, 037, 042, 048, 068, 071, 072 QLD: 078, 079, 084, 085, 094, 097, 099, 105, 111, 112 VIC: 146, 168 WA: 175

233 FAN ALOE NSW: 014, 028, 037, 042, 048, 072 QLD: 079 SA: 116, 117, 121 TAS: 125, 126 VIC: 141, 142, 145, 146, 149, 153, 161 WA: 175

234 BIRD'S NEST FERN NSW: 002, 011, 017, 021, 024, 027, 029, 031, 032, 037, 039, 041, 042, 044, 046, 047, 048, 059, 060, 069, 071, 072 NT: 074 QLD: 079, 080, 081, 085, 086, 090, 094, 099, 107, 112 SA: 113, 115, 116, 117, 119, 124 TAS: 125, 126, 127, 128, 129 VIC: 137, 139, 146, 147, 149, 159, 161, 162 WA: 171, 175, 177

235 SILVER SPEAR NSW: 008, 009, 019, 024, 027, 032, 037, 044, 071, 072 TAS: 125, 129 VIC: 146, 149, 150, 161, 168 WA: 172

236 PONYTAIL NSW: 002, 016, 021, 024, 027, 029, 037, 042, 048, 059, 071, 072 NT: 074 QLD: 079, 080, 085, 089, 094, 099, 107, 109, 110 SA: 115, 116, 117, 121, 124 TAS: 125, 126 VIC: 139, 146, 149, 150, 152, 161, 162 WA: 171, 175, 176, 177

237 BISMARCK PALM NSW: 021, 029, 037, 042, 048, 071, 072 NT: 074 QLD: 085, 089, 092, 094, 099, 107, 110 SA: 116, 117 VIC: 146, 161

238 FISHBONE WATER FERN NSW: 002, 003, 011, 016, 017, 021, 024, 029, 032, 037, 042, 048, 059, 060, 063, 068, 071, 072 QLD: 080, 086, 099, 107 SA: 115 TAS: 125, 126, 127, 128, 129 VIC: 146, 147, 149, 150, 161, 162 WA: 171, 175, 177

239 JAPANESE BOX NSW: 002, 006, 008, 011, 016, 017, 019, 020, 021, 024, 026, 027, 029, 032, 037, 042, 044, 045, 046, 047, 048, 049, 059, 063, 064, 066, 069, 071, 072 QLD: 078, 079, 090, 098, 107, 108 SA: 113, 114, 115, 116, 117, 118, 119, 120, 124 TAS: 125, 126, 127, 128, 129 VIC: 138, 145, 146, 149, 150, 151, 153, 154, 159, 161, 162, 166 WA: 171, 172, 175, 177

240 SAND CYPRESS PINE NSW: 027, 031, 037, 042, 048, 050, 051, 052, 053, 054, 055, 056, 057, 071, 072 QLD: 086, 098 SA: 116, 117, 119 TAS: 125, 128 VIC: 148, 149, 150, 155, 164

241 CAMELLIA NSW: 002, 008, 012, 013, 015, 016, 017, 019, 021, 024, 027, 029, 032, 037, 043, 044, 046, 047, 048, 059, 064, 069, 070, 071, 072 QLD: 090, 103, 107 SA: 113, 115, 116, 117, 119, 120, 124 TAS: 125, 126, 127, 128, 129 VIC: 137, 146, 149, 150, 151, 154, 159, 161, 162, 166, 169 WA: 171, 173, 175, 177

242 MEYER LEMON NSW: 002, 008, 016, 021, 024, 027, 029, 032, 037, 042, 044, 046, 047, 048, 059, 069, 071, 072 QLD: 079, 085, 086, 107 SA: 113, 114, 115, 116, 117, 119, 124 TAS: 125, 126, 127, 128, 129 VIC: 140, 144, 146, 149, 150, 154, 159, 161, 162 WA: 171, 173, 175, 177

243 SILVER TORCH CACTUS NSW: 028, 037 QLD: 107 SA: 121

244 NZ CABBAGE TREE NSW: 001, 002, 006, 008, 009, 011, 016, 017, 019, 021, 024, 027, 029, 032, 037, 042, 044, 045, 046, 047, 048, 059, 061, 064, 069, 071, 072 QLD: 079, 081, 085, 098, 099, 103 SA: 113, 114, 115, 116, 117, 118, 119, 120, 124 TAS: 125, 126, 127, 128, 129 VIC: 134, 137, 139, 140, 144, 145, 146, 149, 150, 153, 154, 159, 161, 162, 168 WA: 171, 172, 175, 176, 177

245 TI PLANT NSW: 011, 016, 017, 021, 024, 027, 029, 037, 041, 042, 045, 046, 047, 048, 059, 069, 071, 072 QLD: 079, 080, 081, 084, 085, 094, 098, 099, 102, 112 SA: 113, 115 TAS: 125, 128 VIC: 146, 150, 161 WA: 171, 175

246 SWAMP LILY NSW: 002, 003, 008, 011, 013, 016, 017, 021, 024, 027, 029, 031, 032, 037, 042, 047, 048, 059, 060, 061, 068, 071, 072 QLD: 078, 080, 085, 086, 092, 094, 098, 099, 107, 111 TAS: 125, 128 VIC: 145, 149, 153, 162

247 PENCIL PINE NSW: 002, 016, 017, 024, 026, 027, 029, 037, 046, 048, 049, 069, 070, 071, 072 QLD: 079, 093, 107 SA: 113, 114, 115, 116, 117, 118, 119, 124 TAS: 125, 126, 127, 128, 129 VIC: 143, 145, 146, 149, 150, 153, 154, 161, 162, 164 WA: 171, 172, 175

248 ROUGH TREE FERN NSW: 002, 011, 012, 016, 017, 024, 027, 029, 031, 032, 037, 042, 047, 048, 050, 051, 052, 053, 054, 055, 056, 057, 059, 061, 071, 072 QLD: 086, 094, 098, 099 SA: 113, 115, 124 TAS: 125, 126, 128, 129 VIC: 146, 147, 149, 150, 157, 159, 161, 162 WA: 171, 172, 175, 177

249 SAGO PALM NSW: 002, 008, 016, 017, 021, 022, 024, 027, 029, 032, 037, 042, 046, 047, 048, 059, 061, 071, 072 NT: 073, 074 QLD: 079, 083, 085, 087, 090, 094, 098, 099, 100, 106, 109, 110 SA: 113, 114, 115, 116, 117, 121, 124 TAS: 125, 128, 129 VIC: 139, 146, 149, 150, 159, 161, 162 WA: 171, 175, 176, 177

250 CYMBIDIUM ORCHID NSW: 002, 021, 024, 027, 029, 037, 039, 044, 046, 048, 059, 062, 071, 072 QLD: 079, 085, 112 SA: 113, 115, 124 TAS: 125, 126, 127, 128 VIC: 138, 141, 142, 146, 149, 150, 156, 159, 161, 162 WA: 171, 175, 177

251 SOFT TREE FERN NSW: 002, 016, 017, 021, 024, 027, 029, 032, 037, 039, 042, 047, 048, 050, 051, 052, 053, 054, 055, 056, 057, 060, 069, 071, 072 QLD: 085, 106 SA: 113, 115, 116, 117, 119, 124 TAS: 125, 129 VIC: 146, 147, 149, 150, 157, 159, 161, 162 WA: 171, 175

252 MEXICAN FERN PALM NSW: 021, 024, 037, 042, 048, 071, 072 NT: 074 QLD: 079, 083, 084, 089, 099, 110 SA: 124, 177

253 GYMEA LILY NSW: 002, 008, 011, 016, 017, 020, 024, 027, 029, 031, 032, 037, 042, 045, 046, 047, 048, 050, 051, 052, 053, 054, 055, 056, 057, 059, 060, 061, 071, 072 QLD: 078, 085, 086, 090, 094 SA: 115, 116, 117, 124 TAS: 128, 129 VIC: 149, 150, 161 WA: 171

254 DRAGON TREE NSW: 002, 009, 011, 016, 018, 021, 024, 027, 029, 037, 042, 048, 059, 069, 071, 072 NT: 074 QLD: 079, 085, 094, 099, 109 SA: 114, 115, 116, 117, 124 TAS: 125, 126 VIC: 139, 141, 142, 144, 146, 149, 152, 159, 161, 162, 168 WA: 171, 175

255 HAPPY PLANT NSW: 002, 016, 021, 024, 027, 029, 037, 042, 046, 048, 071, 072 NT: 074 QLD: 079, 080, 085, 091, 098, 099, 102, 107 SA: 113, 115, 116, 117, 119, 124 TAS: 125, 126, 128, 129 VIC: 139, 146, 149, 150, 159, 161, 162 WA: 171, 175

256 RED EDGE DRACAENA NSW: 002, 016, 017, 021, 024, 027, 029, 037, 039, 042, 044, 046, 048, 069, 071, 072 NT: 074 QLD: 079, 080, 085, 089, 090, 091, 094, 098, 099, 102, 107 SA: 113, 116, 117, 119, 121, 124 TAS: 125, 126, 128, 129 VIC: 139, 146, 149, 150, 159, 161, 162 WA: 171, 175, 177

257 LUCKY BAMBOO NSW: 021, 024, 027, 029, 037, 039, 042, 046, 048, 069, 072 QLD: 079, 080, 085, 091, 098, 099, 112 SA: 113, 115, 116, 117, 124 TAS: 125, 128 VIC: 139, 146, 159 WA: 171

258 TRIANGLE PALM NSW: 002, 021, 024, 029, 037, 042, 048, 071, 072 QLD: 079, 080, 085, 089, 090, 099, 110, 112 SA: 115, 116, 117, 124 TAS: 125 VIC: 139, 146, 161 WA: 171, 177

259 RED EDGE ECHEVERIA NSW: 002, 006, 012, 014, 016, 021, 024, 027, 028, 029, 032, 037, 039, 042, 048, 059, 069, 071, 072 **QLD:** 079, 085, 107, 109 **SA:** 113, 114, 115, 119, 121, 124 **TAS:** 125, 126, 128 **VIC:** 141, 142, 146, 149, 150, 159, 161, 162 **WA:** 175

260 GOLDEN BARREL CACTUS NSW: 002, 024, 028, 037, 048, 071, 072 **QLD:** 079, 085, 109 **SA:** 113, 115, 116, 117, 121, 124 **TAS:** 125, 128, 129 **VIC:** 141, 142, 149, 150, 161

261 PRICKLY CYCAD NSW: 037, 042, 048, 071, 072 QLD: 099, 109 **VIC:** 146, 161

262 ABYSSINIAN BANANA NSW: 008, 037, 059, 071 SA: 113, 115, 116, 117, 124 **VIC:** 161

263 FIDDLE LEAF FIG NSW: 002, 016, 021, 027, 029, 037, 042, 048, 071, 072 NT: 074 QLD: 079 SA: 115, 116, 117, 119, 124 **TAS:** 125 **VIC:** 139, 146, 149

264 RED-FRUITED SAW SEDGE NSW: 001, 008, 011, 017, 020, 024, 031, 032, 037, 042, 060, 067, 071 QLD: 078, 086 SA: 122 TAS: 125, 127 **VIC:** 158

265 HEBE NSW: 002, 008, 016, 017, 021, 024, 027, 029, 032, 037, 044, 046, 048, 049, 059, 069, 071, 072 QLD: 085 SA: 115, 116, 117, 119 TAS: 125, 126, 127, 128, 129 **VIC:** 134, 138, 145, 146, 149, 150, 153, 159, 161, 162, 166, 177

266 EMERALD GREEN HEBE NSW: 002, 006, 009, 016, 017, 019, 021, 024, 027, 029, 037, 046, 048, 049, 059, 071, 072 QLD: 079, 085 SA: 115, 116, 117, 119, 124 TAS: 125, 126, 127, 128, 129 **VIC:** 134, 145, 146, 149, 150, 153, 154, 159, 161, 162 **WA:** 171, 172, 175

267 KENTIA PALM NSW: 002, 011, 013, 016, 017, 021, 022, 024, 027, 029, 034, 037, 042, 046, 047, 048, 059, 060, 071, 072 QLD: 079, 085, 099 SA: 113, 114, 115, 116, 117, 122, 124 TAS: 125, 126, 128, 129 **VIC:** 139, 146, 149, 150, 159, 161, 162 **WA:** 171, 175, 176, 177

268 SPIDER LILY NSW: 004, 008, 024, 029, 037, 048, 071, 072 QLD: 078, 079, 080, 085, 099, 112 TAS: 125 **VIC:** 136, 138, 146, 149, 162 **WA:** 171, 175

269 SKYROCKET JUNIPER NSW: 002, 016, 017, 019, 024, 026, 027, 029, 037, 044, 046, 047, 048, 069, 071, 072 QLD: 079, 107 SA: 115, 116, 117, 118, 119, 124 TAS: 125, 126, 127, 128, 129 **VIC:** 143, 145, 146, 149, 150, 151, 153, 154, 159, 161, 162 **WA:** 171, 177

270 FELT PLANT NSW: 002, 008, 014, 016, 024, 027, 028, 037, 039, 048, 071 QLD: 079, 109 TAS: 125, 128 **VIC:** 141, 142, 144, 146, 149, 152, 161, 168

271 RED HOT POKER NSW: 002, 008, 009, 011, 014, 016, 021, 024, 027, 032, 037, 038, 042, 044, 046, 047, 048, 069, 071, 072 QLD: 078, 096, 103 SA: 116, 117, 118, 119, 124 TAS: 125, 126, 127, 128, 129, 130 **VIC:** 137, 138, 145, 146, 149, 150, 153, 161, 162, 168 **WA:** 171, 172, 175

272 BURRAWANG NSW: 002, 017, 021, 024, 027, 029, 032, 037, 042, 048, 059, 060, 071, 072 QLD: 079, 085, 099, 106 TAS: 125 **VIC:** 149, 161 **WA:** 175

273 LITTLE GEM MAGNOLIA NSW: 002, 008, 011, 013, 014, 016, 017, 019, 021, 024, 027, 029, 032, 037, 042, 044, 046, 047, 048, 059, 064, 069, 070, 071, 072 **QLD:** 079, 085, 093, 103, 107 **SA:** 114, 115, 116, 117, 119, 124 **TAS:** 125, 126, 127, 128, 129 **VIC:** 143, 146, 149, 150, 151, 154, 159, 161, 162, 164, 166 **WA:** 171, 173, 175

274 HONEY BUSH NSW: 008, 024, 038, 044, 048, 071, 072 SA: 113 TAS: 126, 131 **VIC:** 137, 146, 149, 161

275 WEDDING LILY NSW: 014, 030, 048, 060, 071 SA: 113 TAS: 129 **VIC:** 149, 161

276 PINK VELVET BANANA NSW: 042, 071, 072 VIC: 161 WA: 171

277 SACRED LOTUS NSW: 003, 004, 005, 021, 023, 027, 032, 037, 048, 068, 071, 072 QLD: 080, 085, 111 SA: 122 **VIC:** 146, 149

278 MADAGASCAR PALM NSW: 002, 021, 024, 027, 028, 029, 037, 042, 048, 059, 071, 072 NT: 074 QLD: 079, 083, 084, 085, 089 TAS: 125 **VIC:** 139, 141, 142, 149, 161

279 SCREW PINE NSW: 021, 029, 042, 048, 071 QLD: 080, 085, 099 SA: 119 TAS: 125

280 DEVIL'S BACKBONE NSW: 016, 024, 029 SA: 116, 117 TAS: 125 VIC: WA: 171, 175

281 CANARY ISLAND DATE PALM NSW: 002, 016, 017, 021, 022, 024, 029, 032, 041, 042, 048, 059, 071, 072 NT: 074 QLD: 079, 085, 099 SA: 113, 115, 116, 117, 119, 124 TAS: 125, 126, 127, 128, 129 **VIC:** 146, 149, 159, 161, 162 **WA:** 171, 175, 177

282 PYGMY DATE PALM NSW: 002, 013, 016, 017, 021, 022, 024, 029, 032, 037, 041, 042, 047, 048, 059, 071, 072 NT: 074 QLD: 079, 085, 089, 094, 098, 099, 103 SA: 113, 114, 115, 116, 117, 118, 119, 124 TAS: 125, 126, 129 **VIC:** 139, 146, 149, 150, 159, 161, 162 **WA:** 171, 175, 176, 177

283 NZ FLAX NSW: 001, 002, 006, 008, 009, 011, 014, 016, 017, 019, 021, 024, 027, 029, 032, 037, 042, 044, 046, 047, 048, 049, 059, 064, 066, 069, 071, 072 **QLD:** 078, 079, 085, 099, 103, 107 **SA:** 113, 114, 115, 116, 117, 118, 119, 120, 124 **TAS:** 125, 126, 127, 128, 129 **VIC:** 136, 145, 146, 149, 150, 153, 154, 159, 161, 162, 168 **WA:** 171, 172, 175, 176, 177

284 STAGHORN FERN NSW: 002, 021, 024, 027, 029, 037, 039, 042, 048, 059, 060, 069, 071, 072 QLD: 079, 085, 086 SA: 113, 115, 116, 117, 124 TAS: 125, 128 VIC: 139, 146, 147, 149, 150, 159, 161, 162 **WA:** 171, 177

285 FOXTAIL FERN NSW: 002, 016, 029, 037, 048, 069, 071, 072 QLD: 079 SA: 115, 116, 117, 119, 122, 124 TAS: 125, 126, 127, 128 **VIC:** 146, 159, 161, 162 **WA:** 171, 175

286 TASSEL CORD RUSH NSW: 002, 003, 011, 016, 021, 024, 027, 031, 032, 037, 042, 048, 050, 051, 052, 053, 054, 055, 056, 057, 060, 067, 068, 071, 072 QLD: 078, 086 SA: 115, 116, 117, 119, 120, 124 TAS: 125, 126, 127, 128, 129 **VIC:** 149, 150, 154, 158, 159, 161, 162 **WA:** 172

287 MOTHER-IN-LAW'S TONGUE NSW: 008, 011, 016, 021, 024, 027, 029, 032, 035, 037, 042, 046, 048, 059, 071, 072 NT: 074 QLD: 079, 084, 085, 094, 112 SA: 113, 115, 116, 117, 124 TAS: 125, 126, 128, 129 **VIC:** 139, 141, 142, 146, 149, 150, 159, 161, 162 **WA:** 171, 175

288 PEACE LILY NSW: 002, 016, 017, 021, 023, 024, 027, 032, 037, 039, 044, 046, 048, 059, 071, 072 NT: 074 QLD: 079, 085, 094, 102, 103, 112 SA: 113, 115, 116, 117, 119, 124 TAS: 125, 126, 128, 129 **VIC:** 139, 146, 149, 150, 159, 161, 162 **WA:** 171, 175

289 RUSH-LIKE STRELITZIA NSW: 002, 024, 027, 037, 042, 048, 071 QLD: 079, 092, 099 TAS: 125 **VIC:** 146, 161

290 STROMANTHE NSW: 021, 024, 027, 037, 042, 048, 059, 071, 072 QLD: 102 VIC: 139

291 RED AFRICAN MILK BUSH NSW: 008, 037, 048

292 WARATAH NSW: 002, 012, 016, 019, 020, 021, 024, 027, 029, 031, 032, 037, 040, 042, 048, 050, 051, 052, 053, 054, 055, 056, 057, 059, 060, 061, 067, 069, 071, 072 SA: 113, 115, 116, 117 TAS: 125, 126, 127, 128, 129 **VIC:** 132, 146, 149, 150, 155, 159, 161, 162

293 SPANISH MOSS NSW: 002, 007, 010, 021, 024, 027, 029, 032, 037, 039, 042, 044, 048, 059, 071, 072 QLD: 080, 085, 099, 105 SA: 113, 115, 116, 117 TAS: 125, 127 **VIC:** 146, 162

294 CHINESE WINDMILL PALM NSW: 002, 011, 016, 021, 024, 027, 029, 037, 042, 048, 059, 071, 072 NT: 074 QLD: 079, 085, 099 SA: 115, 116, 117, 124 TAS: 125, 128, 129 **VIC:** 139, 146, 149, 150, 161, 162 **WA:** 171, 175

295 VRIESEA BROMELIAD NSW: 002, 007, 010, 021, 024, 027, 029, 037, 039, 048, 059, 071, 072 QLD: 079, 084, 085, 099, 112 TAS: 125 **VIC:** 139, 146, 149, 150, 151, 159, 161, 177

296 GRASS TREE NSW: 001, 002, 008, 016, 017, 021, 022, 024, 027, 029, 032, 037, 042, 046, 048, 050, 051, 052, 053, 054, 055, 056, 057, 059, 060, 061, 071, 072 NT: 073, 074 QLD: 079, 080, 085, 086, 098, 099, 102, 106, 109 SA: 113, 115, 116, 117, 119, 124 TAS: 125 **VIC:** 139, 146, 149, 150, 161, 162 **WA:** 170, 171

297 GIANT YUCCA NSW: 002, 008, 016, 017, 021, 024, 027, 029, 032, 037, 038, 042, 044, 045, 046, 048, 059, 071, 072 NT: 074 QLD: 079, 085, 089, 099, 102 SA: 113, 114, 115, 116, 117, 118, 119, 121, 124 TAS: 125, 126, 127, 128 **VIC:** 139, 141, 142, 144, 146, 149, 150, 154, 159, 161, 162 **WA:** 171, 172, 175, 176, 177

298 CARDBOARD PALM NSW: 002, 021, 024, 027, 029, 037, 042, 048, 071, 072 NT: 073, 074 QLD: 079, 083, 084, 085, 089, 094, 099, 103, 109, 110 SA: 116, 117, 124 VIC: 139, 150, 161 WA: 171, 177

299 ACANTHUS NSW: 002, 006, 008, 011, 016, 017, 019, 021, 024, 027, 029, 032, 037, 038, 042, 044, 046, 047, 048, 049, 059, 069, 071, 072 QLD: 107 SA: 113, 116, 117, 118, 120, 123, 124 TAS: 125, 126, 127, 128, 129 VIC: 134, 137, 144, 145, 146, 149, 150, 153, 154, 159, 161, 162, 168 WA: 171, 172, 175

300 DELTA MAIDENHAIR FERN NSW: 021, 024, 027, 029, 037, 046, 048, 071, 072 SA: 115, 122 TAS: 125, 129 VIC: 146, 147, 159, 161 WA: 171, 175, 176

301 AGAPANTHUS NSW: 002, 006, 008, 009, 011, 013, 016, 017, 019, 021, 024, 027, 029, 032, 037, 039, 042, 044, 045, 046, 047, 048, 059, 063, 069, 071, 072 QLD: 078, 079, 080, 085, 096, 100, 107 SA: 113, 115, 116, 117, 118, 119, 124 TAS: 125, 126, 127, 128, 129, 130 VIC: 134, 136, 137, 138, 144, 145, 146, 149, 150, 153, 154, 159, 160, 161, 162, 168 WA: 171, 172, 175, 176, 177

302 GOLD & SILVER NSW: 037, 059, 071, 072 TAS: 125

303 NATIVE GINGER NSW: 002, 011, 017, 021, 024, 031, 037, 042, 048, 059, 060, 061, 071, 072 QLD: 078, 079, 080, 081, 085, 086, 094, 097, 099, 107 TAS: 125, 126 VIC: 146, 149, 161

304 RED GINGER NSW: 002, 021, 024, 037, 042, 048, 061, 071, 072 NT: 074 QLD: 079, 080, 097, 107 TAS: 125 VIC: 146, 149

305 JAPANESE WIND FLOWER NSW: 002, 008, 011, 012, 016, 017, 019, 021, 024, 027, 032, 037, 038, 042, 044, 047, 048, 049, 069, 071, 072 QLD: 079, 103, 107 SA: 113, 115, 116, 117, 119, 120, 123, 124 TAS: 125, 126, 127, 128, 129, 130, 131 VIC: 134, 137, 144, 146, 149, 150, 159, 160, 161, 162 WA: 175

306 DWARF APPLE NSW: 015, 020, 024, 027, 029, 031, 032, 037, 042, 048, 050, 051, 052, 053, 054, 055, 056, 057, 058, 060, 061, 071, 072 QLD: 079, 086 SA: 119 TAS: 125 VIC: 146, 148, 149, 150, 161, 162

307 KANGAROO PAW NSW: 002, 006, 008, 009, 011, 016, 017, 019, 020, 021, 024, 025, 027, 029, 031, 032, 033, 037, 040, 042, 044, 046, 047, 048, 050, 051, 052, 053, 054, 055, 056, 057, 058, 059, 060, 061, 069, 071, 072 QLD: 079, 085, 086, 097, 107, 112 SA: 113, 115, 116, 117, 118, 119, 120, 121, 124 TAS: 125, 126, 127, 128, 129 VIC: 134, 140, 145, 146, 148, 149, 150, 153, 154, 158, 160, 161, 162, 168 WA: 171, 172, 175, 176, 177

308 PRIDE OF THE CAPE NSW: 002, 008, 016, 019, 021, 024, 029, 037, 042, 048, 059, 071, 072 NT: 074 QLD: 085 SA: 115, 116, 117 TAS: 125 VIC: 146, 162 WA: 171, 172

309 CUT LEAF DAISY NSW: 002, 006, 011, 014, 016, 017, 021, 024, 025, 027, 029, 031, 032, 035, 037, 040, 042, 046, 047, 048, 058, 060, 061, 067, 071, 072 QLD: 079, 080, 085, 086, 098 SA: 115, 116, 117, 118, 120, 124 TAS: 125, 126, 127, 128, 129 VIC: 145, 146, 149, 150, 153, 154, 158, 159, 160, 161, 162 WA: 171, 172, 175, 176

310 ZEBRA PLANT NSW: 002, 016, 021, 024, 027, 029, 037, 041, 042, 048, 071, 072 QLD: 079, 080, 082, 084, 085, 099, 107 SA: 113 TAS: 125, 126, 129 VIC: 139, 146, 149, 150, 159, 162 WA: 171

311 SEDGE NSW: 001, 002, 003, 006, 008, 011, 016, 017, 020, 021, 024, 025, 027, 029, 030, 032, 037, 038, 042, 044, 046, 047, 048, 060, 066, 067, 068, 069, 071, 072 QLD: 078, 079, 080, 085, 086, 111 SA: 113, 114, 115, 116, 117, 118, 119, 120, 124 TAS: 125, 127, 128, 129 VIC: 134, 144, 145, 146, 148, 149, 150, 153, 154, 158, 159, 161, 162, 168 WA: 170, 171, 172, 175

312 PARLOUR PALM NSW: 002, 016, 021, 024, 027, 029, 032, 037, 042, 046, 048, 071, 072 NT: 074 QLD: 079, 085, 090, 094, 099, 103 SA: 113, 115, 116, 117, 119, 124 TAS: 125, 126, 128, 129 VIC: 139, 146, 149, 150, 159, 161, 162 WA: 171, 175, 177

313 CLIVIA NSW: 002, 006, 008, 011, 013, 016, 017, 019, 021, 022, 024, 026, 027, 029, 032, 037, 039, 042, 044, 046, 047, 048, 059, 069, 071, 072 QLD: 079, 081, 085, 090, 092, 099, 100, 103, 107 SA: 113, 115, 116, 117, 118, 119, 120, 124 TAS: 125, 126, 127, 128, 129, 130 VIC: 136, 144, 145, 146, 149, 150, 153, 154, 159, 161, 162, 167 WA: 171, 175, 177

314 SILVERBUSH NSW: 002, 006, 008, 011, 014, 016, 017, 019, 024, 027, 029, 032, 037, 042, 044, 046, 047, 048, 049, 059, 069, 071, 072 QLD: 079, 085, 107 SA: 114, 115, 116, 117, 118, 120, 124 TAS: 125, 126, 127, 128, 129 VIC: 134, 137, 138, 140, 144, 145, 146, 149, 150, 153, 154, 159, 160, 161, 162, 168 WA: 171, 172, 175, 176

315 SMALL LEAFED LOOKING GLASS PLANT NSW: 002, 008, 017, 021, 024, 027, 029, 037, 048, 049, 071, 072 QLD: 079 SA: 113, 115, 116, 117, 119, 120 TAS: 125, 126, 127, 128, 129 VIC: 134, 140, 145, 146, 149, 150, 153, 161, 162 WA: 171, 175

316 SLENDER PALM LILY NSW: 002, 011, 016, 017, 019, 021, 024, 027, 029, 031, 032, 037, 039, 042, 045, 046, 047, 048, 059, 060, 069, 071, 072 QLD: 078, 079, 080, 081, 085, 086, 098, 099 SA: 115, 116, 117 TAS: 125 VIC: 137, 145, 146, 149, 150, 151, 153, 161, 162, 168 WA: 175

317 CTENANTHE NSW: 002, 021, 024, 027, 032, 037, 041, 042, 044, 046, 048, 059, 071, 072 QLD: 080, 085, 094, 099, 102 TAS: 125 VIC: 146, 149 WA: 171

318 UMBRELLA SEDGE NSW: 002, 003, 004, 005, 021, 024, 027, 029, 030, 037, 044, 046, 048, 059, 068, 071, 072 QLD: 079, 111 SA: 113, 115, 116, 117, 124 TAS: 125, 126, 127, 129 VIC: 149, 150, 161

319 FLAX LILY NSW: 001, 002, 008, 021, 024, 027, 029, 042, 046, 048, 059, 069, 071, 072 NT: 074 QLD: 078, 079, 085, 103, 107 SA: 115, 119, 124 TAS: 126, 128, 129 VIC: 146, 148, 149, 150, 161 WA: 171

320 VARIEGATED FLAX LILY NSW: 001, 002, 008, 011, 012, 016, 017, 020, 021, 024, 025, 027, 029, 031, 032, 035, 037, 042, 044, 046, 047, 048, 050, 051, 052, 053, 054, 055, 056, 057, 058, 059, 060, 061, 067, 069, 071, 072 NT: 074 QLD: 078, 079, 080, 085, 086, 094, 097, 098, 103, 107 SA: 113, 114, 115, 116, 117, 118, 119, 120, 124 TAS: 125, 126, 127, 128, 129, 130 VIC: 134, 137, 145, 146, 148, 149, 150, 153, 154, 155, 158, 159, 161, 162 WA: 170, 171, 172, 175, 176

321 BLUE GINGER NSW: 002, 008, 011, 021, 024, 027, 029, 037, 042, 044, 048, 071, 072 QLD: 078, 079, 080, 081, 084, 085, 098, 099, 107 VIC: 146, 149, 161 WA: 171

322 WILD IRIS NSW: 002, 008, 011, 014, 017, 021, 024, 027, 030, 037, 039, 042, 044, 045, 047, 048, 069, 071, 072 QLD: 078, 079, 080 SA: 115 TAS: 125, 127, 128, 129 VIC: 138, 146, 149, 150, 154, 161 WA: 171, 172, 175, 177

323 CARDAMOM NSW: 008, 011, 021, 037, 039, 042, 071, 072 VIC: 139

324 BLUE SAGE NSW: 002, 008, 048, 071, 072 SA: 113, 119 TAS: 125 VIC: 146, 161

325 LEOPARD PLANT NSW: 003, 008, 027, 048, 068, 071, 072 QLD: 079, 112 TAS: 125 VIC: 146, 161 WA: 175

326 BLUE FESCUE NSW: 002, 006, 008, 011, 017, 021, 024, 025, 027, 029, 032, 037, 038, 042, 044, 046, 047, 048, 059, 069, 071, 072 QLD: 079, 098 SA: 113, 115, 116, 117, 119, 120, 122, 124 TAS: 125, 126, 127, 128, 129 VIC: 134, 137, 138, 144, 145, 146, 148, 149, 150, 153, 154, 159, 160, 161, 162, 168 WA: 171, 172, 175, 176

327 BUTTERFLY PLANT NSW: 002, 008, 016, 017, 019, 021, 024, 025, 027, 029, 032, 037, 042, 044, 046, 047, 048, 059, 069, 071, 072 QLD: 079, 085, 103 SA: 113, 114, 115, 116, 117, 119, 120, 124 TAS: 125, 126, 127, 128, 129 VIC: 134, 137, 140, 145, 146, 149, 150, 153, 154, 159, 160, 161, 162, 168 WA: 171, 172, 175

328 NATIVE SARSAPARILLA NSW: 002, 006, 008, 011, 016, 017, 020, 021, 024, 027, 031, 032, 035, 037, 040, 042, 044, 046, 047, 048, 050, 051, 052, 053, 054, 055, 056, 057, 058, 059, 060, 067, 069, 071, 072 QLD: 078, 079, 085, 086, 097 SA: 113, 115, 116, 117, 118, 119, 120, 124 TAS: 125, 126, 127, 128, 129 VIC: 140, 145, 146, 149, 150, 153, 154, 155, 159, 160, 161, 162 WA: 171, 172, 175

329 HEBE NSW: 002, 006, 016, 017, 021, 024, 027, 029, 037, 042, 044, 047, 048, 049, 059, 069, 071, 072 SA: 113, 115, 116, 117, 119, 120 TAS: 125, 126, 127, 128, 129 VIC: 134, 140, 145, 146, 149, 150, 151, 153, 154, 159, 161, 162 WA: 175

330 **KAHILI GINGER** NSW: 002, 008, 011, 016, 017, 019, 021, 024, 027, 037, 039, 042, 044, 048, 071 NT: 074 QLD: 079, 081, 094, 099, 105, 112 TAS: 125 VIC: 136, 146, 149, 161 WA: 171

331 **LICORICE PLANT** NSW: 002, 008, 011, 021, 024, 025, 037, 042, 044, 048, 071, 072 TAS: 125, 129 VIC: 134, 145, 146, 149, 153, 154, 161, 162 WA: 171, 175

332 **HELIOTROPE** NSW: 002, 006, 008, 016, 021, 024, 025, 027, 029, 032, 037, 044, 048, 071, 072 QLD: 078, 079, 085 SA: 113, 115, 116, 117, 124 TAS: 125, 126, 128, 129 VIC: 134, 146, 149, 150, 154, 159, 161, 162

333 **HELLEBORE** NSW: 002, 008, 016, 019, 024, 027, 029, 032, 037, 042, 044, 047, 048, 049, 069, 071, 072 SA: 114, 115, 116, 117, 118, 119, 120, 123 TAS: 125, 126, 127, 128, 129, 130, 131 VIC: 134, 135, 136, 137, 140, 144, 145, 146, 149, 150, 153, 159, 160, 161, 162 WA: 175

334 **JAPANESE BLOOD GRASS** NSW: 001, 002, 003, 008, 017, 020, 021, 024, 025, 027, 029, 032, 037, 048, 068, 071, 072 QLD: 077, 078, 079, 085, 099 SA: 115, 116, 117, 120, 124 TAS: 125, 126, 128, 129 VIC: 134, 144, 145, 146, 149, 150, 153, 161, 162 WA: 171, 172, 175

335 **BEARDED IRIS** NSW: 002, 008, 012, 024, 027, 029, 037, 039, 044, 046, 048, 069, 071, 072 QLD: 085 SA: 113, 115, 119, 120, 121, 124 TAS: 125, 128, 129 VIC: 136, 137, 138, 146, 149, 150, 159, 161, 162, 165 WA: 171, 175

336 **KNOBBY CLUB RUSH** NSW: 001, 002, 003, 008, 016, 017, 020, 024, 025, 027, 029, 031, 032, 037, 042, 048, 059, 060, 068, 071, 072 QLD: 078, 086 SA: 113, 115, 116, 117 TAS: 125, 127, 129 VIC: 145, 149, 153, 154, 161, 162 WA: 170, 172, 175

337 **BROAD-LEAFED DRUMSTICKS** NSW: 002, 016, 021, 024, 027, 029, 031, 032, 040, 042, 046, 048, 050, 051, 052, 053, 054, 055, 056, 057, 058, 060, 061, 071, 072 SA: 119 TAS: 125, 127, 129 VIC: 146, 149, 159, 161, 162 WA: 172, 175

338 **DOUBLE ARABIAN JASMINE** NSW: 021, 024, 027, 029, 037, 044, 048, 071, 072 QLD: 078, 079, 094, 105 SA: 115, 116, 117, 119, 124 TAS: 125, 129 VIC: 145, 146, 149, 153, 159, 161 WA: 171, 175

339 **FLAMING KATY** NSW: 002, 008, 014, 016, 021, 024, 027, 029, 037, 039, 044, 046, 048, 071 QLD: 079, 085, 101 SA: 115, 116, 117, 118, 121, 124 TAS: 125, 126, 127, 128, 129 VIC: 139, 141, 142, 146, 149, 152, 161, 162, 168 WA: 171, 177

340 **PANDA PLANT** NSW: 016, 024, 027, 028, 037, 039, 042, 048, 066, 071 TAS: 125 VIC: 134, 141, 142, 146, 149, 161, 168 WA: 171, 175

341 **SPINY-HEADED MAT RUSH** NSW: 001, 002, 006, 008, 011, 016, 017, 020, 021, 024, 025, 027, 029, 031, 032, 033, 035, 037, 042, 046, 047, 048, 050, 051, 052, 053, 054, 055, 056, 057, 058, 059, 060, 061, 063, 067, 069, 071, 072 QLD: 078, 079, 080, 085, 090, 094, 097, 098 SA: 113, 115, 116, 117, 118, 120, 124 TAS: 125, 126, 127, 128, 129 VIC: 134, 145, 146, 148, 149, 150, 153, 154, 155, 158, 159, 161, 162 WA: 171, 172, 175, 176

342 **MISCANTHUS** NSW: 002, 003, 004, 008, 011, 016, 021, 024, 027, 037, 038, 048, 068, 071, 072 QLD: 078, 085 SA: 113, 115, 116, 117, 119 TAS: 125, 127, 128, 129, 131 VIC: 134, 137, 144, 145, 146, 149, 150, 153, 161

343 **ZEBRA GRASS** NSW: 002, 003, 004, 008, 011, 016, 021, 024, 027, 029, 032, 037, 048, 068, 071, 072 QLD: 078, 085, 094, 099 SA: 113, 115, 116, 117, 119, 121 TAS: 125, 129, 130, 131 VIC: 137, 146, 149, 150, 161

344 **FRUIT SALAD PLANT** NSW: 002, 016, 024, 027, 029, 032, 037, 039, 042, 048, 071, 072 QLD: 079, 080, 085, 099, 102 SA: 113, 115, 116, 117, 119, 124 TAS: 125, 126, 128, 129 VIC: 139, 146, 149, 150, 159, 161, 162 WA: 171

345 **NEOREGELIA BROMELIAD** NSW: 007, 010, 021, 024, 027, 029, 032, 037, 039, 046, 048, 059, 071, 072 QLD: 079, 080, 081, 084, 085, 094, 099 SA: 115 TAS: 125, 128 VIC: 139, 146, 149, 150, 161 WA: 171, 175

346 **CATMINT** NSW: 002, 008, 016, 017, 021, 024, 025, 027, 029, 032, 037, 038, 039, 044, 046, 047, 048, 069, 071, 072 QLD: 079, 085 SA: 113, 114, 115, 116, 117, 119, 120, 124 TAS: 125, 126, 127, 128, 129 VIC: 134, 137, 144, 145, 146, 149, 150, 153, 159, 161, 162 WA: 171, 174, 175

347 **MONDO GRASS** NSW: 001, 002, 008, 011, 014, 016, 017, 019, 021, 024, 027, 029, 032, 037, 039, 042, 044, 046, 047, 048, 059, 064, 069, 071, 072 NT: 074 QLD: 078, 079, 080, 084, 085, 087, 094, 098, 099, 100, 103, 107 SA: 113, 114, 115, 116, 117, 118, 119, 120, 121, 124 TAS: 125, 126, 127, 128, 129 VIC: 134, 138, 139, 144, 145, 146, 149, 150, 153, 154, 159, 161, 162 WA: 171, 175, 176, 177

348 **OX-EYE DAISY** NSW: 002, 006, 008, 016, 017, 021, 024, 027, 029, 037, 042, 044, 046, 047, 048, 071, 072 QLD: 103 SA: 113, 115, 119 TAS: 125, 126, 127, 128, 129 VIC: 134, 137, 145, 146, 149, 150, 153, 154, 161, 162, 168 WA: 171, 172, 175, 176

349 **IVY LEAFED GERANIUM** NSW: 002, 008, 021, 024, 027, 029, 032, 037, 044, 046, 048, 069, 071, 072 QLD: 079, 080, 085, 104 SA: 115, 119, 124 TAS: 125, 126, 127, 128, 129 VIC: 146, 149, 159, 161, 162, 168 WA: 171, 172, 175

350 **SWAMP FOXTAIL GRASS** NSW: 001, 002, 008, 016, 017, 020, 021, 024, 025, 027, 031, 032, 037, 038, 042, 044, 046, 047, 048, 050, 051, 052, 053, 054, 055, 056, 057, 060, 067, 071, 072 QLD: 078, 085, 086 SA: 113, 115, 120, 124 TAS: 125, 126, 127, 128, 129 VIC: 134, 144, 145, 146, 148, 149, 150, 153, 154, 159, 161, 162, 168 WA: 175

351 **TREE PHILODENDRON** NSW: 002, 011, 016, 017, 021, 024, 027, 029, 032, 037, 042, 048, 071, 072 NT: 074 QLD: 079, 080, 094, 099, 107 SA: 113, 116, 117, 118, 124 TAS: 125, 126, 127 VIC: 139, 146, 149, 159, 161, 162 WA: 171, 175, 177

352 **SILVER SPUR FLOWER** NSW: 002, 008, 011, 021, 024, 027, 029, 032, 037, 044, 048, 071, 072 QLD: 085 SA: 116, 117, 119 TAS: 125, 128 VIC: 134, 146, 149, 160, 161, 162 WA: 171, 172, 175

353 **TUSSOCK GRASS** NSW: 001, 002, 008, 011, 016, 017, 020, 024, 025, 027, 032, 037, 042, 044, 047, 048, 050, 051, 052, 053, 054, 055, 056, 057, 059, 060, 067, 071, 072 QLD: 078, 079, 085, 086 SA: 115, 116, 117, 118, 120 TAS: 125, 126, 127, 128, 129 VIC: 134, 137, 145, 146, 149, 150, 153, 154, 155, 159, 161, 162 WA: 171, 175

354 **CORAL CACTUS** NSW: 024, 027, 037, 039, 048, 066, 071 SA: 122 TAS: 125 VIC: 149

355 **ROSEMARY** NSW: 002, 006, 008, 011, 016, 017, 021, 024, 025, 027, 029, 032, 037, 042, 044, 046, 047, 048, 049, 059, 066, 069, 071, 072 QLD: 079, 080, 085, 100, 103, 105, 107 SA: 113, 114, 115, 116, 117, 118, 119, 120, 124 TAS: 125, 126, 127, 128, 129 VIC: 140, 145, 146, 149, 150, 153, 154, 159, 160, 161, 162 WA: 171, 172, 174, 175, 176, 177

356 **CORAL PLANT** NSW: 002, 008, 011, 016, 017, 021, 024, 027, 032, 037, 042, 047, 048, 071, 072 NT: 074 QLD: 078, 080, 082, 085, 094 SA: 113, 115, 116, 117, 118, 119, 120, 124 TAS: 125 VIC: 146, 149, 150, 159, 160, 161 WA: 171, 172, 175, 176

357 **SINALOA SAGE** NSW: 002, 008, 012, 027, 029, 042, 048, 065, 072 QLD: 079 SA: 114, 119, 120, 122, 123 TAS: 125 VIC: 134, 145, 146, 148, 153, 160, 161, 162 WA: 175

358 **VARIEGATED STAR JASMINE** NSW: 002, 008, 011, 016, 017, 019, 021, 024, 027, 029, 032, 037, 042, 044, 046, 047, 048, 059, 061, 066, 069, 071, 072 QLD: 078, 079, 085, 100, 107 SA: 119, 120 TAS: 125, 126 VIC: 146, 149, 150, 161, 162 WA: 172, 175

359 **RHOEO** NSW: 002, 011, 017, 021, 024, 027, 029, 037, 047, 048, 059, 066, 071, 072 NT: 074 QLD: 078, 079, 080, 085, 094, 099 SA: 113, 115, 116, 117, 124 TAS: 125, 126, 127 VIC: 139, 146, 149, 162 WA: 171, 175, 177

360 **GREATER PERIWINKLE** NSW: 002, 008, 011, 016, 017, 024, 027, 029, 037, 042, 046, 048, 071, 072 QLD: 078, 085 SA: 113, 115, 116, 117, 119, 124 TAS: 125, 127, 128, 129 VIC: 146, 149, 161 WA: 171, 172, 175

361 **BLUE TARO** NSW: 003, 029, 037, 048, 068, 071, 072 QLD: 078, 079 VIC: 149

362 **CHOCOLATE VINE** NSW: 002, 008, 019, 021, 027, 029, 032, 037, 044, 048, 069, 071 SA: 115 TAS: 125, 127, 128, 129 VIC: 144, 145, 149, 150, 153, 159, 161 WA: 172, 175

363 GOLDEN TRUMPET NSW: 002, 021, 024, 027, 029, 037, 042, 046, 048, 071, 072 NT: 074 QLD: 079, 080, 085, 094 SA: 115, 116, 117, 119 TAS: 125 VIC: 149, 150, 161 WA: 171, 172

364 PORCELAIN VINE NSW: 002, 006, 008, 037, 048, 066 TAS: 125 VIC: 145, 146, 149, 153 WA: 172

365 GUM VINE NSW: 016, 042, 048, 060, 071 QLD: 079, 086 TAS: 125, 126 VIC: 146, 159, 161

366 BOUGAINVILLEA NSW: 002, 006, 017, 019, 021, 024, 027, 029, 032, 037, 042, 044, 046, 047, 048, 059, 071, 072 NT: 074 QLD: 079, 085, 094, 103, 112 SA: 113, 115, 116, 117, 119, 120, 124 TAS: 125, 126, 128, 129 VIC: 146, 149, 150, 159, 161 WA: 171, 175, 176, 177

367 WATER VINE NSW: 031, 042, 048, 072 TAS: 125 VIC: 161

368 FLAMING GLORYBOWER NSW: 016, 024, 027, 029, 048, 069, 071, 072 QLD: 078, 085 TAS: 125, 128 VIC: 146, 150, 159, 161 WA: 171

369 ARGENTINE TRUMPET VINE NSW: 002, 008, 016, 037, 044, 048, 071, 072 QLD: 079 SA: 119 TAS: 126 VIC: 149

370 CREEPING FIG NSW: 002, 006, 011, 016, 017, 021, 024, 027, 029, 032, 037, 042, 044, 046, 047, 048, 059, 069, 071, 072 NT: 074 QLD: 078, 079, 085 SA: 113, 114, 116, 117, 124 TAS: 125, 126, 129 VIC: 137, 139, 140, 146, 149, 150, 159, 161, 162 WA: 171, 175

371 CAROLINA JASMINE NSW: 002, 006, 016, 017, 021, 024, 027, 029, 032, 037, 044, 047, 048, 069, 071, 072 QLD: 109 SA: 113, 115, 116, 117, 124 TAS: 125, 126, 127, 128, 129 VIC: 140, 145, 146, 149, 150, 153, 159, 161 WA: 172, 175

372 SNAKE VINE NSW: 002, 006, 008, 011, 016, 017, 020, 021, 024, 027, 029, 032, 035, 037, 042, 046, 047, 048, 050, 051, 052, 053, 054, 055, 056, 057, 060, 061, 071, 072 QLD: 078, 079, 085, 086, 097 SA: 115, 116, 117, 118, 119, 120 TAS: 125, 126, 127, 128, 129 VIC: 140, 145, 146, 149, 150, 151, 153, 154, 159, 161, 162 WA: 171, 172, 175

373 WAX FLOWER NSW: 002, 016, 021, 024, 027, 029, 037, 039, 042, 046, 048, 059, 071, 072 QLD: 078, 079, 085, 103, 112 SA: 113, 115, 116, 117, 119, 120, 121, 122, 124 TAS: 125, 126, 127, 128, 129 VIC: 146, 149, 150, 159, 161, 162 WA: 171, 175, 176

374 CHILEAN JASMINE NSW: 002, 016, 021, 024, 027, 029, 032, 037, 042, 044, 046, 048, 059, 061, 071, 072 QLD: 079, 085, 094, 101, 103 SA: 113, 115, 116, 117, 119, 120, 124 TAS: 125, 126, 128, 129 VIC: 146, 149, 150, 159, 161, 162 WA: 171, 172, 175

375 BOWER OF BEAUTY VINE NSW: 002, 006, 008, 011, 012, 016, 017, 019, 020, 021, 024, 026, 027, 029, 031, 032, 037, 040, 042, 046, 047, 048, 050, 051, 052, 053, 054, 055, 056, 057, 059, 060, 061, 063, 067, 069, 071, 072 QLD: 078, 079, 085, 086, 094, 097 SA: 113, 114, 115, 116, 117, 118, 120, 124 TAS: 125, 126, 127, 128, 129 VIC: 145, 146, 149, 150, 151, 153, 154, 155, 159, 161, 162 WA: 171, 172, 175

376 SILVER VEIN CREEPER NSW: 016, 019, 024, 037, 043, 044, 048, 049, 069, 072 SA: 113, 116, 117 TAS: 125, 126, 128, 129 VIC: 137, 146, 149, 150, 161, 162 WA: 171

377 BOSTON IVY NSW: 002, 008, 011, 016, 017, 019, 024, 027, 037, 044, 046, 047, 048, 049, 069, 071, 072 SA: 113, 116, 117, 124 TAS: 125, 126, 127, 128, 129 VIC: 134, 137, 140, 145, 146, 149, 150, 153, 159, 161, 162 WA: 171

378 RED FLOWERING PASSIONFRUIT NSW: 002, 021, 024, 029, 037, 042, 044, 046, 048, 071, 072 NT: 074 QLD: 079, 085 SA: 115, 116, 117 TAS: 125, 129 VIC: 146, 149, 161 WA: 175

379 ELKHORN FERN NSW: 002, 021, 024, 027, 029, 037, 039, 042, 048, 059, 060, 071, 072 QLD: 079, 085, 086, 103, 112 SA: 113, 115, 116, 117, 124 TAS: 125, 128 VIC: 139, 146, 147, 149, 150, 159, 161, 162 WA: 171, 175, 177

380 MADAGASCAR JASMINE NSW: 002, 016, 021, 024, 027, 029, 032, 037, 042, 044, 048, 059, 071, 072 NT: 074 QLD: 078, 079, 094 SA: 115, 116, 117, 124 TAS: 125 VIC: 146, 149, 150, 159, 161, 162 WA: 171, 172, 175, 176

381 SKYFLOWER NSW: 002, 008, 019, 024, 029, 037, 044, 048, 071, 072 SA: 116, 117 TAS: 125 VIC: 146, 149, 150, 161 WA: 171

382 STAR JASMINE NSW: 002, 006, 008, 009, 011, 013, 014, 016, 017, 019, 021, 024, 026, 027, 029, 032, 037, 042, 044, 046, 047, 048, 059, 061, 066, 069, 071, 072 NT: 074 QLD: 078, 079, 085, 094 SA: 113, 114, 115, 116, 117, 118, 119, 120, 124 TAS: 125, 126, 127, 128, 129 VIC: 134, 140, 145, 146, 149, 150, 151, 153, 154, 159, 161, 162 WA: 171, 172, 175, 176

383 SNAIL FLOWER NSW: 027, 029, 037, 048, 072 QLD: 079 VIC: 146, 149, 161

384 ORNAMENTAL GRAPE NSW: 002, 008, 016, 019, 024, 027, 029, 037, 048, 049, 069, 071, 072 SA: 113, 116, 117, 119, 124 TAS: 125, 126, 128, 129 VIC: 134, 146, 149, 150, 159, 161, 162

385 CHINESE WISTERIA NSW: 002, 006, 008, 014, 016, 017, 019, 021, 024, 027, 029, 032, 037, 044, 046, 047, 048, 059, 069, 070, 071, 072 QLD: 107 SA: 113, 114, 115, 116, 117, 118, 120, 124 TAS: 125, 126, 127, 128, 129 VIC: 137, 146, 149, 150, 151, 159, 161, 162 WA: 171, 172, 175

386 JAPANESE RUSH NSW: 003, 008, 011, 012, 016, 021, 024, 025, 027, 030, 037, 042, 044, 045, 048, 059, 063, 066, 068, 071, 072 QLD: 078, 085, 111 SA: 113, 116, 117, 119, 120, 124 TAS: 125, 126, 127, 128, 129 VIC: 144, 145, 146, 149, 150, 153, 159, 161, 168 WA: 171, 172, 175

387 FAIRY MOSS NSW: 003, 025, 027, 032, 037, 068, 071, 072 QLD: 107, 111 SA: 124 TAS: 125, 128 VIC: 162

388 TARO NSW: 002, 003, 004, 008, 021, 023, 024, 027, 029, 032, 037, 039, 042, 048, 059, 068, 071, 072 QLD: 078, 079, 080, 085, 094, 099, 105, 112 SA: 113, 119, 124 TAS: 125 VIC: 144, 146, 149, 150, 161, 168 WA: 171, 175, 177

389 PAPYRUS NSW: 002, 003, 004, 005, 008, 011, 021, 024, 027, 032, 037, 039, 044, 048, 059, 068, 071, 072 NT: 074 QLD: 078, 079, 080, 085, 099, 111 SA: 115, 116, 117, 119, 124 TAS: 125, 126, 127, 129 VIC: 137, 146, 149, 150, 159, 161, 162 WA: 171, 175, 176

390 DWARF PAPYRUS NSW: 002, 003, 004, 005, 008, 021, 023, 024, 025, 027, 029, 030, 032, 037, 048, 059, 068, 071, 072 QLD: 078, 079, 080, 085, 099, 111 SA: 113, 115, 124 TAS: 125, 126, 129 VIC: 146, 149, 150, 161, 162 WA: 171, 175

391 LOUISIANA IRIS NSW: 002, 003, 004, 008, 012, 014, 021, 023, 024, 025, 027, 029, 030, 032, 037, 039, 044, 046, 048, 068, 069, 071, 072 QLD: 078, 079, 085, 100, 111 SA: 113, 115, 116, 117, 119, 120 TAS: 125, 128, 129 VIC: 138, 146, 149, 150, 161, 162, 165 WA: 171, 175

392 TUSSOCK RUSH NSW: 001, 002, 003, 005, 016, 017, 020, 024, 027, 032, 037, 042, 048, 067, 068, 071, 072 QLD: 078 SA: 115 TAS: 125, 127, 129 VIC: 149, 161 WA: 175

393 PICKEREL WEED NSW: 003, 004, 005, 023, 025, 027, 030, 032, 037, 048, 068, 071, 072 QLD: 078 SA: 113

394 MATTED PRATIA NSW: 002, 003, 016, 021, 024, 025, 027, 029, 032, 037, 042, 044, 046, 047, 048, 050, 051, 052, 053, 054, 055, 056, 057, 059, 060, 067, 068, 069, 071, 072 QLD: 078, 079, 086 SA: 113, 115, 116, 117, 118, 119, 120, 124 TAS: 125, 126, 127, 128, 129 VIC: 134, 140, 145, 146, 149, 150, 153, 159, 161, 162 WA: 171, 172, 175

395 WATER CANNA NSW: 003, 004, 021, 025, 027, 032, 037, 048, 059, 068, 072 QLD: 078, 099, 111 TAS: 129 VIC: 149 WA: 175

396 CUMBUNGI NSW: 021, 023, 027, 048, 071, 072 VIC: 161

397 ARUM LILY NSW: 002, 003, 004, 006, 008, 011, 019, 021, 024, 025, 027, 029, 030, 032, 037, 038, 039, 042, 044, 046, 047, 048, 059, 068, 069, 071, 072 QLD: 078, 079, 085, 111 SA: 113, 114, 115, 116, 117, 119, 120, 123, 124 TAS: 125, 126, 127, 128, 129 VIC: 136, 138, 140, 145, 146, 149, 150, 153, 154, 159, 161, 162 WA: 175

PLANTS: SUPPLIERS

NO.	COMPANY	SALES	EMAIL / WEB	PHONE / FAX	ADDRESS	COMMENT
001	Abulk Pty Ltd	W	info@abulk.com.au www.abulk.com.au	P:02 4577 5912 F:02 4577 5736	Lot 3 Cupitts Lane Clarendon NSW 2756	Ornamental compact grass-like plants: low water users
002	Alpine Nurseries	W	sales@alpinenurseries.com.au www.alpinenurseries.com.au	P:02 9651 2444 F:02 9651 2835	PO Box 3140 Dural NSW 2158	Quality growers of advanced to semi-mature trees & shrubs
003	Aqua World Enterprises	W	watergarden@mBox.com.au www.watergardenparadise.com.au	P:02 9211 0071 F:02 9281 9128	PO Box 81 Yagoona NSW 2199	
004	Arcadia Lily Ponds	W R	arcadia.lily.ponds@bigpond.com www.arcadia-lily-ponds.com	P:02 9655 1670 F:02 9655 1060	151 Arcadia Rd Arcadia NSW 2159	
005	Austral Watergardens	R	australwatergardens@bigpond.com australwatergardens.citysearch.com.au	P:02 9985 7370 F:02 9985 7024	1295 Pacific Hwy Cowan NSW 2081	3 acres of display gardens: waterlilies, lotus, iris, waterbowls
006	Bails Nursery	W		P:02 9653 2003 F:02 9653 2004	48 Knights Rd Galston NSW 2159	175mm climbers & 140mm shrubs & groundcovers
007	Bamboo World	W R	bamboo@bambooworld.com.au www.bambooworld.com.au	P:02 6628 6988 F:02 6628 6987	1053 Teven Rd Tuckombil NSW 2477	Clumping non-invasive bamboo. Freight to Sydney, Melb, Ad, Bris
008	Belrose Nursery	R	felicity@belrosenursery.com www.belrosenursery.com	P:02 9450 1484 F:02 9986 3519	Bundaleer St Belrose NSW 2085	Unusual perennials, shrubs & ornamental grasses
009	Bournda Plants	W		P:02 6495 9999 F:02 6495 0047	Widgeram Rd Merimbula NSW 2548	
010	Bromeliad Garden Nursery	W R	bromeliadgarden@yahoo.com	P:02 9489 2063 F:02 9489 2063	15 Spurgin St Wahroonga NSW 2076	The only specialist bromeliad growers, retailers & w'salers in Sydney
011	Cabbage Tree Nursery	W		P:02 9651 1851 F:02 9651 1132	64 Quarry Rd Dural NSW 2158	
012	Carroll's Country Gardens Nursery	W R		P:02 4782 7744	23A Megalong St Katoomba NSW 2780	Mountain grown plants for cool climates
013	Civic Trees Pty Ltd	W		P:02 9651 2833 F:02 9651 2849	Dural NSW 2158	Growers of trees and palms from 1m to 9m
014	Coachwood Nursery	W	coachnsy@coachwoodnurseries.com.au www.coachwoodnurseries.com.au	P:02 4372 1770 F:02 4372 1899	900 Wisemans Ferry Rd Somersby NSW 2250	Great flaxes, succulents, conifers & camellias etc
015	Cowra Advanced Trees	W R		P:02 6341 2959 F:02 6341 2958	PO Box 465 Cowra NSW 2794	Accredited nursery: plants above ground in root pruning containers
016	The Delivered Garden	@	carol@deliveredgarden.com.au www.deliveredgarden.com.au	P:02 9653 2424 F:02 9653 3949	Galston NSW 2159	Formal garden specialists, from acreage to a terrace: delivered
017	Downes Wholesale Nursery	W	info@downesnursery.com.au www.downesnursery.com.au	P:02 9606 5044 F:02 9606 5234	41 Wynyard Ave Rossmore NSW 2171	Large scale grower native, exotics: 150mm to 400lt containers
018	Dragon Trees Australia	W	banora@norex.com.au	P:02 6674 1516 F:02 6674 0747	13 Waugh St Chinderah NSW 2487	The ultimate in architectural planting: a rare succulent
019	Drue Wholesale Nursery	W	druenursery@ozemail.com.au	P:02 4464 1830 F:02 4464 2296	PO Box 51 Berry NSW 2535	Growers: Japanese maples, camellias, magnolias, azaleas & rarer plants
020	Eastwood Nurseries	W	eastwood@eastwoodnurseries.com.au www.eastwoodnurseries.com.au	P:02 4374 1399 F:02 4374 1699	91 Pembertons Hill Rd Mangrove Mountain NSW 2250	
021	Eden at Byron	R		P:02 6685 6874 F:02 6680 8874	140 Bangalow Rd Byron Bay NSW 2481	Winner Best Small Garden Centre NSW (2004 AGIA)
022	Ellison Horticultural Pty Ltd	W R	ellisonhort.com.au	P:02 6629 5788 F:02 6629 5766	267 Rous Rd Alstonville NSW 2477	
023	Everglades Watergarden Supplies	✉	ponds@midcoast.com.au www.everglades.com.au	P:02 6553 0700 F:02 6553 0744	216 Abbotts Rd Bootwa NSW 2430	Australia-wide mail order: pond equipment, plants, fish
024	Flower Power–Enfield	R	dearflowerpower@flowerpower www.flowerpower.com.au	P:02 9747 5555 F:02 9747 5533	27 Mitchell St Enfield NSW 2136	

W Wholesale   R Retail   ✉ Mail order   @ Internet sales

NO.	COMPANY	SALES	EMAIL / WEB	PHONE / FAX	ADDRESS	COMMENT
025	Glenfield Wholesale Nursery	W	glenwho@bigpond.com.au	P:02 9605 2266 F:02 9605 3110	63 Wills Rd Macquarie Fields NSW 2564	Small pot grower of ground covers & new releases
026	Glenleigh Wholesale Nursery	W	nursery@glenleigh.com.au www.glenleigh.com.au	P:02 4733 3243 F:02 4733 3022	427 Mulgoa Rd Regentville NSW 2745	Growers: conifers, trees, shrubs, screening and hedging plants
027	Greenshades Nursery	R	enquiries@greenshades.com.au www.greenshades.com.au	P:02 9653 2200 F:02 9653 2200	353 Galston Rd Galston NSW 2159	Boutique nursery: unusual plants & garden design service
028	Hamilton's World of Cacti	W R	hamiltonscacti@bigpond.com	P:02 4777 4876 F:02 4777 5077	Lot 2 Fourth Ave Llandilo NSW 2747	Mon–Sat, 8.30am to 4.30pm, closed public holidays
029	Hickmans Nursery	R	hickmansnursery@optusnet.com.au	P:02 6552 4065 F:02 6552 4022	PO Box 4100 Taree Delivery Centre, Taree NSW 2430	Accredited NGINA nursery: plants, topsoil, blocks & pavers
030	Iris Haven	✉	irishaven@pip.com.au www.irishaven.com.au	P:02 9144 3805 F:02 9440 0663	PO Box 83 Pennant Hills NSW 1715	Australia-bred Louisiana irises, shipped Australia-wide & export
031	Jamberoo Native Nursery	W	mail@jamberoonatives.com.au	P:02 4236 0445 F:02 4236 0621	127 Currarmore Rd Jamberoo NSW 2533	
032	Kangarutha Nursery	W R	info@kangarutha.com.au www.kangarutha.com.au	P:02 6494 1500 F:02 6494 1738	PO Box 15 Tathra NSW 2550	Best Medium Garden Centre in Australia 2003
033	Killuke Nursery	W	killuke.com.au	P:02 6566 0141 F:02 6566 0600	299 Maria River Rd Crescent Head NSW 2440	Grevillea specialist: weekly deliveries to Sydney & Newcastle
034	Lord Howe Island Nursery	W R	kentia_lhib@bigpond.com	P:02 6563 2164 F:02 6563 2323	Middle Beach Rd Lord Howe Island NSW 2898	
035	Mole Station Native Nursery	W	caldnsy@halenet.com.au www.molestationnursery.com	P:02 6737 5429 F:02 6737 5443	Mole Station Tenterfield NSW 2372	
036	Mr Bamboo	W R	mrbamboo@mrbamboo.com.au www.mrbamboo.com.au	P:02 9486 3604 F:02 9450 0125	18 Myoora Rd Terrey Hills NSW 2084	Hide the neighbours: bamboo for the urban landscape
037	North Manly Garden Centre	R	nmgc@bigpond.net.au	P:02 9905 5202 F:02 9905 5620	510/512 Pittwater Rd North Manly NSW 2100	
038	Nutshell Perennial Nursery and Plant Farm	W R	nutshellperennials@ix.net.au	P:02 6368 1035 F:02 6368 1035	Campbell St Newbridge NSW 2795	Bare root plants: dividable & highly cost effective
039	Orchid Images	W R	info@orchidimages.com.au www.orchidimages.com.au	P:02 4465 1655 F:02 4465 1655	PO Box 6108 Kangaroo Valley NSW 2577	High quality plants, inspiration, innovation & information
040	Ozgraft Native Nursery	W		P:02 4577 2831 F:02 4577 8694	107 Pitt Town Rd McGraths Hill NSW 2756	Grafted native plants: 200+ varieties of grevilleas yearly
041	Palm Park Wholesale Nursery	W	www.palmpark.com	P:07 5590 9498 F:07 5590 9408	69 Omiah Way Pigabeen NSW 2486	
042	PalmLand Nursery	R	www.palmland.com.au	P:02 9450 1555 F:02 9450 0215	327 Mona Vale Rd Terrey Hills NSW 2084	Extensive range of native plants, trade discount
043	Paradise Plants	W	sales@paradiseplants.com.au		Kulnura NSW 2250	Producing new varieties for Australian conditions
044	Parkers of Turramurra	R	purchasing@parkersnursery.com.au	P:02 9487 3888 F:02 9489 3081	45–47 Tennyson Ave Turramurra NSW 2074	Semi-advanced trees & shrubs, unusual perennials, roses and topiary
045	Plants That Please in assoc. with Landscapes	W	info@plantsthatplease.com www.plantsthatplease.com	P:02 4653 1770 F:02 4647 6675	PO Box 102 Cobbitty NSW 2570	Hedging specialists & drought tolerant garden planning
046	Regal Nursery	R		P:02 9679 1901 F:02 9679 0490	249 Annangrove Rd Annangrove NSW 2156	
047	Rossmore Nurseries	W R	sales@rossmorenurseries.com.au www.rossmorenurseries.com.au	P:02 9606 5298 F:02 9606 5499	104 Barry Ave Catherine Field NSW 2171	Grower: natives, exotics, conifers, trees, shrubs & groundcovers
048	Simply d'vine Garden & Gift Gallery	R	admin@simplydvine.com.au	P:02 4990 4291 F:02 4990 7285	Nulkaba via Cessnock NSW 2325	Largest display of working fountains in Australia
049	Springrove Wholesale Nursery	W		P:02 6366 3131 F:02 6366 3434	PO Box 45 Millthorpe NSW 2798	
050	State Forest Nurseries – Cumberland	R	Free call 1800 000 123 forest.nsw.gov.au/business/nurseries	P:02 9871 3222 F:02 9871 3456	95 Castle Hill Rd West Pennant Hills NSW 2119	Specialising in Australian plants – tubestock to advanced sizes

See page 171 for how to deal with wholesalers and retailers.

NO.	COMPANY	SALES	EMAIL / WEB	PHONE / FAX	ADDRESS	COMMENT
051	State Forest Nurseries – Dubbo	R	Free call 1800 000 123 forest.nsw.gov.au/business/nurseries	P:02 6884 5319	Wellington Rd Dubbo NSW 2830	Specialising in Australian plants – tubestock to advanced sizes
052	State Forest Nurseries – Forbes	R	Free call 1800 000 123 forest.nsw.gov.au/business/nurseries	P:02 6852 1924	67 Reyond St Forbes NSW 2871	Specialising in Australian plants – tubestock to advanced sizes
053	State Forest Nurseries – Gunnedah	R	Free call 1800 000 123 forest.nsw.gov.au/business/nurseries	P:02 6742 0618	Cnr Martin & Mullaley Gunnedah NSW 2380	Specialising in Australian plants – tubestock to advanced sizes
054	State Forest Nurseries – Inverell	R	Free call 1800 000 123 forest.nsw.gov.au/business/nurseries	P:02 6721 0103	Warialda Rd Inverell NSW 2360	Specialising in Australian plants – tubestock to advanced sizes
055	State Forest Nurseries – Muswellbrook	R	Free call 1800 000 123 forest.nsw.gov.au/business/nurseries	P:02 6543 2622	New England Hwy Muswellbrook NSW 2333	Specialising in Australian plants – tubestock to advanced sizes
056	State Forest Nurseries – Narrandera	R	Free call 1800 000 123 forest.nsw.gov.au/business/nurseries	P:02 6959 1223	Lake Drive Narrandera NSW 2700	Specialising in Australian plants – tubestock to advanced sizes
057	State Forest Nurseries – Wagga Wagga	R	Free call 1800 000 123 forest.nsw.gov.au/business/nurseries	P:02 9631 2600	Olympic Way Wagga Wagga NSW 2650	Specialising in Australian plants – tubestock to advanced sizes
058	Stocks Native Nursery	R	bsto@bigpond.com.au	P:02 6386 2682 F:02 6386 3995	Lot 3 Simmonds Rd Harden NSW 2587	2004 State Award Winning 1.5 ha Australian Native Display Garden
059	Sunrise Nursery	W R	sunrisenursery@bigpond.com	P:02 4294 1307 F:02 4294 3373	336 Princes Hwy Helensburgh NSW 2506	Four acres of growing area with shop, cafe & giftwear
060	Sydney Wildflower Nursery West	R	swnw@bigpond.com www.australian-natives.com	P:02 9628 4448 F:02 9628 4043	241 South St Marsden Park NSW 2765	Native plant specialists, est 1983, nursery industry accredited
061	Tarara Nursery	W R		P:02 6553 6140 F:02 6553 6140	1688 The Lakesway Rainbow Flat NSW 2430	Specialising in Australian native plants: 140mm & 200mm pots
062	Tinonee Orchid Nursery	W R	clement@tpg.com.au www.tinoneeorchids.com	P:02 6553 1012 F:02 6553 1012	768 Tinonee Rd Tinonee NSW 2430	Free Orchid Growers Guide available on request
063	Tropical Ornamentals	W		P:02 6562 8439 F:02 6562 2139	Yabsleys Lane Kempsey NSW 2440	
064	Uki Tree Nurseries	W	info@ukitreenursery.com www.ukitreenursery.com	P:02 6679 5237 F:02 6679 5010	1666 Kyogle Rd Uki NSW 2484	Modern production nursery: designer plants
065	Unlimited Perennials	R	templeton@albury.net.au www.salviaspecialist.com	P:02 6025 4585	369 Boomerang Drive Lavington NSW 2641	Specialising in salvias: new varieties & mail order
066	Valley View Nursery	W R	valleyvu@idx.com.au	P:02 9655 1550 F:02 9655 1218	19 Bay Rd Arcadia NSW 2159	Specialising in succulents, hanging baskets, buxus & bonsai
067	Wariapendi Nursery	W R	sales@wariapendi.com.au www.wariapendi.com.au	P:02 4889 4327 F:02 4889 4092	Church Ave Colo Vale NSW 2575	Cold climate native trees, shrubs, groundcovers, grasses
068	Watergarden Paradise Aquatic Nursery	✉	watergarden@mBox.com.au www.watergardenparadise.com.au	P:02 9727 2622 F:02 9281 9128	PO Box 7039 Bass Hill NSW 2197	
069	Welby Garden Centre	W R	welbygc@challengesh.org.au	P:02 4872 1244 F:02 4872 1228	Cnr Old Hume Highway & Bendooley St, Welby NSW 2577	Specialist in plants ideal for Southern Highlands gardens
070	Winter Hill Tree Farm	W R	annie@winterhill.com.au www.winterhill.com.au	P:02 4878 9193 F:02 4878 9109	Canyonleigh Rd Canyonleigh NSW 2577	Specialising in quality advanced trees for the home & landscape
071	Wirreanda Nursery	W R		P:02 9450 1400 F:02 9450 2664	169 Wirreanda Rd Ingleside NSW 2101	Hedge & screening, advanced trees & shrubs, Sydney delivery
072	Wyee Nursery	R	wyeenursery@bigpond.com www.wyeenursery.com.au	P:02 4357 1335 F:02 4357 1536	103 Wyee Rd Wyee NSW 2259	
073	Cycad Gardens Nursery	W R	cycadnurserynt@bigpond.com www.cycadgardensnursery.com.au	P:08 8971 1335 F:08 8971 2689	PO Box 435 Katherine NT 0851	
074	Darwin Plant Wholesalers	W	info@darwinplants.com.au www.darwinplants.com.au	P:08 8988 1888 F:08 8988 2110	PO Box 39196 Winnellie NT 0821	
075	Frangipani Farm	W	frangipanifarm@bigpond.com	P:08 8988 6029 F:08 8988 6346	PO Box 1217 Palmerston NT 0831	*Plumeria* flowers & newly developed *Heliconia psittacorum* rhizomes
076	Bamboo Australia	W R	bamboo@bamboo-oz.com.au www.bamboo-oz.com.au	P:07 5447 0299 F:07 5447 0299	1171 Kenilworth Rd Belli Park QLD 4562	Bamboo specialist: large & small plants & handicrafts, to all states

W Wholesale   R Retail   ✉ Mail order   @ Internet sales

NO.	COMPANY	SALES	EMAIL / WEB	PHONE / FAX	ADDRESS	COMMENT
077	Bamboos Wholesale	W	enquiries@bamboos.com.au www.bamboos.com.au	P:07 4975 0343 F:07 4975 0022	75 Pikes Crossing Rd Benaraby QLD 4680	Quality clumping bamboo, direct from grower, delivery Australia-wide
078	Beantree Nursery	W	beantree@bigpond.com www.beantree.com.au	P:07 4096 6515 F:07 4096 6039	PO Box 137 Malanda QLD 4885	Specialists in ornamental grasses, strap-leaf plants & Louisiana iris
079	Botanix Lifestyle Garden Centre	R	info@botanix.com.au www.botanix.com.au	P:07 3822 1111 F:07 3822 8055	Nelson Rd Wellington Point QLD 4160	Unique combination of art, design, education & quality plants
080	Boundary Nursery	W		P:07 4939 7663 F:07 4939 7663	407 Byfield Rd Yeppoon QLD 4703	
081	Buderim Ginger Flower Nursery	R	buderimg@buderimginger.com www.buderimginger.com	P:07 5446 7100 F:07 5446 7520	50 Pioneer Rd Yandina QLD 4561	Specialists in gingers and heliconias; Ginger Flower Festival late January
082	Delta Nursery	W	delta@winshop.com.au	P:07 5537 2299 F:07 5537 1246	378 Pine Ridge Rd Coombabah QLD 4216	Wholesale supplier of quality indoor & house plants
083	Denby Cycads	W	sales@denbycycads.com.au www.denbycycads.com.au	P:07 4780 4275 F:07 4780 4375	1 Alligator Creek Rd Townsville QLD 4816	Extensive range of 20+ species of native and exotic cycads
084	Equatorial Exotics	✉	sales@equatorialexotics.com www.equatorialexotics.com	P:07 4039 1135 F:07 4039 1199	PO Box 79R Redlynch Crystal Cascades QLD 4870	We source beautiful and unusual plants from the tropical world
085	Evergreen Nursery	R	evergreen@evergreengardencentre.com.au www.evergreengardencentre.com.au	P:07 5531 7895 F:07 5538 8174	Cnr Ashmore & Bundall Rd Surfers Paradise QLD 4217	The quintessential gift/garden centre, renowned for its unique items
086	Fairhill Native Plants	W R	fairhill@bigpond.com www.fairhillnursery.com	P:07 5446 7088 F:07 5446 7379	Fairhill Rd Yandina QLD 4561	Native plant specialist, 10 acre botanic garden, shop, gallery, restaurant
087	Fortune-8 Nurseries	W	mieke@fortune-8.com	P:0418 708 304 F:07 5447 6804	PO Box 840 Cooroy QLD 4563	
088	Frangipani Heaven	@	frangipaniheaven@bigpond.com users.bigpond.com/clewis1955		PO Box 444 Coolangatta QLD 4225	100s of colours, mail order worldwide, growing info & support
089	Fronds Wholesale Nursery	W	fronds@iig.com.au www.fronds.com.au	P:07 4093 7348 F:07 4093 9866	PO Box 82 Kuranda QLD 4881	Palm specialists tropical Nth Qld, also foliage to go with palms & yuccas
090	Garrad's Nursery	W		P:07 5442 1355 F:07 5442 1402	PO Box 116 Woombye QLD 4559	Home of Syzygium Tiny Trev & Murraya Min-A-Min
091	Glass House Mountains Nursery	W		P:07 5496 9104 F:07 5496 9704	PO Box 22 Glasshouse Mountains QLD 4518	Specialist grower of Dracaenas
092	Greendale Nursery	W	greendalenursery@bigpond.com www.greendalenursery.com	P:07 3289 7062 F:07 3289 7060	998 Mt Glorious Rd Highvale QLD 4520	Specialise in unusual landscape & drought resistant plants
093	Lake Devon Nursery	W		P:07 5573 4482 F:07 5573 6395	743 Tamborine Oxenford Rd Upper Coomera QLD 4209	Quality rainforest plants & natives, suppliers of Magnolia Little Gems
094	Mad About Plants Wholesale Nursery	W	madaboutplants@bigpond.com.au www.madaboutplants.com.au	P:07 4045 2777 F:07 4055 5469	PO Box 468 Edmonton QLD 4869	Palms & trees in larger bags
095	Martins Creek Tree Farm	W	jb.mctf@bigpond.com www.martinscreektreefarm.com.au	P:07 5445 4283 F:07 5445 3721	PO Box 8113 Maroochydore QLD 4558	
096	Mountain View Daylily Nursery	✉	daylily@bigpond.com www.daylily.com	P:07 5494 2346 F:07 5499 9774	PO Box 458 Maleny QLD 4552	
097	Natives 'R' Us Nursery	W	nativesrus@spiderweb.com.au	P:07 5485 1800 F:07 5485 1700	97 Thomason Rd Traveston QLD 4570	Wide variety of Australian natives, transportation no problem
098	Noosa Lakes Nursery	W	www.noosalakesnursery.com.au	P:07 5442 4454 F:07 5442 4154	PO Box 435 Tewantin QLD 4565	Advanced trees, shrubs, palms & topiary
099	Palms for Brisbane	R	pfb@gil.com.au www.palmsforbrisbane.com.au	P:07 3899 8925 F:07 3899 9905	451 Lytton Rd Morningside QLD 4170	Tropical plant specialists: heliconia, gingers, bromeliad, cordylines etc
100	Pine Mountain Nursery	W ✉	www.pinemountainnursery.com.au	P:07 5464 3976 F:07 5464 3700	PO Box 5016 Brassall QLD 4035	Specialist breeders of exotic clivias & agapanthus
101	P.R. Nursery	W R		P:07 4093 3794 F:07 4093 3794	PO Box 252 Tolga QLD 4882	A large range of succulents in small numbers available
102	QLD Indoor Foliage	W		P:07 5497 5324 F:07 5497 5024	825 Bribie Island Rd Ningi QLD 4511	Where the quality of stock is really all that matters

See page 171 for how to deal with wholesalers and retailers.

NO.	COMPANY	SALES	EMAIL / WEB	PHONE / FAX	ADDRESS	COMMENT
103	Redlands Nursery	W	www.redlandsnursery.com.au	P:07 3206 7611 F:07 3206 7502	905–907 German Church Rd Redland Bay QLD 4165	Growing 'Plants that Perform for You'™ since 1958 for Australian gardens
104	The Retreat Pelargoniums	✉	www.ozgeraniums.com	P:07 4166 7151	PO Box 247 Monto QLD 4630	Over 400 Pelargoniums cultivars of all your favourites & more
105	Shipards Herb Farm	R	isabellshipard@hotmail.com	P:07 5441 1101	PO Box 66 Nambour QLD 4560	Retail culinary, medicinal herbs, rare edible plants & seeds*
106	Station Creek Tree Farm	W		P:07 5426 7366 F:07 5426 7564	PO Box 10 Fernvale QLD 4306	
107	Tamborine Mountain Wholesale Nursery	W		P:07 5545 4999 F:07 5545 0264	176 Long Rd Eagle Heights QLD 4271	Rare & unusual plants, collectors & importers, 100mm to 100lt
108	Topiary Grove Formal Gardens	W R ✉	devitth@optusnet.com.au	P:07 5494 2049 F:07 5494 3932	7 Lawrence Pl Maleny QLD 4552	Specialises in hedge plants, mail order Australia & NZ (except WA)
109	Trevisan's Tropical Gardens Nursery	W		P:07 3823 2321 F:07 3245 6657	PO Box 891 Capalaba QLD 4157	Cycads & succulents, *Draceana draco*, *Rhapis*, *Xanthorrhoea glauca*, agaves
110	Utopia Palms & Cycads	W R	utopia@babe.net.au www.utopiapalmsandcycads.com	P:07 5446 6205 F:07 5446 6205	38 Ninderry Slopes Rd Valdora QLD 4561	Only open by appointment
111	Waterlily Acres	✉	lillyput@technet2000.com.au www.waterlilyacres.com.au	P:07 5543 5566 F:07 5543 5566	23b Lamington National Park Rd Canungra QLD 4275	A specialist watergarden nursery that knows and grows all its own plants
112	Xepermoon Exotics	@	xepermoon@kooee.com.au www.xepermoonexotics.com	P:07 4955 0911	QLD	Frangipani *Plumeria* specialists, rare colours & fragrances
113	Conboy's Nurseries	W R	www.conboysnurseries.com.au	P:08 8725 3301 F:08 8725 6661	PO Box 9012 Mt Gambier West SA 5291	Largest variety of plants in the area, plus lots of pots
114	The Flower Garden	W R	flgarden@bigpond.com www.flowergarden.com.au	P:08 8388 6126 F:08 8388 0450	Shakes Rd Nairne SA 5252	Outdoor furniture & garden design service
115	Garden Grove Supplies	R	gargrove@senet.com.au	P:08 8251 1111 F:08 8251 3435	1150 Golden Grove Rd Garden Grove SA 5125	9+ acres of gardening, building & landscape supplies
116	Heyne's Garden Centre – Beulah Park	R	garden-centre@heyne.com.au www.heyne.com.au/gardencentre	P:08 8332 2933 F:08 8332 4332	283–289 The Parade Beulah Park SA 5067	Wide range of plants, great customer service
117	Heyne's Garden Centre – Klemzig	R	klemzig@heyne.com.au www.heyne.com.au/gardencentre	P:08 8369 1085 F:08 8369 2096	216–220 North East Rd Klemzig SA 5087	Wide range of plants, great customer service
118	Heyne's Wholesale Nursery	W	wholesale@heyne.com.au	P:08 8280 8088 F:08 8280 6322	Lot 5 Bolivar Rd Burton SA 5110	Environmentally aware wholesale production nursery
119	Newman's Nursery & Topiary Tea House	R	garden@newmansnursery.com.au www.newmansnursery.com.au	P:08 8264 2661 F:08 8396 2124	PO Box 10 Tea Tree Gully SA 5097	Camellia specialists, old-fashioned service & advice
120	The Plant People SA	W R	phil@goglobaltrading.com	P:08 8389 1393 F:08 8389 1398	PO Box 110 Gumeracha SA 5233	One of the largest ranges of any mobile nursery
121	Potavations	W R	potavations@bigpond.com	P:08 8586 4011 F:08 8586 3366	Ral Ral Ave Renmark SA 5341	Quaint nursery: cacti, succulents, suntuff plants and daylilies
122	Precision Nursery	W	precision_nursery@bigpond.com	P:08 8337 1442 F:08 8337 1192	18 North St Hectorville SA 5073	Established 60 years: shade, indoor & patio plants
123	Sheringa Perennial Plants	R	sheringa@bigpond.com	P:08 8390 3153	Greenhill Rd Carey Gully SA 5144	Growers of Hellebores and rare perennials
124	Vadoulis Garden Centre	R		P:08 8522 3400 F:08 8523 0104	554 Main North Rd Gawler SA 5118	Wide range of plants, giftware, garden architecture
125	Allans Garden Centre Prospect	W R	allansprospect@hotkey.net.au	P:03 6344 6257 F:03 6344 8795	285 Westbury Rd Launceston TAS 7250	Professional friendly service every day of the week
126	Chandlers Nursery	R	chandlers@southcom.com.au	P:03 6223 5688 F:03 6224 1161	75 Queen St Sandy Bay TAS 7005	
127	Cloverlea Plants Plus	W R	clover@southcom.com.au	P:03 6435 1391 F:03 6435 2793	PO Box 148 Somerset TAS 7322	
128	Grow Master Howrah	R	Growmaster.Howrah@bigpond.com www.growmaster.com.au	P:03 6247 1382 F:03 6247 1382	Howrah Garden Centre 469 Rokeby Rd Howrah TAS 7018	Garden consultancy/design & landscaping services

W Wholesale   R Retail   ✉ Mail order   @ Internet sales

for catalogue send 12 x 50c stamps

NO.	COMPANY	SALES	EMAIL / WEB	PHONE / FAX	ADDRESS	COMMENT
129	Stoneman's Garden Centre	R	www.stonemans.com.au	P:03 6273 0611 F:03 6272 3569	94 Grove Rd Glenorchy TAS 7011	
130	Woodbridge Nursery	W ✉	woodbridge@southcom.com.au www.woodbridgenursery.com.au	P:03 6267 4437 F:03 6267 4437	PO Box 90 Woodbridge TAS 7162	Helleborus, geranium, campanula, kniphofia, primula, salvia & iris
131	Wychwood	R	enquiries@wychwoodtasmania.com www.wychwoodtasmania.com	P:03 6363 1210 F:03 6363 1210	PO Box 161 Mole Creek TAS 7304	Unusual perennials, ornamental grasses, 2.5 acre display
132	Ausflora Pacific Pty Ltd	W @	ausflora@satlink.com.au	P:03 5968 1650 F:03 5968 1676	PO Box 72 Gembrook VIC 3783	Proteaceae & Gembrook Waratah for gardens, rockeries and tubs
133	Azalea Park Nursery	W		P:03 9551 1843 F:03 9558 1335	142 Kingston Rd Heatherton VIC 3202	Standard azaleas in 8" & 13" tubs: big range
134	Batesford Plant Nursery	W		P:03 5276 1347 F:03 5276 1522	34 Cullinan Rd Batesford VIC 3221	
135	Border Gateway Bulbs	R	users.bigpond.com/dirkwallace/	P:02 6056 1430 F:02 6056 1430	4/1 Skipton Court Wodonga VIC 3690	Bulbs & seeds for conservation & waterwise gardening
136	Broersen Bulbs	W R	sales@broersen.com.au www.broersen.com.au	P:03 9737 9202 F:03 9737 9707	365–367 Monbulk Rd Silvan VIC 3795	
137	Buda Historic Home and Garden Nursery	R	buda@castlemaine.net www.budacastlemaine.org	P:03 5472 1032 F:03 5472 1032	42 Hunter St Castlemaine VIC 3450	Hardy, water-conserving & unusual ornamental plants
138	Bulb Express	✉	info@bulbexpress.com.au www.bulbexpress.com.au	P:1800 677 437 F:1800 063 739	PO Box 6 Monbulk VIC 3793	Quality mail order bulbs, plants & products
139	Cassaboo Nursery PL	W	sales@cassaboo.com.au www.cassaboo.com.au	P:03 9720 4300 F:03 9720 4013	11 Newcastle Rd Bayswater VIC 3153	Advanced palms & quality indoor foliage plants
140	Clyde Plant Nursery	W		P:03 5998 5546 F:03 5998 5586	95 Moores Rd Clyde VIC 3978	Exclusive Dwf 'Lots A Lemon', roses, ground covers, climbers
141	Collectors Corner (retail)	R	webmaster@collectorscorner.com.au www.collectorscorner.com.au	P:03 9798 5845 F:03 9706 3339	810 Springvale Rd Braeside VIC 3195	Australia's largest range of succulents, orchids, bromeliads and other rarities
142	Collectors Corner (wholesale)	W	webmaster@collectorscorner.com.au www.collectorscorner.com.au	P:03 9700 4888 F:03 9706 1425	VIC	Australia's largest range of succulents orchids, bromeliads and other rarities
143	Conifer Gardens Nursery	W R	conifernursery@bigpond.com users.bigpond.com/conifer_gardens	P:03 9755 1793 F:03 9755 2677	252–6 Mt Dandenong Tourist Rd Ferny Creek VIC 3786	Conifers, Japanese maples, *Magnolia*, *Cornus*, *Cotinus* & *Buxus*, advanced size
144	The Digger's Club	R	info@diggers.com.au www.diggers.com.au	P:03 5987 1877 F:03 5981 4298	105 La Trobe Parade Dromana VIC 3936	
145	Di's Delightful Plants	✉	Di@disdelights.com.au www.disdelights.com.au	P:03 9735 3831 F:03 9739 6370	PO Box 567 Lilydale VIC 3140	Mail order for Larkman Plants, weekly dispatches Australia-wide
146	Essendon Garden Centre	R	info@e-plants.com.au www.e-plants.com.au	P:03 9379 0555 F:03 9379 6941	1060 Mt Alexander Rd Essendon VIC 3040	Best garden centre in Vic: for service, range, quality
147	Fern Acres Nursery	W R	sales@fernacres.com.au www.ferns.com.au	P:03 5786 5031 F:03 5786 5031	1052 Whittlesea-Kinglake Rd Kinglake West VIC 3757	Specialist fern & native orchids, in bush setting
148	Floriana	W	sales@floriana.com.au www.floriana.com	P:03 9798 9155 F:03 9798 9177	365 Greens Rd Keysborough VIC 3142	One of the largest wholesale nurseries: seedlings, herbs and potted colour
149	Gardenworld	R	gardenworld@hotkey.net.au www.gardenworld.com.au	P:03 9798 8095 F:03 9798 6777	810 Springvale Rd Braeside VIC 3195	Melb's largest range of plants & garden products
150	Grevillea Nursery & Landscaping	R	grevillea@21century.com.au www.grevilleanursery.com.au	P:03 9741 3100 F:03 9742 5356	63 Railway Ave Werribee VIC 3030	Plants, display gardens, garden imaging & plant placement services
151	Humphris Nursery	W		P:03 9761 9688 F:03 9728 6763	220 Cardigan Rd Mooroolbark VIC 3138	
152	Kapitany Concepts	W R	gecko@connexus.net.au	P:03 9729 7059 F:03 9738 0431	3 Norwich St Boronia VIC 3155	books, consultation
153	Larkman Nurseries	W	larkman@larkmannurseries.com.au www.larkmannurseries.com.au	P:03 9735 3831 F:03 9739 6370	PO Box 567 Lilydale VIC 3140	Home of Larkman Plants: innovative plants from around the world
154	Meredith Wholesale Nursery	W	www.meredithnursery.com.au	P:03 5286 1397 F:03 5286 1280	PO Box 50 Meredith VIC 3333	One stop nursery for all gardening & revegetation needs

See page 171 for how to deal with wholesalers and retailers.

NO.	COMPANY	SALES	EMAIL / WEB	PHONE / FAX	ADDRESS	COMMENT
155	Mildura Native Nursery	W R	tim@nativenursery.com.au www.nativenursery.com.au	P:03 5021 4117 F:03 5023 0607	PO Box 565 Mildura VIC 3502	Order native plants online, delivered to your door
156	Mount Beenak Orchids	✉ R	mtbeenak@valylink.net.au www.nurseriesonline.com.au	P:03 5966 7253 F:03 5966 7253	27 Hacketts Creek Rd Three Bridges VIC 3797	Mail order cool growing orchids, accredited to send plants Australia wide
157	Mr. Fern Pty Ltd	W	www.mrfern.com.au	P:03 5237 3216 F:03 5237 3270	260 Amiets Rd Wyelangta VIC 3237	Leading fern nursery with world's first sustainable tree fern plantation
158	Neerim Native Flora	W R	mikeh@sympac.com.au members.dcsi.net.au/neerimnativeflora	P:03 5628 1419	PO Box 95 Neerim South VIC 3831	Propagating West Gippsland indigenous plants. Only open by appointment.
159	Pinewood Quality Nursery	R	pinewoodnurs@ains.net.au	P:03 5560 8711 F:03 5561 8241	478 Blackburn Rd Glen Waverley VIC 3150	
160	Plant Growers Australia	W	www.pga.com.au	P:03 9722 1444 F:03 9722 1018	3 Harris Rd Wonga Park VIC 3115	
161	Plants Central	W	www.plantscentral.com.au	P:03 9560 7601 F:03 9560 7352	Glen Waverley VIC 3150	
162	Rosemont Nursery	W R	rosemont@pacificorp.com.au www.pacificorp.com.au	P:03 9728 2222 F:03 9728 1822	960 Mt Dandenong Tourist Rd Montrose VIC 3765	35 years of gardening, landscape & inspiration
163	Specialist Plant Growers	W	spg@foxall.com.au	P:03 5964 9295 F:03 5964 9420	PO Box 95 Coldstream VIC 3770	
164	Speciality Trees	W R		P:03 9796 8308 F:03 9796 8222	PO Box 66 Narre Warren North VIC 3804	Hardy advanced evergreens for landscaping & municipal plants
165	Tempo Two	W R	tempotwo@bigpond.com www.tempotwo.com.au	P:03 5978 6980 F:03 5978 6235	PO Box 1109 Pearcedale VIC 3912	Largest, most modern listing of irises in Australia
166	Toolangi Wholesale Nurseries	W		P:03 5962 9286 F:03 5962 9466	1141 Myers Creek Rd Toolangi VIC 3777	Specialist grower of rare & unusual trees & shrubs
167	Valley Clivia Nursery	W		P:03 9807 9141 F:03 9807 9141	40 Bruce St Mt Waverley VIC 3149	Specialising in cream-yellow clivias from world renowned breeders
168	Warren Park Nurseries	W		P:03 9796 8916 F:03 9796 8239	100 Boundary Rd Narre Warren East VIC 3804	
169	Wiseman Nursery	W		P:03 9737 9234 F:03 9737 9366	20 Wiseman Rd Silvan VIC 3795	Quality flowering plants
170	Apace Aid Inc	W R	apace@apacewa.org.au www.argo.net.au/apace	P:08 9336 1262 F:08 9430 5729	1 Johannah St North Fremantle WA 6159	Specialises in plant species of the Swan Coastal Plain, Darling Scarp & Range
171	Botanica Trading	R		P:08 9433 1675 F:08 9384 8834	Shop 261 Queen Victoria St North Fremantle WA 6159	
172	Domus Nursery	W	sales@domusnursery.com.au www.domusnursery.com.au	P:08 9293 1768 F:08 9293 3786	50 Bahen Rd Hacketts Gully WA 6076	Growers: extensive range of native & exotic plants
173	Ellenby Tree Farm	W R	ellenby@iinet.net.au	P:08 9405 4558 F:08 9405 3759	439 Sydney Rd Gnangara WA 6065	WA's premier tree farm, large range of quality trees
174	Heavenscent Herbs	W	www.thepottedwok.com.au	P:08 6278 4581 F:08 6278 4781	Lot 23 Benara Rd Caversham WA 6055	Growers: 'Herbaceous' herbs and 'The Potted Wok' Asian vegetables
175	Hort Marketing	W R		P:08 9306 3933 F:08 9306 3913	7 Stoney Rd Gnangara WA 6065	
176	Swanview Plant Farm	W	orders@swanviewplantfarm.com.au	P:08 9454 6341 F:08 9454 4229	29 Sorensen Rd High Wycombe WA 6057	
177	Tony & Sons Nursery and Orchid Farm	W R	www.tonyandsons.cjb.net	P:08 9302 1137 F:08 9302 1771	713 Gnangara Rd Lexia WA 6065	Quality stock: palms, orchids, frangipani, topiary & hedging plants

W Wholesale   R Retail   ✉ Mail order   @ Internet sales

NO.	COMPANY	SALES	EMAIL / WEB	PHONE / FAX	ADDRESS	COMMENT
178	Aeria Country Floors		via website www.aeria.com.au	P:02 9326 2444 F:02 9327 8559	28 Moncur St Woollahra NSW 2025	Call 02 9362 0900 for stockists
179	African Thatch Australia		info@african-thatch.com.au www.african-thatch.com.au	P:08 9255 4466 F:08 9255 2294	PO Box 215 Midland WA 6936	Four styles of fire retardant Cape Reed thatching from South Africa
180	Alloy		sydney@alloydesign.com.au www.alloydesign.com.au	P:02 9565 2422 F:02 9565 2522	PO Box 74 Paddington NSW 2021	metal mosaics + metalware + personal + design
181	Amber		via website www.ambertiles.com.au	P:1300 362 241	outlets in NSW, ACT & QLD	Extensive range of tiles, pavers & retaining walls – many exclusive
182	Ausgum Furniture		sales@ausgum.com www.ausgum.com.au	P:07 4987 7222 F:07 4987 6444	1 Cliffe Street Emerald QLD 4720	100% Australian, quality, award winning, environmentally certified
183	Austimber Supplies		sales@austimbersupplies.com.au www.austimbersupplies.com.au	P:02 9627 5001 F:02 9627 5002	8 Windsor Rd Box Hill NSW 2765	Ezydeck & Australian & imported kiln-dried hardwoods
184	Australian Garden Furniture Co.		agfc@optusnet.com.au	P:07 3865 4277 F:07 3965 4755	PO Box 180 Wilston QLD 4051	Durable & practical furniture, commercial or domestic commissions
185	Axolotl Metal Finishes		info@axolotl.com.au www.axolotl.com.au	P:02 9666 1207 F:02 9666 1210	6/73 Beauchamp Rd Matraville NSW 2036	Application of semi-precious metals to any substrate
186	Bauwerk Colour		info@bauwerk.com.au www.bauwerk.com.au	P:08 9433 1008 F:08 9433 1009	271 South Terrace South Fremantle WA 6162	Complete range of contemporary & environmentally friendly products
187	Beech Wood Fired Ovens Australia		sales@beechovens.com.au www.beechovens.com	P:07 3397 0277 F:07 3397 0030	36 Gladys St Stones Corner QLD 4126	Australia's largest manufacturer of wood fired ovens
188	Bisanna Tiles			P:02 9310 2500 F:02 9310 3621	423 Crown St Surry Hills NSW 2010	
189	Cast In Stone		sales@castinstone.com.au www.castinstone.com.au	P:03 9763 2442 F:03 9763 2443	59 Rushdale St Knoxfield VIC 3180	Handcrafted large format pavers using no pigments/oxides
190	Cotterstone		sales@cotterstone.com.au www.cotterstone.com.au	P:02 4871 3435 F:02 4871 3435	225 Old Hume Hwy Mittagong NSW 2575	Hand made garden and architectural cast stone pieces
191	CSR PGH		via website www.pghpavers.com.au	P:1800 012 121 F:02 9826 1237	Lot 7 Cecil Rd Cecil Park NSW 2171	Natural clay pavers in a full range of colours & textures
192	Daniel Robertson		sales@danielrobertson.com.au www.danielrobertson.com.au	P:03 9875 3000 F:03 9894 1804	58–74 Station St Nunawading VIC 3131	Family business crafting unique clay bricks & paving
193	De Pot Man		depotman@ozemail.com.au	P:07 4639 4721 F:07 4632 4782	Cnr Herries & Clifford St Toowoomba QLD 4350	QLD's No. 1 pot store for price, quality and service
194	Décor Pebble		sales@decorpebble.com.au www.decorpebble.com.au	P:03 9888 9888 F:03 9888 9884	84–90 Highbury Rd Burwood VIC 3125	Australia's largest range and best value imported decorative pebbles
195	Domo Collections		sales@domo.com.au www.domo.com.au	P:03 9882 8788 F:03 9882 8789	55 Camberwell Rd Hawthorn VIC 3122	Traditional & contemporary, highest quality & exclusivity
196	Dura-Stone		david@durastone.com.au www.durastone.com.au	P:02 9905 5677 F:02 9905 4703	PO Box 299 Terrey Hills NSW 2084	Check website for retail outlets
197	E H Brett & Sons P/L		sailshades@brettproducts.com.au www.brettproducts.com.au	P:02 9648 5622 F:02 9648 5699	1 River Street Silverwater NSW 2128	Australian made canvas & PVC shade sails, blinds and awnings
198	Emac & Lawton Pty Ltd		sales@emac-lawton.com.au www.emac-lawton.com.au	P:02 9700 0188 F:02 9700 0188	76 Bay Street Botany NSW 2109	Importers of impressive decorator pieces for interior & exterior spaces
199	Eureka Tiles		sales@eurekatiles.com www.eurekatiles.com	P:1800 800 672 F:1800 653 190	62 Belmore Road Punchbowl NSW 2196	Australia's largest floor tile manufacturer of glazed & unglazed tiles
200	Fabulous Foliage Plantscaping		info@fabfol.com www.fabfol.com	P:07 3871 0592 F:07 3700 9325	Auchenflower QLD 4066	Planters, plants, pebbles: contemporary plantscaping solutions
201	Feast Watson			P:1800 252 502 F:03 9757 9590	1330 Ferntree Gully Rd Scoresby VIC 3179	Stunning timber finishes for outstanding quality & protection

SALES column (vertical text): PHONE OR VISIT THE COMPANY'S WEBSITE TO FIND YOUR NEAREST RETAILER

See page 171 for how to deal with wholesalers and retailers.

NO.	COMPANY	SALES	EMAIL / WEB	PHONE / FAX	ADDRESS	COMMENT
202	Freedom		via website www.freedom.com.au	P:1300 135 588	see website	
203	Gardens at Night		sales@gan.com.au www.gan.com.au	P:03 9824 4937 F:03 9824 4936	1316 Malvern Rd Malvern VIC 3144	Dedicated team of landscape lighting professionals
204	Granite Works		info@graniteworks.com.au www.graniteworks.com.au	P:03 9813 5999 F:03 9813 5399	see website for VIC, ACT & QLD offices	Natural architectural stone: granite, bluestone, sandstone & limestone
205	Haymes Paint		info@haymespaint.com.au www.haymespaint.com.au	P:1800 033 431 F:03 5338 1868	Waringa Drive, Wendouree Industrial Park Ballarat VIC 3350	Family owned paint manufacturer, in Ballarat since 1935
206	House of Bamboo		info@houseofbamboo.com.au www.houseofbamboo.com.au	P:02 9666 5703 F:02 9666 5693	13 Erith St Botany NSW 2109	Natureed & bamboo related materials for screens, fences & shade
207	Hunza		hunza@hunza.co.nz www.hunza.co.nz		see website	Lights from aluminium, copper & 316 stainless steel
208	IKEA		www.IKEA.com.au	P:02 9418 2744	see website	Beautiful, functional designs that everyone can afford
209	Industree		industree@conceptual.net.au www.industree.com.au	P:08 9433 6632 F:08 9433 6632	PO Box 58 North Fremantle WA 6159	Contemporary, functional & versatile aluminium planters & containers
210	IN-EX Living		diriddell@in-ex.com.au www.in-ex.com.au	P:03 9813 4550 F:03 9813 4513	PO Box 151 Toorak VIC 3142	Custom made furniture & mirrors with meticulous design detail
211	Issey Sun Shade Systems		sales@issey.com.au www.issey.com.au	P:1800 070 000 F:02 9810 0900	84 Justin Street Lilyfield NSW 2040	Premium external, retractable quality sunshades for the discerning
212	Jungle Fever		info@junglefever.com.au www.junglefever.com.au	P:07 4725 0788 F:07 4725 0788	5/52 Keane St Currajong QLD 4812	Everything for your tropical home & garden makeover
213	Kevin Free			P:03 5356 9203	Burke St Landsborough VIC 3384	Sculptor
214	Ke-Zu		info@kezu.com.au www.kezu.com.au	P:02 9571 8200 F:02 9571 8300	179 Harris St Pyrmont NSW 2009	Creating better environments to live, work & relax in
215	Korban/Flaubert		info@korbanflaubert.com.au www.korbanflaubert.com.au	P:02 9557 6136 F:02 9557 6136	8/8–10 Burrows Rd Alexandria NSW 2044	Furniture, lighting & installations from a Sydney laboratory
216	Leisure Central		sales@leisurecentral.com.au www.leisurecentral.com.au	P:1800 003 095 F:07 3865 6244	103 Copperfield St Geebung QLD 4034	The Azzurra range of furniture is on our web site
217	Leisure Structures P/L		info@natureshade.com www.natureshade.com	P:02 9666 5703 F:02 9666 5693	13 Erith St Botany NSW 2109	Imaginative, versatile shade & other leisure structures
218	Littlehampton Clay Bricks and Pavers		sales@littlehamptonbrick.com.au www.littlehamptonbrick.com.au	P:08 8391 1855 F:08 8398 2218	Main Rd Littlehampton SA 5250	Character in Clay with 113 years of experience
219	Longlife Bamboo		info@longlifebamboo.com www.longlifebamboo.com	P:07 5483 4810 F:07 5483 4851	8 & 13 Jerry Creek Rd Langshaw QLD 4570	Pressure preserved to last for decades in external situations
220	Louis Poulsen Australia Pty Ltd		lplm@lplm.com.au www.louis-poulsen.com.au	P:02 8399 1611 F:02 8399 2944	71–77 Regent St Redfern NSW 2016	Leading developer of design lighting solutions, outdoor & indoor
221	Lumascape Lighting		sales@lumascape.com.au www.lumascape.com.au	P:07 3286 2299 F:07 3286 6599	38–44 Enterprise St Cleveland QLD 4163	Australian made, corrosion resistant outdoor & underwater lighting
222	Lumeah Limestone		lumeah@lumeah.com.au www.lumeah.com.au	P:08 9204 1400 F:08 9204 1044	1/7 Guthrie St Osborne Park WA 6017	Hand crafted, insitu poured, reconstituted natural limestone
223	Made in Concrete		info@madeinconcrete.com www.madeinconcrete.com	P:03 9391 3317 F:03 9391 3001	6 Ramsay St Spotswood VIC 3015	Beautiful contemporary concrete products for home and garden use
224	Makinstone		dmakin@makinstone.com.au www.makinstone.com.au	P:02 9838 8030 F:02 9838 8002	Unit 7/16 Anvil Rd Seven Hills NSW 2147	Australian made statues, birdbaths, waterfeatures, pots & planters
225	ME Lighting Pty Ltd		loretta.maitland@melighting.com.au www.melighting.com.au	P:02 9700 9204 F:02 9700 9699	3/25 Ossary St Mascot NSW 2020	Lights hand made in Australia for quality & longevity
226	Mediterranean Woodfired Ovens		lifestyle@woodfiredovens.com.au www.woodfiredovens.com.au	P:1300 883 909 F:08 9403 3178	PO Box 3061 Joondalup WA 6027	Woodfired ovens for lifestyle & entertaining throughout the year
227	Moondani Glass Design		info@moondaniglass.com.au www.moondaniglass.com.au	P:02 9519 9520 F:02 9519 9420	146 Edinburgh Rd Marrickville NSW 2204	Custom designed glass water features

PHONE OR VISIT THE COMPANY'S WEBSITE TO FIND YOUR NEAREST RETAILER

See page 171 for how to deal with wholesalers and retailers.

NO.	COMPANY	SALES	EMAIL / WEB	PHONE / FAX	ADDRESS	COMMENT
228	Motyaj Pty Ltd		sales@motyaj.com.au www.motyaj.com.au	P:1300 668 925 F:02 9829 3688	30 Williamson Rd Ingleburn NSW 2565	Wholesaling quality unique planters & garden décor products
229	NorStone		sales@norstone.com.au www.norstone.com.au	P:02 9944 6711 F:02 9944 6747	PO Box 824 Narrabeen NSW 2101	Custom made natural stone products including rock panels
230	Papaya		shop@papaya.com.au www.papaya.com.au	P:02 9386 9980 F:02 9386 9920	Shop 5015, lvl 5 Westfield Bondi 500 Oxford St Bondi NSW 2022	Homewares harmonising raw materials & contemporary design
231	Parterre Garden		warehouse@parterre.com.au www.parterre.com.au	P:02 9356 4747 F:02 9356 4050	493 Bourke St Surry Hills NSW 2010	European contemporary exterior furniture & modern garden accesssories
232	The Pebble People		pebblepeople@dodo.com.au	P:07 5448 5722 F:07 5884 5722	931 Yandina Bli Bli Rd, PO 206 Bli Bli QLD 4560	Suppliers of quality tumbled & natural Australian pebble
233	Pine Solutions Australia – Ironwood®		enquiries@pinesolutions.com.au www.pine.com.au	P:02 9496 9155 F:02 9496 9150	Ground Floor, 71 Ridge St Gordon NSW 2072	Ironwood® for outdoor structures such as decks, fences & pergolas
234	Porch	PHONE OR VISIT THE COMPANY'S WEBSITE TO FIND YOUR NEAREST RETAILER	sales@porch.com.au www.porch.com.au	P:02 9565 2717 F:02 9565 2718	Unit 8a, 32–60 Alice St Newtown NSW 2042	Beautiful, contemporary outdoor furniture, made in Australia
235	Porter's Paints		enquiries@porters.com.au www.porterspaints.com	P:02 9698 5322 F:02 9699 5332	895 Bourke St Waterloo NSW 2017	Over 30 different products all low in VOC's for a healthier environment
236	Pottery Pavilion		pottery@benara.com.au www.potterypavilion.com	P:08 9405 0011 F:08 9405 0012	Lot 31 Vincent Rd Wanneroo WA 6065	Features, pottery, floristry vases & designer planters for stockists only
237	Quantum Stone		info@quantumstone.com.au www.quantumstone.com.au	P:08 8234 8911 F:08 8234 7918	325 Richmond Rd Netley SA 5037	Extensive range of reconstituted stone: texture–colour–quality–style
238	Radial Timber Sales		sales@radialtimber.com www.radialtimber.com	P:03 9558 4111 F:03 9558 4155	60–72 Garden Rd Clayton VIC 3168	Native hardwood decking, cladding, linings & screens
239	Rock 'n Stone		sales@rocknstone.com.au www.rocknstone.com	P:1300 553 612 F:03 9523 0400	693 Glenhuntly Rd South Caulfield VIC 3162	Natural stone products & like-minded support for your design journey
240	Sareen Stone (NSW) Pty Ltd		duncan@sareenstone.com.au www.sareenstone.com.au	P:02 9884 8802 F:02 9411 5609	23 Findlay Ave Roseville NSW 2069	Limestone, marble, granite, travertine, sandstone, basalt, pebbles
241	Smartrock		jan@smartrock.com.au www.smartrock.com.au	P:03 5981 0755 F:03 5981 0886	PO Box 223 Sorrento VIC 3943	Proudly Australian, authentic & affordable light weight rock veneer
242	Spirit Level Designs		inspired@spiritlevel.com.au www.spiritlevel.com.au	P:02 8399 0660 F:02 8399 0554	194 Devonshire St Surry Hills NSW 2010	Landscape design company with a gallery and shop
243	Superior Steel Lattice		info@superiorsteellattice.com.au www.superiorsteellattice.com.au	P:1300 766 799 F:07 3843 5762	PO Box 3265 Norman Park QLD 4070	Privacy screens, gables, gates, fencing, louvres, maxi-slat & balustrades
244	Tait		info@tait.biz www.tait.biz	P:03 9416 0909 F:03 9416 0964	15–17 Easey St Collingwood VIC 3066	Leading design house delivering innovative ideas with passion & quality
245	Taiyo Membrane Corporation		info@taiyomc.com www.taiyomc.com	P:07 3633 5900 F:07 3633 5999	570 Curtin Ave East Eagle Farm QLD 4009	High quality, cost-effective shade structures
246	Terrastone		service@terrastone.com.au www.terrastone.com.au	P:02 9666 7725 F:02 9666 7723	10/12 Anderson St Banksmeadow NSW 2019	Exquisite, functional & decorative handcarved stone garden artistry
247	Tessac Pty Ltd		info@tessac.com www.tessac.com	P:03 9338 0088 F:03 9338 0021	9A International Square Tullamarine VIC 3043	15% off retail price for presenting Jamie's book at purchase
248	Tovo Lighting		sales@tovolighting.com.au	P:02 9939 1122 F:02 9905 0206	726 Pittwater Rd Brookvale NSW 2100	Consult, Design, Manufacture
249	Urban Stone		manager@urbanstone.com.au www.urbanstone.com.au	P:08 9417 2444 F:08 9417 7060	27 Jandakot Rd Perth WA 6164	New & exciting Ultra Premium range of paving & landscaping products
250	Wild Duck Garden Creations		info@wildduck.com.au www.wildduck.com.au	P:02 4567 2222 F:02 4567 2233	PO Box 3028 Bilpin NSW 2758	Columns, blocks, pavers: sandstone look without the price
251	Wistow Stone Quarries		wsq@chariot.net.au www.chariot.net.au/~wsq	P:08 8398 2960 F:08 8398 3077	PO Box 946 Mount Barker SA 5251	Wistow Bluestone for pools, patios, paving & walling
252	Yardware		sales@yardware.com.au www.yardware.com.au	P:02 8353 3882 F:02 9358 4500	CDA Centre, 513 Sth Dowling St Surry Hills NSW 2010	Designer outdoor furniture & decorative landscaping products
253	Dulux Australia		email: via website www.dulux.com.au	P:13 25 25	see website	Products available from all leading hardware & paint retailers
254	Wattyl		wattyl@wattyl.com.au www.wattyl.com.au	P:13 21 01	see website	Our Colour Visualiser helps devise your own colour scheme

Australian Institute of Horticulture (Inc)

In this crazy, full-on world it is sometimes hard to find a quiet activity to do such as gardening. Then when you do, it seems impossible to find out how to go about doing it. Not only do you have to find the time for the activity, but also the time to run around to find what you need to do it!

In this book, Jamie has helped both the professional and the homemaker to easily find what they need horticulturally. The reader will find assistance on design, but also a comprehensive list of where to find plants and related materials.

Like Jamie, The Australian Institute of Horticulture (Inc.) is committed to helping those either working or playing with plants. For both horticulturist and home gardeners we provide workshops that help them either learn how to do something or extend skills they already have.

We would like to congratulate Jamie on producing this book. Its emphasis on enjoying the greener environment is to be commended. This book will be of great benefit to anyone wishing to get their hands dirty and relieve a little stress, while not wanting to waste time precious time on finding what is needed to have fun.

Bernard A. Chapman
B.A. Dip. Ed. Dip T (E.C.E.) Cert Hort. M.A.I.H.
NATIONAL PRESIDENT
THE AUSTRALIAN INSTITUTE OF HORTICULTURE (INC.)

www.aih.org.au

Botanic Gardens Trust

Sydney's Botanic Gardens Trust is committed to what has become known as 'sustainable horticulture'. As a 190-year old organisation devoted to the study and display of plants, the Trust manages some of the most striking cultural and historical landscapes in Australia: the Royal Botanic Gardens and Domain on Sydney Harbour, Mount Tomah Botanic Garden in the Blue Mountains, and Mount Annan Botanic Garden in rapidly developing western Sydney. As one of the world's leading botanic gardens we take long-term stewardship of our land and landscapes seriously.

If you like Jamie's book, you'll be keen to visit our gardens where you'll see innovative planting, modern design, practical approaches to water conservation, integrated pest management, soil improvement, and fascinating interpretation. Alternatively, visit the Trust's website (www.rbgsyd.nsw.gov.au) for fact sheets on plant pests and diseases, a vast database of information on native and garden plants, or to become an active supporter by joining the Friends of the Gardens.

Dr Tim Entwisle
EXECUTIVE DIRECTOR
BOTANIC GARDENS TRUST

www.rbgsyd.nsw.gov.au

Parks and Leisure Australia

Parks and Leisure Australia is a key professional association which promotes cooperation and mutual assistance between persons and organisations in the parks and leisure industry. For over 70 years, PLA has supported members in the development of quality environments for the enjoyment of leisure for Australian society.

Recent horticultural lifestyle programs have further heightened the awareness to individuals on how they can improve their own private environments to enhance their leisure pursuits. The industry is quite diverse but equally passionate in its outcome. The contribution to lifestyle horticultural through the publications of Jamie Durie and the PATIO team is regarded as significant and complimentary to the Parks and Leisure Industry.

Stephen Bourke
NATIONAL PRESIDENT
PARKS & LEISURE AUSTRALIA

www.parks-leisure.com.au

Landscape Industries Association of Australia

The Landscape Industries Association of Australia is the recognised national industry peak body that has the responsibility of coordinating the collective efforts of the six dedicated state-based landscape associations (Victoria, Queensland, South Australia, Western Australia, New South Wales, and Tasmania). These six state-based landscape associations are made up of a collection of landscape professionals including commercial and residential landscape contractors, landscape designers, and landscape suppliers, that share the common goal of providing a quality product and a world class service. Contact your recognised state based Landscape Association (refer websites) to access the most appropriate landscape professional for your landscape project.

SOUTH AUSTRALIA
www.lasa.org.au

WESTERN AUSTRALIA
www.landscapewa.com.au

QUEENSLAND
www.qali.asn.au

VICTORIA
www.liav.com.au

NEW SOUTH WALES
www.lcansw.com.au

TASMANIA
03 6274 1284

Nursery and Garden Industry Australia

Nursery and Garden Industry Australia wholeheartedly supports Jamie's initiative in producing this handbook. Our industry is tremendously varied with thousands of suppliers and producers and literally tens of thousands of products. A book such as this assists us all in finding exactly the right product for every situation.

Richard de Vos
CHIEF EXECUTIVE OFFICER
NGIA

Nursery & Garden Industry Australia

www.ngia.com.au

Australian Institute of Landscape Architects

On behalf of the Australian Institute of Landscape Architects, I would like to welcome Jamie as an affiliate member of this institute as well as to wish him well with this publication.

Jamie's publications and other promotional work have become important to the development of a national attitude towards improving our residential and open spaces. While always encouraging good design, Jamie has also encouraged people to consider important environmental and health issues as part of their own residential environments. For this, Jamie is to be commended. I look forward to working more with him on such issues in the future.

Paul Costigan
EXECUTIVE DIRECTOR
AILA

www.aila.org.au

Planet Ark

Planet Ark's aim is to show people and business the many ways they can reduce their day-to-day impact on the environment – at home, at work and within the community. Planet Ark is proud to have had Jamie Durie as a supporter for over ten years.

Jon Dee
FOUNDER & MANAGING DIRECTOR
PLANET ARK

www.planetark.com

PLANT INDEX

If you know which plant you are after, use the index below to find information available in this book. The plants are listed alphabetically by genus, and include the common name. The number given is the plant number: use it to look up the picture and horticultural details (starting on page 14) and where to get it in Australia (plants suppliers start on page 184).

Abelia x *grandiflora* GLOSSY ABELIA **061**

Abies spp. FIR **001**

Acacia baileyana COOTAMUNDRA WATTLE **002**

Acacia binervia COASTAL MYALL **003**

Acacia cognata 'Lime Magik' BOWER WATTLE **112**

Acacia elata CEDAR WATTLE **004**

Acacia pravissima 'Kuranga Cascade' OVENS WATTLE **182**

Acacia vestita HAIRY WATTLE **062**

Acanthus mollis ACANTHUS **299**

Acca sellowiana PINEAPPLE GUAVA **063**

Acer palmatum JAPANESE MAPLE **005**

Acer platanoides 'Globosum' NORWAY GLOBE MAPLE **225**

Acmena smithii var. *minor* SMALL LEAFED LILLYPILLY **113**

Acmena smithii CREEK LILLYPILLY **064**

Acokanthera oblongifolia WINTER SWEET **065**

Acorus gramineus JAPANESE RUSH **386**

Adenium obesum IMPALA LILY **226**

Adiantum raddianum DELTA MAIDENHAIR FERN **300**

Aechmea spp. & cvs BROMELIAD **114**

Aeonium arboreum AEONIUM **227**

Agapanthus praecox AGAPANTHUS **301**

Agave americana CENTURY PLANT **228**

Agave attenuata AGAVE **229**

Agave parryi PARRY'S AGAVE **230**

Agonis flexuosa 'After Dark' AFTER DARK AGONIS **115**

Ajania pacifica GOLD & SILVER **302**

Ajuga reptans CARPET BUGLE WEED **183**

Akebia quinata CHOCOLATE VINE **362**

Allamanda cathartica GOLDEN TRUMPET **363**

Alluaudia comosa ALLUAUDIA **231**

Alocasia brisbanensis CUNJEVOI **232**

Aloe arborescens CANDELABRA ALOE **116**

Aloe plicatilis FAN ALOE **233**

Alpinia coerulea NATIVE GINGER **303**

Alpinia purpurata RED GINGER **304**

Alpinia zerumbet SHELL GINGER **066**

Alternanthera dentata cvs JOY WEED **117**

Ampelopsis glandulosa var. *brevipedunculata* PORCELAIN VINE **364**

Anemone x *hybrida* JAPANESE WIND FLOWER **305**

Angophora costata SYDNEY RED GUM **006**

Angophora hispida DWARF APPLE **306**

Anigozanthos flavidus hybrids KANGAROO PAW **307**

Anthurium spp. FLAMINGO FLOWER **118**

Aphanopetalum resinosum GUM VINE **365**

Aptenia cordifolia HEARTLEAF ICE PLANT **184**

Araucaria bidwillii BUNYA BUNYA **007**

Araucaria heterophylla NORFOLK ISLAND PINE **008**

Arbutus unedo STRAWBERRY TREE **009**

Archontophoenix alexandrae ALEXANDRA PALM **010**

Artemisia 'Powis Castle' POWIS CASTLE WORMWOOD **119**

Arthropodium cirratum RENGA LILY **120**

Aspidistra elatior CAST IRON PLANT **121**

Asplenium australasicum BIRD'S NEST FERN **234**

Astelia chathamica SILVER SPEAR **235**

Aucuba japonica GOLD DUST PLANT **122**

Azolla spp. FAIRY MOSS **387**

Backhousia anisata ANISEED MYRTLE **067**

Backhousia citriodora LEMON SCENTED MYRTLE **068**

Bambusa multiplex cvs HEDGE BAMBOO **069**

Banksia ericifolia HEATH BANKSIA **070**

Banksia integrifolia COAST BANKSIA **011**

Banksia spinulosa & cvs HAIRPIN BANKSIA **123**

Banksia spinulosa 'Birthday Candles' BIRTHDAY CANDLES BANKSIA **185**

Bauhinia galpinii PRIDE OF THE CAPE **308**

Bauhinia variegata ORCHID TREE **012**

Beaucarnea recurvata PONYTAIL **236**

Berberis thunbergii JAPANESE BARBERRY **124**

Bergenia spp. & cvs BERGENIA **186**

Betula pendula SILVER BIRCH **013**

Bismarckia nobilis BISMARCK PALM **237**

Blechnum nudum FISHBONE WATER FERN **238**

Bougainvillea cvs BOUGAINVILLEA **366**

Brachychiton acerifolius ILLAWARRA FLAME TREE **014**

Brachychiton rupestris QLD BOTTLE TREE **015**

Brachyscome multifida CUT LEAF DAISY **309**

Brunfelsia australis 'Sweet & Petite' YESTERDAY TODAY TOMORROW **125**

Buckinghamia celsissima IVORY CURL FLOWER **016**

Burchellia bubalina SOUTH AFRICAN POMEGRANATE **126**

Buxus microphylla var. *japonica* JAPANESE BOX **239**

Buxus sempervirens 'Suffruticosa' DUTCH BOX **127**

Calathea zebrina ZEBRA PLANT **310**

Calliandra haematocephala POWDERPUFF TREE **071**

Callistemon viminalis 'Little John' LITTLE JOHN BOTTLEBRUSH **128**

Callistemon viminalis WEEPING BOTTLEBRUSH **017**

Callitris columellaris SAND CYPRESS PINE **240**

Calodendrum capense CAPE CHESTNUT **018**

Camellia japonica CAMELLIA **241**

Camellia sasanqua SASANQUA CAMELLIA **072**

Carex spp. SEDGE **311**

Castanospermum australe BLACK BEAN **019**

Cephalotaxus harringtonia JAPANESE PLUM YEW **073**

Cerastium tomentosum SNOW IN SUMMER **187**

Ceratopetalum gummiferum NSW CHRISTMAS BUSH **074**

Chaenomeles speciosa FLOWERING QUINCE, JAPONICA **129**

Chamaedorea elegans PARLOUR PALM **312**

Chamaerops humilis MEDITERRANEAN FAN PALM **075**

Choisya ternata MEXICAN ORANGE BLOSSOM **130**

Chorizema cordatum HEART-LEAFED FLAME PEA **131**

Chrysocephalum apiculatum YELLOW BUTTONS **188**

Cissus antarctica KANGAROO VINE **189**

Cissus hypoglauca WATER VINE **367**

Citrus cvs CITRUS **020**

Citrus x *meyeri* 'Meyer' MEYER LEMON **242**

Cleistocactus straussii SILVER TORCH CACTUS **243**

Clerodendrum splendens FLAMING GLORYBOWER **368**

Clivia miniata CLIVIA **313**

Clytostoma callistegioides ARGENTINE TRUMPET VINE **369**

Codiaeum variegatum CROTON **132**

Coleonema pulchellum DIOSMA **133**

Colocasia esculenta TARO **388**

Convolvulus cneorum SILVERBUSH **314**

Convolvulus sabatius ssp. *mauritanicus* GROUND MORNING GLORY **190**

Coprosma repens LOOKING GLASS PLANT **076**

Coprosma x *kirkii* SMALL LEAFED LOOKING GLASS PLANT **315**

Cordyline australis NZ CABBAGE TREE **244**

Cordyline fruticosa cvs TI PLANT **245**

Cordyline stricta SLENDER PALM LILY **316**

Correa alba WHITE CORREA **134**

Crassula ovata JADE PLANT **135**

Crinum pedunculatum SWAMP LILY **246**

Ctenanthe setosa 'Grey Star' CTENANTHE **317**

Cuphea hyssopifolia MEXICAN HEATHER **136**

Cupressus glabra ARIZONA CYPRESS **077**

Cupressus sempervirens PENCIL PINE **247**

x *Cuprocyparis leylandii* LEYLAND CYPRESS **078**

Cyathea australis ROUGH TREE FERN **248**

Cycas revoluta SAGO PALM **249**

Cymbidium Hybrid Cultivars CYMBIDIUM ORCHID **250**

Cyperus involucratus UMBRELLA SEDGE **318**

Cyperus papyrus PAPYRUS **389**

Cyperus prolifer DWARF PAPYRUS **390**

Dianella ensiformis hybrids FLAX LILY **319**

Dianella spp. & cvs FLAX LILY **320**

Dichondra repens KIDNEY WEED **191**

Dichorisandra thyrsiflora BLUE GINGER **321**

Dicksonia antarctica SOFT TREE FERN **251**

Dietes bicolor YELLOW PEACOCK FLOWER **137**

Dietes vegeta WILD IRIS **322**

Dioon edule MEXICAN FERN PALM **252**

Dodonea viscosa 'Purpurea' PURPLE STICKY HOP BUSH **138**

Doodia aspera PRICKLY RASP FERN **192**

Doryanthes excelsa GYMEA LILY **253**

Dracaena draco DRAGON TREE **254**

Dracaena fragrans 'Massangeana' HAPPY PLANT **255**

Dracaena marginata RED EDGE DRACAENA **256**

Dracaena sanderiana LUCKY BAMBOO **257**

Duranta erecta 'Sheena's Gold' PIGEON BERRY **139**

Dypsis decaryi TRIANGLE PALM **258**

Dypsis lutescens GOLDEN CANE PALM **079**

Echeveria agavoides RED EDGE ECHEVERIA **259**

Echeveria elegans MEXICAN SNOWBALL **193**

Echinocactus grusonii GOLDEN BARREL CACTUS **260**

Echium fastuosum PRIDE OF MADEIRA **140**

Elaeocarpus reticulatus BLUEBERRY ASH **021**

Elettaria cardamomum CARDAMOM **323**

Encephalartos altensteinii PRICKLY CYCAD **261**

Ensete ventricosum ABYSSINIAN BANANA **262**

Eranthemum pulchellum BLUE SAGE **324**

Erigeron karvinskianus SEASIDE DAISY **194**

Escallonia spp. & cvs ESCALLONIA **141**

Eucalyptus citriodora LEMON SCENTED GUM **022**

Eucalyptus ficifolia & hybrids RED FLOWERED GUM **023**

Eucalyptus haemastoma SCRIBBLY GUM **024**

Eucalyptus maculata SPOTTED GUM **025**

Eucalyptus sideroxylon ssp. *sideroxylon* MUGGA IRON BARK **026**

Euphorbia milii CROWN OF THORNS **142**

Euphorbia pulcherrima POINSETTIA **080**

Euryops pectinatus BRIGHT EYES **143**

Evolvulus glomeratus BLUE DAZE **195**

Farfugium japonicum 'Aureomaculatum' LEOPARD PLANT **325**

Fatsia japonica FATSIA **144**

Festuca glauca BLUE FESCUE **326**

Ficus benjamina WEEPING FIG **081**

Ficus lyrata FIDDLE LEAF FIG **263**

Ficus pumila CREEPING FIG **370**

Fraxinus angustifolia 'Raywood' CLARET ASH **027**

Fraxinus excelsior 'Jaspidea' GOLDEN ASH **028**

Gahnia sieberiana RED-FRUITED SAW SEDGE **264**

Gardenia augusta GARDENIA **145**

Gaura lindheimeri BUTTERFLY PLANT **327**

Gazania Hybrid Cultivars TREASURE FLOWER **196**

Gelsemium sempervirens CAROLINA JASMINE **371**

Ginkgo biloba MAIDENHAIR TREE **029**

Gleditsia triacanthos 'Sunburst' GOLDEN HONEY LOCUST **030**

Gordonia axillaris GORDONIA **031**

Graptopetalum paraguayense MOTHER OF PEARL PLANT **197**

Grevillea 'Bronze Rambler' BRONZE RAMBLER GREVILLEA **198**

Grevillea 'Moonlight' MOONLIGHT GREVILLEA **082**

Gunnera manicata GIANT RHUBARB **083**

Hardenbergia violacea NATIVE SARSAPARILLA **328**

Hebe albicans HEBE **265**

Hebe diosmifolia HEBE **329**

Hebe 'Emerald Green' EMERALD GREEN HEBE **266**

Hebe 'Wiri Mist' WIRI MIST HEBE **146**

Hedera helix ENGLISH IVY **199**

Hedychium gardneranum KAHILI GINGER **330**

Helichrysum petiolare LICORICE PLANT **331**

Heliotropium arborescens HELIOTROPE **332**

Helleborus orientalis HELLEBORE **333**

Hemerocallis Hybrid Cultivars DAY LILY **147**

Hibbertia scandens SNAKE VINE **372**

Hibiscus rosa-sinensis HIBISCUS **084**

Hibiscus tiliaceus COTTONWOOD **085**

Howea forsteriana KENTIA PALM **267**

Hoya carnosa HOYA, WAX FLOWER **373**

Hydrangea macrophylla HYDRANGEA **148**

Hymenocallis spp. SPIDER LILY **268**

Imperata cylindrica 'Rubra' JAPANESE BLOOD GRASS **334**

Iresine herbstii BEEFSTEAK PLANT **149**

Iris Louisiana Hybrids LOUISIANA IRIS **391**

Iris x *germanica* BEARDED IRIS **335**

Isolepis nodosa KNOBBY CLUB RUSH **336**

Isopogon anemonifolius BROAD-LEAFED DRUMSTICKS **337**

Isopogon formosus ROSE CONEFLOWER **150**

Ixora Hybrid Cultivars JUNGLE FLAME **151**

Jacaranda mimosifolia JACARANDA **032**

Jasminum sambac 'Grand Duke of Tuscany' DOUBLE ARABIAN JASMINE **338**

Juncus usitatus TUSSOCK RUSH **392**

Juniperus chinensis 'Spartan' SPARTAN JUNIPER **086**

Juniperus conferta SHORE JUNIPER **200**

Juniperus horizontalis 'Douglasii' WAUKEGAN JUNIPER **201**

Juniperus virginiana 'Skyrocket' SKYROCKET JUNIPER **269**

Kalanchoe beharensis FELT PLANT **270**

Kalanchoe blossfeldiana FLAMING KATY **339**

Kalanchoe pumila FLOWER DUST PLANT **202**

Kalanchoe tomentosa PANDA PLANT **340**

Kniphofia spp. & hybrids RED HOT POKER **271**

Lagerstroemia indica CREPE MYRTLE **033**

Lamium maculatum cvs DEAD NETTLE **203**

Lampranthus spp. ICE PLANT **204**

Lantana montevidensis TRAILING LANTANA **205**

Laurus nobilis BAY LAUREL **087**

Lavandula stoechas ITALIAN LAVENDER **152**

Leucadendron spp. & cvs LEUCADENDRON **153**

Leucophyta brownii SILVER CUSHION BUSH **154**

Liriodendron tulipifera TULIP TREE **034**

Liriope muscari LILY TURF **155**

Lomandra longifolia SPINY-HEADED MAT RUSH **341**

Lonicera nitida BOX LEAFED HONEYSUCKLE **156**

Lophomyrtus x *ralphii* LOPHOMYRTUS **157**

Loropetalum chinense 'Rubrum' CHINESE FRINGE FLOWER **158**

Luma apiculata TEMU **088**

Macadamia tetraphylla MACADAMIA **035**

Macrozamia communis BURRAWANG **272**

Magnolia denudata YULAN MAGNOLIA **036**

Magnolia grandiflora 'Little Gem' LITTLE GEM MAGNOLIA **273**

Magnolia grandiflora BULL BAY MAGNOLIA **037**

Magnolia x *soulangeana* MAGNOLIA **038**

Malus x *floribunda* JAPANESE FLOWERING CRABAPPLE **039**

Mammillaria spp. PINCUSHION CACTUS **206**

Mandevilla sanderi CHILEAN JASMINE **374**

Megaskepasma erythrochlamys BRAZILIAN RED CLOAK **089**

Melaleuca quinquenervia BROAD LEAFED PAPER BARK **040**

Melia azedarach WHITE CEDAR **041**

Melianthus major HONEY BUSH **274**

Mentha suaveolens APPLE MINT **207**

Mespilus germanica MEDLAR **042**

Metrosideros kermadecensis KERMADEC POHUTUKAWA **090**

Michelia figo PORT WINE MAGNOLIA **091**

Miscanthus sinensis cvs MISCANTHUS **342**

Miscanthus sinensis 'Zebrinus' ZEBRA GRASS **343**

Molineria capitulata WEEVIL LILY **159**

Monstera deliciosa FRUIT SALAD PLANT **344**

Moraea robinsoniana WEDDING LILY **275**

Murraya paniculata MURRAYA 092
Musa velutina PINK VELVET BANANA 276
Myrtus communis MYRTLE 160
Nandina domestica 'Nana' DWARF SACRED BAMBOO 161
Nandina domestica SACRED BAMBOO 093
Nelumbo nucifera SACRED LOTUS 277
Neoregelia spp. & cvs BROMELIAD 345
Nepeta x *faassenii* CATMINT 346
Nerium oleander OLEANDER 094
Nymphaea spp. & cvs WATERLILY 208
Odontonema strictum FIRESPIKE 162
Olea europaea var. *communis* OLIVE 043
Ophiopogon japonicus MONDO GRASS 347
Ophiopogon planiscapus 'Nigrescens' BLACK MONDO GRASS 209
Origanum vulgare OREGANO 210
Osteospermum Hybrid Cultivars OX-EYE DAISY 348
Pachypodium lamerei MADAGASCAR PALM 278
Pandanus tectorius SCREW PINE 279
Pandorea jasminoides BOWER OF BEAUTY VINE 375
Parrotia persica PERSIAN IRONWOOD 044
Parthenocissus henryana SILVER VEIN CREEPER 376
Parthenocissus tricuspidata BOSTON IVY 377
Passiflora coccinea RED FLOWERING PASSIONFRUIT 378
Pedilanthus tithymaloides DEVIL'S BACKBONE 280
Pelargonium peltatum IVY LEAFED GERANIUM 349
Pelargonium x *hortorum* ZONAL GERANIUM 163
Pennisetum alopecuroides SWAMP FOXTAIL GRASS 350
Persoonia pinifolia PINE-LEAFED GEEBUNG 095
Philodendron selloum TREE PHILODENDRON 351
Philodendron 'Xanadu' XANADU PHILODENDRON 164
Phlomis fruticosa JERUSALEM SAGE 165
Phoenix canariensis CANARY ISLAND DATE PALM 281
Phoenix roebelenii PYGMY DATE PALM 282
Phormium cookianum MOUNTAIN FLAX 166
Phormium tenax NZ FLAX 283
Photinia glabra 'Rubens' SMALL LEAFED PHOTINIA 096
Phyllostachys nigra BLACK BAMBOO 097
Pieris japonica JAPANESE PIERIS 167
Pittosporum tenuifolium cvs PITTOSPORUM 098
Pittosporum tobira JAPANESE MOCK ORANGE 168
Pittosporum undulatum SWEET PITTOSPORUM 045
Platycerium bifurcatum ELKHORN FERN 379
Platycerium superbum STAGHORN FERN 284
Plectranthus argentatus SILVER SPUR FLOWER 352
Plumbago auriculata PLUMBAGO 099

Plumeria obtusa WHITE FRANGIPANI 046
Plumeria rubra FRANGIPANI 047
Poa labillardieri TUSSOCK GRASS 353
Podocarpus elatus PLUM PINE 048
Pogonatherum paniceum MINIATURE BAMBOO GRASS 169
Pontederia cordata PICKEREL WEED 393
Pratia pedunculata MATTED PRATIA 394
Protasparagus densiflorus 'Myersii' FOXTAIL FERN 285
Protea neriifolia OLEANDER LEAFED PROTEA 170
Prunus cerasifera 'Nigra' PURPLE LEAFED PLUM 049
Punica granatum 'Nana' DWARF POMEGRANATE 171
Punica granatum POMEGRANATE 100
Pyrus calleryana 'Capital' CAPITAL CALLERY PEAR 050
Reineckea carnea REINECKEA 211
Restio tetraphyllus TASSEL CORD RUSH 286
Rhaphiolepis indica cvs INDIAN HAWTHORN 172
Rhaphis excelsa LADY PALM 101
Rhipsalis cereuscula CORAL CACTUS 354
Rhododendron Indica & Kurume Hybrids AZALEA 173
Rhododendron Large Leaf Hybrids RHODODENDRON 102
Robinia psuedoacacia 'Frisia' GOLDEN ROBINIA 051
Rosmarinus officinalis ROSEMARY 355
Russelia equisetiformis CORAL PLANT 356
Sagina subulata PEARLWORT 212
Salvia corrugata RIBBED SAGE 174
Salvia sinaloensis SINALOA SAGE 357
Sansevieria trifasciata MOTHER-IN-LAW'S TONGUE 287
Santolina chamaecyparissus COTTON LAVENDER 175
Sapium sebiferum CHINESE TALLOW TREE 052
Scaevola aemula cvs FAN FLOWER 213
Schefflera actinophylla QLD UMBRELLA TREE 053
Schefflera arboricola MINIATURE UMBRELLA TREE 103
Schinus molle var. *areira* PEPPER TREE 054
Scleranthus biflorus SCLERANTHUS 214
Sedum rubrotinctum JELLY BEAN PLANT 215
Sempervivum tectorum HOUSELEEK 216
Senecio serpens BLUE CHALK STICKS 217
Soleirolia soleirolii BABY'S TEARS 218
Spathiphyllum Hybrid Cultivars PEACE LILY 288
Spathodea campanulata AFRICAN TULIP TREE 055
Stachys byzantina LAMBS' EARS 219
Stenocarpus sinuatus QLD FIREWHEEL TREE 056
Stephanotis floribunda MADAGASCAR JASMINE 380
Strelitzia nicolai GIANT BIRD OF PARADISE 104
Strelitzia reginae var. *juncea* RUSH-LIKE STRELITZIA 289
Strelitzia reginae BIRD OF PARADISE 176

Stromanthe sanguinea STROMANTHE 290
Synadenium compactum 'Rubrum' RED AFRICAN MILK BUSH 291
Syzygium australe SCRUB CHERRY 105
Syzygium leuhmannii RIBERRY 106
Telopea speciosissima WARATAH 292
Teucrium fruticans BUSH GERMANDER 177
Thalia dealbata WATER CANNA 395
Thevetia spp. YELLOW OLEANDER 107
Thuja plicata WESTERN RED CEDAR 108
Thunbergia grandiflora SKYFLOWER 381
Thymus spp. & cvs THYME 220
Tibouchina 'Jules' JULES TIBOUCHINA 178
Tibouchina lepidota 'Alstonville' ALSTONVILLE TIBOUCHINA 057
Tillandsia usneoides SPANISH MOSS 293
Trachelospermum jasminoides 'Tricolor' VARIEGATED STAR JASMINE 358
Trachelospermum jasminoides STAR JASMINE 382
Trachycarpus fortunei CHINESE WINDMILL PALM 294
Tradescantia pallida 'Purpurea' PURPLE HEART 221
Tradescantia spathacea RHOEO 359
Tradescantia zebrina SILVER INCH PLANT 222
Tristaniopsis laurina WATER GUM 058
Tulbaghia violacea SOCIETY GARLIC 179
Typha spp. CUMBUNGI 396
Ulmus parvifolia CHINESE WEEPING ELM 059
Viburnum odoratissimum SWEET VIBURNUM 109
Viburnum tinus LAURISTINUS 110
Vigna caracalla SNAIL FLOWER 383
Vinca major GREATER PERIWINKLE 360
Vinca minor LESSER PERIWINKLE 223
Viola hederacea NATIVE VIOLET 224
Vitis vinifera 'Alicante Bouchet' ORNAMENTAL GRAPE 384
Vriesea spp. & cvs BROMELIAD 295
Washingtonia spp. COTTON PALM 060
Waterhousia floribunda WEEPING LILLYPILLY 111
Westringia fruticosa COAST ROSEMARY 180
Wisteria sinensis CHINESE WISTERIA 385
Xanthorrhoea spp. GRASS TREE 296
Xanthosoma violaceum BLUE TARO 361
Yucca guatemalensis GIANT YUCCA 297
Zamia furfuracea CARDBOARD PALM 298
Zantedeschia aethiopica ARUM LILY 397
Zephyranthes candida STORM FLOWER 181